7/01

Kubrick's *2001:*
A Triple Allegory

Leonard F. Wheat

The Scarecrow Press, Inc.
Lanham, Maryland, and London
2000

SCARECROW PRESS, INC.

Published in the United States of America
by Scarecrow Press, Inc.
4720 Boston Way, Lanham, Maryland 20706
www.scarecrowpress.com

4 Pleydell Gardens, Folkestone
Kent CT20 2DN, England

British Cataloguing in Publication Information Available

Library of Congress Cataloging-in-Publication Data

Wheat, Leonard F.
  Kubrick's 2001 : a triple allegory / Leonard F. Wheat
    p. cm.
  Includes bibliographical references and index.
  ISBN 0-8108-3796-X (alk. paper)
  1. 2001, a space odyssey (Motion picture). I. Title.
PN1997.T86 W49   2000
791.43'72—dc21   00-027997

Printed in the United States of America

♾™ The paper used in this publication meets the minimum requirements of
American National Standard for Information Sciences—Permanence of
Paper for Printed Library Materials, ANSI/NISO Z39.48–1992.
Manufactured in the United States of America.

To Kitty

Contents

1   **Introduction**   1

Where the Answers Lie
Allegory and Kubrick's Allegorical Symbols
A Preview of Coming Attractions

2   **The Surface Story**   17

The Basic Narrative
Fuzzy Areas of the Narrative

3   **The Odysseus Allegory**   41

Dave Bowman's Name
The African Monolith
The Judgment of Paris
Heywood R. Floyd's Name
Heywood Floyd as Paris
Heywood Floyd as Menelaus
The Trojan Horse and the Fall of Troy
The City of Ismarus and Lotus Land
The Cyclops Monster
The Laestrygonian Rock Attack
The Sirens
The Surf, Charybdis, and Scylla
Hyperion and Zeus
Seven Years with Calypso
Phaeacian Hospitality
Pallas Athene
Penelope, Her Suitors, and the Great Bow
Slaying the Suitors
Reunion with Penelope

4 The Man-Machine Symbiosis Allegory   63

Overview of the Allegory
The Dawn of Man
The Evolution of Humanoid Machines
Hal-Discovery as a Genuine Humanoid
The Death of Homo Machinus
The Evolution of Homo Futurus
What About Freud and Jung?

5 The Zarathustra Allegory: Background and Cast   87

Nietzsche's Characters and Themes
Interpretive Progress
The Monoliths as Human Attributes
Frank Poole as the Rope Dancer
Heywood Floyd as the Young Zarathustra
Dave Bowman as the Older Zarathustra and Overman
Hal-Discovery as God

6 The Zarathustra Allegory: The Action   109

The Death of God
The Immediate Aftermath
Man into Overman
Eternal Recurrence
Appendix A: Fallacies in Zarathustra's Eternal Recurrence Argument
Appendix B: List of the Zarathustra Allegory's 160 Symbols

7 Evaluation   139

2001's Critical Stature in the Absence of Allegory
The Quality of the Allegory and Symbolism
One Man's Opinion

Bibliography   163

Index   167

About the Author   181

Chapter 1

Introduction

Stanley Kubrick's *2001: A Space Odyssey* is one of the most, if not *the* most, controversial and thought-provoking movies ever filmed. Released in 1968, it has inspired the writing of six previous books, not counting Arthur Clarke's novel, which is based on the movie.[1] It has been panned by some critics, praised by others, and puzzled over by just about everyone. The naysayers have reacted to its ponderously slow, boring plot development; its lack of character development; its confusing exposition; its substitution of special effects for story; and its enigmatic, frustratingly symbolic, surrealistic conclusion. *2001*'s admirers have countered by hailing its plot sophistication (no Buck Rogers stuff here); its substitution of concepts for characters as dramatic substance; its imaginative use of symbols; its stimulating ambiguities; and its breathtaking visual images, superbly enhanced by classical music.

The admirers seem to be winning. Roger Ebert, probably America's best-known film critic and surely among the most respected (Pulitzer prize), places *2001* on his all-time list of "My Ten Great Films."[2] *2001*, he says, evokes a "sense of wonder"[3] and is one of "only a few films [that] are transcendent."[4] Other critics have tended to agree. *Sight and Sound*, the highly respected journal of the British Film Institute, conducts an International Critics Poll every ten years. Critics are asked to list the ten greatest films of all time. In the most recent poll, conducted in 1992, *2001* ranked tenth.[5] The American Film Institute conducted a similar but less critic-centered poll in 1998. The Institute's archivists and film historians compiled a list of 400 great American movies. AFI then asked more than 1,500 critics, producers, directors, actors, film photographers, film executives, and exhibitors to pick the 100 best. The resulting list of the "100 greatest American movies" had *2001* ranked twenty-second.[6]

The public has also given *2001* a resounding endorsement. A movie guide published by the editors of Consumer Reports Books lists movies that

1

have been rated excellent or very good (the two highest of five categories) on the basis of opinion-votes submitted by the generally highly educated readers of *Consumer Reports*. *2001* is among the movies listed and is described by the editors as a "classic science fiction essay."[7] Piers Bizony points out that *2001* "turned out to be one of MGM's five most famous and successful creations, along with *Gone with the Wind*, *Lawrence of Arabia*, *The Wizard of Oz*, and *Doctor Zhivago*."[8]

But even the admirers have been unable to fathom the film's mysteries. Bizony is one of *2001*'s strongest champions. He calls *2001* "the epitome of science fiction film-making" (21). Yet writing in 1994, a quarter century after *2001* was released, and having the benefit of three years of research, including the reading of numerous reviews, articles, and books, he was forced to admit that the plot is "confusing" (15) and "unapologetically ambiguous" (16). Bizony is unable to clarify the plot. He maintains that the film's greatness lies in its being "an extraordinary exercise in totally visual cinema" (21) and that the plot hardly matters: "You're just meant to *watch* it" (9). Needless to say, the earlier reviews, articles, and books Bizony read—including those written by admirers of *2001*—also failed to come up with very many answers.

Some people doubt that *2001*'s mysteries *can* be explained. Bizony's quoted remarks suggest as much. And Pauline Kael, writing from the opposite end of the critical spectrum (she loathes *2001*), accuses Kubrick of being too focused on special effects and of lacking enough imagination to create a story to go with his special effects.[9] She says Kubrick failed to make a movie; she seems to imply that Kubrick himself doesn't know the answers. Geduld, who is critically neutral, likewise implies that Kubrick doesn't know the answers: "For Kubrick, the story is just another cinematic tool. It is used to create a receptive mood for a vision that is basically beyond narrative."[10] *Time* says about the same thing: "The ambiguous ending . . . leaves doubt that the film makers themselves knew precisely what they were flying at."[11] Glenn Man believes that "the film's essential characteristic [is] its ambiguity" and that *2001*'s "open-endedness" permits "different and *equally valid*" interpretations.[12] He clearly rejects the idea that Kubrick has or intends that there be definitive answers.

WHERE THE ANSWERS LIE

Rest assured, Kubrick does have the answers. But to find them you must look beneath the visible plot—confusing, ambiguous, clouded by surrealism—and discover the deeper, and very different, stories that lie hidden. You must refuse to take everything you see on the screen literally. You must instead search for the symbolic meanings of a multitude of plot elements. For *2001* is only superficially a futuristic story about space travel. Beneath the surface story is a wondrously complex allegorical structure that both hides and reveals the answers. More than *an* allegory, *2001* is a *triple* allegory—three allegories in one. Each allegory uses the space voyage narrative to represent an entirely different narrative that is hidden in symbols. This book explains the three allegories—and the movie.

The three allegories are based on stories and ideas from (1) the Greek poet Homer, (2) the science-fiction writer Arthur Clarke, and (3) the German philosopher Friedrich Nietzsche. Kubrick's first allegory is a symbolic retelling, in far more detail than has been imagined, of Homer's epic poem *The Odyssey*. *The Odyssey* relates the adventures of a Greek king, Odysseus, during his ten-year voyage home from Troy after the Trojan War. The second allegory takes Clarke's theory of a future man-machine symbiosis, caricatures it, and inflates it into a spoofy three-evolutionary-leaps scenario. Leap number two—the leap from man to a species of humanoid machines—is abortive: the bad guy, symbolizing the new species, gets spiked in the forehead. The third allegory uses the surface story to symbolize the main themes of Nietzsche's *Thus Spake Zarathustra*. This allegory, the main one, again deals with evolution, so it shares considerable symbolism with the second allegory. But now there are just two evolutionary leaps—ape to man, man to overman. Between man and overman is a major subplot in which God stands in man's way. Man finally kills God, clearing the way for the evolution of a new supreme being—overman (a race)—and allowing Zarathustra to deliver the message for which Nietzsche is famous: "God is Dead!"[13]

The above capsule summaries provide general orientation to the three allegories. But to really understand what Kubrick has done, we need to examine each allegorized narrative in more detail.

The Odysseus Allegory

The Odysseus allegory is partially out in the open: it is revealed in *2001*'s subtitle, *A Space Odyssey*. People generally understand that Kubrick is using one voyage to symbolize another: Dave Bowman's space voyage from earth to a distant corner of the universe and back symbolizes Odysseus's ocean voyage (complete with plenty of land action) from Troy back to Ithaca after the Trojan War. Many people also recognize another connection, which has been openly mentioned by Arthur Clarke, co-author (with Kubrick) of *2001*'s screenplay. The reason all of Bowman's crewmen must die is that all of Odysseus's crewmen died.[14] Geduld has figured out that Hal's red eye identifies him as the cyclops monster that Odysseus disabled by plunging a stake into the eye in its forehead.[15] What is not public knowledge is the presence of many other symbolic connections between Bowman's odyssey and Odysseus's. People haven't caught onto the two connections involving Bowman's first and last names, for example, and they haven't seen the multitude of parallels between things and incidents in the space voyage and their Homerian antecedents.

A large part of the problem is that most of the people who have seen Kubrick's movie are either unfamiliar with or only superficially familiar with *The Odyssey*. A quick review of its plot is therefore in order. The summary that follows is necessarily general. Particular incidents will be described in more detail at appropriate points in chapter 3, which deals with the Odysseus allegory.

Before Odysseus's voyage home begins, the Trojan War occurs. The Trojans are the residents of the city of Troy, located a few miles from the Dardanelles in what is now Turkey.[16] Kubrick's allegory covers not only (*a*) the events of *The Odyssey*—the voyage—but (*b*) the events leading up to the war and (*c*) the climactic event of the war. In the pre-*Odyssey* events (1) Odysseus receives the gift of the Great Bow, (2) a golden apple is offered as a prize for being the fairest, (3) Zeus arranges for Paris, a prince of Troy, to judge a beauty contest among three goddesses, (4) one of them, Aphrodite, bribes Paris to choose her by promising him the loveliest woman in the world, (5) Paris meets that woman, Helen, wife of Menelaus, king of Sparta, (6) Paris seduces Helen and takes her to Troy while Menelaus is off on a trip to the Mediterranean, (7) Menelaus returns to Sparta, (8) he is briefed on what has happened, (9) he raises an army and launches a thousand ships to take the army to Troy, (10) the Greeks lay siege to Troy for ten years, and (11) the Greeks finally conquer Troy through a ruse that involves the Trojan Horse, a huge wooden horse with Greek soldiers hidden inside. The Trojan Horse is Odysseus's idea. Odysseus is another Greek king. His kingdom is the island of Ithaca, on the west side of Greece, and he is bound by an oath to help Menelaus.

After Troy falls, Odysseus spends another ten years getting back home. *The Odyssey* is the story of his return voyage, which involves a long string of episodes or adventures. Homer's story actually starts near the end and relates most of these adventures as flashbacks. But for our purposes it is better to list them in the order in which they occur. Odysseus (1) sacks the city of Ismarus, (2) visits the country of the Lotus-eaters, where three of his crewmen become incapacitated by lotus, (3) goes to the island of the giant cyclopes, where he battles the one-eyed, man-eating cyclops monster, (4) visits the island of Aeolia, where his host, Aeolus, king of the winds, gives him a leather bag of winds as a present, (5) gets within sight of Ithaca but then is blown far across the sea when his rascally crew, thinking the bag holds gold, unties it and lets the winds out, (6) loses all ships except his own in a rock attack by the Laestrygonians, (7) outwits and then befriends the sorceress Circe, (8) visits Hades, the kingdom of the dead, (9) manages to escape the Sirens, whose sultry voices lure sailors to their doom, (10) also escapes some raging surf, (11) avoids the whirlpool Charybdis, (12) loses six men to the six-headed monster Scylla, (13) has a run-in with the sun god Hyperion, (14) loses his ship in an attack by Zeus, who is helping Hyperion, (15) almost loses his life to Charybdis in a second encounter, (16) floats on a timber to the island of the goddess Calypso, who keeps him a virtual prisoner for seven years, (17) builds and departs in a small boat after Athene and Zeus intervene with Calypso, (18) loses the boat in an attack by Poseidon, (19) swims ashore to the country of the Phaeacians, where he enjoys Phaeacian hospitality and—here are the flashbacks— relates his adventures, (20) sails home to Ithaca under Phaeacian escort, (21) perceives the distress of his wife, Penelope, (22) gets help from Athene, (23) regains his Great Bow, which he left behind when he sailed for Troy, (24) slays the obnoxious suitors, who have been harassing Penelope, and (25) enjoys a reunion with Penelope.

Kubrick doesn't have time to symbolize all of these adventures, but he does treat most of them. For three of the adventures—the Lotus-eaters, the cyclops, and the rock attack—the symbolism is remarkably obvious. Also symbolized is the pre-*Odyssey* material involving the Great Bow, the three-goddess beauty contest, Paris, Helen, Menelaus, the thousand ships (launched by Helen's face), the Trojan Horse, and the downfall of Troy. (See if you can find hints of three of these in the symbolic name Heywood R. Floyd.)

The Man-Machine Symbiosis Allegory

In the second allegory, Kubrick does not use a previously written narrative. Rather, he takes an *idea* and constructs his own narrative around it. The idea comes from none other than Arthur Clarke, who is not only co-author of *2001*'s screenplay but author of both the short story on which *2001* is loosely based ("The Sentinel") and the novel that is based on the movie. Clarke has theorized that, in the future, man and machine will become a symbiotic (interdependent) whole. He sneaks this idea into the novel, where he writes, "Bowman [the hero] had established a virtual symbiosis with the ship."[17] Later, Bowman ponders the idea that all organic body parts could be replaced by "metal and plastic" ones and that "even the brain might go." Electronic intelligence, he muses, suggests that "the conflict between mind and machine might be resolved at last in the eternal truce of complete symbiosis"—a machine replica of a man.[18]

Kubrick caricatures man-machine symbiosis by creating the symbiotic creature Hal-Discovery. Hal, symbolizing man, is a very human-sounding and human-acting computer; Discovery, symbolizing machine, is Dave Bowman's spaceship—and happens to have a lot of cleverly disguised human features. Together, Hal and Discovery constitute an essentially living organism that *symbolizes* a hypothetical new humanoid species, humanoid machines. In other words, although Hal-Discovery is a single entity—an individual—in the surface story, he symbolizes an entire *race* of machines in the man-machine symbiosis allegory.

In this allegory, Kubrick takes a partly serious but mostly playful jab at this exaggerated representation of Clarke's theory. He does this by constructing a *three*-evolutionary-leaps scenario that imitates but expands the *two*-evolutionary-leaps scenario of Nietzsche. Nietzsche spoke of evolution from ape to man to overman (a superior being). Almost everyone who sees *2001* perceives the two Nietzscheian evolutionary leaps: (1) ape to man (the Dawn of Man episode) and (2) man to star-child (the hotel-room episode). But everyone seems to have missed a third leap, which occurs between the first two and is thus really the second in sequence. This unrecognized leap is an evolutionary near-disaster, an abortive leap from man to humanoid machine.

Each leap is preceded by the appearance of a mysterious, upright, domino-shaped black monolith. It symbolizes (in this allegory only) a milestone along the road of humanoid evolution. Just beyond each milestone a new humanoid species evolves—first, *Homo sapiens*; second, *Homo machinus*; and third, *Homo futurus*. *Homo sapiens* and *Homo machinus* are both imperfect, malevolent, warlike. They turn upon and kill or try to kill their predecessors. *Homo sapiens* succeeds, killing *Australopithecus* in the Battle at the Waterhole. But *Homo machinus* fails, losing to *Homo sapiens* in the Battle in Outer Space.

Homo sapiens, which had started down the wrong fork in the road of evolution, then switches to the right fork. This fork leads to the third upright monolith and, beyond it, to the third new race, *Homo futurus* (represented by the star-child). *Homo futurus* is benevolent. It does not try to kill its predecessor. And here, from a man who is sometimes accused of pessimism, we might read an optimistic message: whatever comes after man will be better, not worse.

Because the man-machine symbiosis allegory gets its basic outline from Nietzsche's ape-man-overman sequence, most of the *2001* symbolism depicting elements of this second allegory also depicts elements of the third. A major difference between the second and third allegories concerns what Hal-Discovery symbolizes. In the second allegory he symbolizes a new humanoid species that figuratively evolves from (is created by) man. In the third allegory, Hal-Discovery symbolizes God—but a reinterpreted Nietzscheian God who is created by man in his (man's) own image, rather than vice versa.

The Zarathustra Allegory

The third allegory uses symbols that represent characters, concepts, and events from Nietzsche's best-known work, *Thus Spake Zarathustra.* Nietzsche was deeply influenced by Darwin's theory of evolution. But he carried evolution one step beyond Darwin by positing the future evolution of a higher species than man—overman (*übermensch*). Overman, a morally and intellectually superior being, would be the fourth stage in an evolutionary progression that went from (1) worm to (2) ape to (3) man to (4) overman. Here worm isn't to be taken literally; it is a representative primitive species that stands for everything that preceded ape. Most of the time Nietzsche ignores the worm and treats the ape as the real starting point of evolution.

Nietzsche's philosophy is a combination of evolution and atheism, with a liberal dose of psychology ("the will to power") thrown in for good measure. Nietzsche is remembered for the chilling announcement, taken from the book being allegorized, that God is dead. This refers to cessation of belief in God; it does not imply that God once lived and then died. Nietzsche integrated his God-is-dead philosophy with his version of evolution by subdividing the third stage of evolution—man—into two parts: (1) lower man and (2) higher man. Lower man comes first, before God comes into being.

Lower man—the masses, the populace, the crowd in the marketplace—creates God. And the God he creates is the image of man: Nietzsche rejects the Bible's claim that God created man in his own image. "In his own image" is a crucial concept in Kubrick's allegory. Kubrick makes his God symbol, Hal-Discovery, just as mentally *and physically* manlike as he can. God even makes mistakes, tells lies, blows bubbles, and uses bathrooms! Not that he is exactly like man: he has three mouths rather than just one, and his arms are detachable.

Higher man is smarter than lower man, which is why the prophet Zarathustra has such a hard time finding higher men. Higher man—actually a progression of increasingly higher higher men—is the next step (beyond lower man) in the evolution of man into overman. But God stands between lower man and higher man, blocking progress. As long as God is supreme, man cannot evolve to supremacy. God's rules—the "blackest will" of God—stifle human thought, creativity, and intellectual development.[19] Hence, to progress, higher man must kill God: God must die. That is, man must stop believing in God and subjecting himself to the imaginary will of God.

When higher man achieves the death of God, he unleashes the will to power. This is an intense psychological drive that propels higher man higher and higher—and makes his intellect brighter and brighter—until "the great noontime" arrives.[20] When higher man can go no higher, and his wisdom can be no brighter, he will have become overman. Overman will be a figurative child, a new beginning. He will also be a figurative noontime sun—maximum height, maximum brightness.

Thus Spake Zarathustra covers the wanderings and encounters of the prophet Zarathustra. As a young man he created God ("that God whom I created").[21] But when he was thirty, doubt filled his mind, and he spent ten years in the mountains nourishing his soul. Then he came down the mountain from his high cave and went forth to teach. His words—words like "God is Dead!" and "Lo, I teach you the overman!"—sound for all the world like Nietzsche's.[22]

In Kubrick's Zarathustra allegory, two characters share the role of Zarathustra. The first character represents lower man. He is Heywood R. Floyd, the scientist who creates Hal-Discovery (God). The second character represents higher man. He is Dave Bowman, the astronaut who, for all practical purposes, kills Hal (kills God). After winning the struggle for supremacy, he symbolically sets his sights above the height of the highest previous higher man and—driven by his will to power—struggles upward. Finally, he reaches out and somehow grasps the unreachable—power. And he is reborn as the brightly glowing, globe-enclosed star-child, symbolizing both overman and the overman metaphor, "the great noontime" sun.

ALLEGORY AND KUBRICK'S ALLEGORICAL SYMBOLS

Before going any further, we need to review what *allegory* means. The clearest definition comes from Bernstein. He defines allegory as "a metaphorical narrative . . . in which the surface story and characters are intended to be taken as symbols pointing to an underlying, more significant meaning."[23] An allegory can be a novel, a short story, a poem, a play, or a motion picture. The symbols can be just about anything: people, creatures, inanimate objects, events, names, titles and subtitles, dialogue, appearance, sounds, music, colors, dates, and so on. The things symbolized (allegorized) are ideas, principles, characters, places, things, and events. These are generally organized into an entirely different narrative, hidden below the surface. Loosely speaking, one story symbolizes another.

Friedman provides more detail: "We have allegory when the events [I would say *elements*] of a narrative obviously and continuously refer to another simultaneous structure of events or ideas."[24] Continuity, he adds, distinguishes allegory from ambiguity or allusion. Allegory displays a *continuing* series of incidents or other symbols that represent other incidents or ideas. If the symbols are only occasional (as *2001*'s symbols have been regarded up until now), we have something different: allegorical tendency.

Kubrick's narrative qualifies as full-fledged allegory, as opposed to mere allegorical tendency. Symbolism, sometimes multiple symbolism, is in almost every scene other than some preceding the first monolith. *2001* displays a steady parade of symbolic characters, symbolic objects, symbolic names with hidden meanings, symbolic events, and other symbols. The characters include the prehuman apes, the tool-user ape-men, Heywood R. Floyd, the Russian woman Elena, Dave Bowman, Frank Poole, the renegade computer Hal, the three hibernating astronauts, the octahedron-aliens (the glittering "diamonds" flying in V-formation), and the star-child. The objects include the bone-club, the four monoliths, the sun, the earth, the moon, the orbiting nuclear bombs, the space shuttle, the space station, the moon lander, the moon bus, the moon crater Tycho, the spaceship Discovery and its appendages, the elongated key Bowman uses to lobotomize Hal, Jupiter and its five moons, the first and third utility pods, the tunnel of lights, the celestial objects seen by Bowman beyond the tunnel, Bowman's blinking eye, the surrealistic hotel room, the room's lit-from-beneath glass floor, the wine glass, the black clothing worn by Bowman while dining, the white clothing worn by Bowman in bed, and the glow surrounding the starchild. The symbolic events come one after another. They include such things as human contact with the three upright monoliths, the space shuttle's penetrating the space station, the moon lander's entering the moon, the briefing given to Heywood Floyd on the moon, the moon monolith's emitting a powerful signal, Hal's making a mistake, the not-so-private conversation Bowman and Poole hold inside the utility pod, Hal's killing Frank Poole, Bowman's picking up Poole's body, Bowman's lobotomizing Hal, the recorded briefing Bowman hears when he arrives at Jupiter, Jupiter's five moons' aligning themselves vertically above the planet, Bowman's chasing the monolith, Bowman's dramatic ride through the tunnel of lights, Bowman's seeing older versions of himself, and Bowman's slowly shifting his gaze from the broken wine glass to the bed.

Some of the symbols represent different things in different allegories. The moon monolith is the Trojan Horse in the first allegory, a milestone marking the evolution of symbiotic man-machine humanoids in the second, and superstition in the third. Hal-Discovery (the computer-spaceship synthesis) is the one-eyed cyclops monster in the Odysseus allegory, a new species of humanoid machines in the symbiosis allegory, and the God created by man in his own image in the Zarathustra allegory. Heywood R. Floyd is both Paris and Menelaus in the Odysseus allegory, nobody in the symbiosis allegory, and the young Zarathustra (who creates God) in the Zarathustra allegory. Dave Bowman is Odysseus in the first allegory, surviving humanity in the second, and the older Zarathustra (who proclaims the death of God) in the third. Frank Poole is one of the crewmen of Odysseus who are eaten by the cyclops monster in the first allegory, a nonsurviving human in the second, and the rope dancer (from a Nietzsche parable) in the third. The tunnel of lights is the trip past the Sirens in the first allegory and a cosmic fallopian tube up which the pod-sperm travels in the last two allegories. The star-child is Odysseus, reunited with Penelope (the earth), in the first allegory; a higher species beyond man in the second; and both the overman and the "great noontime" sun in the third. With three allegories going on at once, you really have to pay close attention.

2001's fans and reviewers are superficially aware that the movie has a certain amount of symbolism. I have already mentioned three out-in-the-open symbols referring to *The Odyssey*: (1) the space voyage as a symbol of Odysseus's ocean voyage, (2) the death of all of Bowman's crewmen as the death of all Odysseus's crewmen, and (3) Hal's red eye as the eye of the one-eyed cyclops. Almost everyone seems to understand the symbolic meaning of the bone the first man uses as a club: it symbolizes tools, the use of which turns ape into man. Several movie critics, along with Birx, have referred to *2001*'s symbolization of ape, man, and overman—Nietzsche's three main stages of evolution (not counting worm).[25] Reviewers and analysts have made many people aware of the sexual symbolism in the earth-to-moon sequence.[26] One unpublished thinker—I'll discuss his ideas later—has more or less correctly identified Hal (the sinister computer) as God, although the spaceship Discovery should have been mentioned as part of the divine package. The breaking of the wine glass, definitely symbolic, has come up for discussion, even if no previous analyst has correctly discerned that it represents the death of a certain snake. And in a vague sort of way, thousands of moviegoers have surely guessed that *2001* has lots of other symbols, hidden or inscrutable though they may seem to be.

But these insights barely scratch the surface of *2001*'s symbolism. Neither the depth and breadth of Kubrick's symbolism nor the meanings of the most important symbols have been recognized. Even in the few cases where specific symbols have been detected, the interpretations have generally been oversimplified, often to the point of superficiality. Modest oversimplification occurs when an interpreter identifies Hal as the cyclops but overlooks related symbols depicting (*a*) the stake with which Odysseus put out the monster's eye, (*b*) the jabbing and twisting—a la Odysseus—of the stake symbol, (*c*) a biblical character who toppled another giant the same way—by attacking its forehead—and (*d*) the monster's victims. Massive oversimplification occurs when Kubrick's symbolization of Nietzsche's evolutionary progression is reduced to (1) non-tool-using ape symbolizes ape, (2) tool-using ape and Bowman symbolize man, and (3) star-child symbolizes overman. Nietzscheian evolution is much more involved than that, and Kubrick's symbolization of it is far more detailed, intricate, complicated, multifaceted, and subtle than the simple 1-2-3 sequence.

Other symbols have been recognized but misinterpreted. Contrary to what Geduld writes, the spherical moon lander that goes from the space station to the moon is not an ovum; it is a sperm cell that is about to fertilize (enter) the ovum, which is *the moon*.[27] And contrary to what Agel suggests, the wine glass's breaking at Bowman's last supper is not a Jewish symbol.[28] Agel is wrong when he writes (in shorthand for a picture caption): "While breaking of wine glass may have been to keep illusion of reality—Earthian Still Makes Mistakes—breaking of glass at wedding ceremony has long Judaic history, symbolizing destruction of Jerusalem temple in 70 A.D. *2001* could be viewed as a marriage of past, present, and future." But the wine glass symbolism is nothing remotely resembling that. The wine glass's falling and breaking (in a black-white-brilliant transformational context) symbolizes (1) God's fall from man's grace—Kubrick's upside down version of The Fall (God's casting man out of Eden)—and (2) a Zarathustran parable—a man decapitates a black serpent and then becomes brilliantly illuminated—that depicts the death of God and man's subsequent deification.

A PREVIEW OF COMING ATTRACTIONS

Lest there be doubt that *2001* really is as profoundly laden with allegorical symbols as I claim it is, let us preview three examples—one from each allegory. (I will discuss these symbols again, in more detail, in subsequent chapters so that those chapters can remain comprehensive.) The first allegory symbolically retells Homer's *The Odyssey*. We have already seen that, for purposes of this allegory, Hal (the malevolent computer) is the cyclops. Odysseus dispatches it with a stake through the eye in its forehead: the red-eyed computer that Bowman repeatedly stabs (with an elongated key, a stake symbol) inside the spaceship's forehead is the one-eyed monster that Odysseus stabs in the eye in its forehead.

But did you know that immediately before Odysseus went to the monster's land he stopped off at the country of the Lotus-eaters? Three of his crew went inland to *survey* the situation. They met the Lotus-eaters, ate the honeyed lotus, lost the will to return, and had to be dragged back to the ship and placed in irons. Now where do you suppose we can find symbols for three out-of-action crewmen in *2001*? Hint: In the televised BBC interview that astronauts Bowman and Poole watch while eating dinner, Bowman's three out-of-action crewmen are identified as "the survey team."

The second allegory pokes fun at Clarke's theory that a symbiosis—a thoroughgoing interdependency—of man and machine will arise in the future. Kubrick caricatures this theory by creating Hal-Discovery, the brain-body symbiosis in which the brain (the computer) is essentially human and the body (the spaceship) is a machine, though a remarkably human-looking one. Kubrick makes Hal-Discovery humanoid in many ways. One of these is sexual *conception, gestation, and birth*. After the coupling of the phallic earth shuttle *Orion* with the female space station, a sperm cell (spherical moon lander) travels to the ovum (moon); the ovum opens and takes the sperm inside. *Conception*. A few scenes later Act 2 begins. "JUPITER MISSION: 18 MONTHS LATER" appears on the screen against a field of stars. Then an abstracted human form—the spaceship Discovery, with its bulbous head, three mouths (each one capable of sticking out its tongue), mod sunglasses, segmented spine, tailbone, and three pairs of excretory orifices (one pair per mouth)—slowly cruises into the universe, headfirst, from the left side of the screen. The words "18 months later" symbolize *gestation*: the postconception gestation period of the newborn male humanoid was 18 months! And his slowly cruising into view—headfirst, horizontally, in the usual human manner—is his *birth*, his dramatic entry into the starry universe. In case your arithmetic is a bit rusty,

$18 = 2 \times 9$, where 9 months is the gestation period of humans. Hal is twice as smart as humans, so naturally he took twice as long to ripen. (Yes, Kubrick does have a sense of humor.)

The third allegory depicts Nietzsche's book *Thus Spake Zarathustra*. One of the book's characters is called the rope dancer. A rope dancer is a person who *walks*, dances, or performs acrobatics on a tightrope. In *2001*, Frank Poole (Bowman's colleague, second in command) is the rope dancer. How do we know? There are several symbolic clues, but the one I will use as an example of a Kubrick symbol is his ten-letter name. It is what I call a 90 percent anagram. An anagram is a word or phrase formed by rearranging the letters of another word or phrase. Rearrange the last 9 of the 10 letters of [F]rank Poole and you get the last 9 of the 10 letters of "[W]alk on rope." Incidentally, hidden meanings can also be found in the names of Heywood R. Floyd, Elena, Dave Bowman, and Hal, although none of these names is another anagram. Moreover, TMA-1 (= TMA-ONE), the official name of the moon monolith, *is* another anagram. It alludes to a wooden horse, contrasted with a flesh-and-blood horse. (Why not stop and work that one out by yourself right now? Hint: The fourth and fifth letters can be used to spell NO.)

The three symbols just revealed are meant to whet your appetite. Over 200 others wait to be savored. Four of the next five chapters will be devoted to identifying *2001*'s symbols, explaining them and (where applicable) their literary antecedents, and fitting them together in coherent narrative patterns. For a few symbols, complete confidence about their reality or interpretation is not possible; the interpretations are tentative. But once you catch onto what Kubrick is doing and learn what to look for, you can see unmistakable symbols everywhere. And you can recognize (from the literature) or deduce (from the context and from analogy) their meanings. Watching *2001* becomes great fun. The next time you see the movie, you're going to enjoy it as you've never enjoyed it before. Also, you're going to understand it. Before probing deeper into the three allegories and analyzing their symbols, we need to review the surface story—the movie taken at face value. We also need to clarify the obscure and ambiguous events, particularly those of part 3, which deviates from literalism to tell the *surface* story symbolically and surrealistically. (This is not what allegories normally do.) Chapter 2 handles these tasks. The next four chapters explain the three allegories and explore their symbols; the Zarathustra material is voluminous and requires two chapters. Chapter 3 deals with the Odysseus allegory, chapter 4 with the man-machine symbiosis allegory, and chapters 5 and 6 with the Zarathustra allegory. The last chapter, chapter 7, presents my evaluation of *2001*.

NOTES

1. Jerome Agel, ed., *The Making of Kubrick's* 2001 (New York: New American Library, 1970); Carolyn Geduld, *Filmguide to* 2001: A Space Odyssey (Bloomington: Indiana University Press, 1973); Arthur C. Clarke, *The Lost Worlds of* 2001 (Boston: Gregg Press, 1979); Piers Bizony, 2001*: Filming the Future* (London: Aurum Press, 1994); David G. Stork, ed., *Hal's Legacy:* 2001*'s Computer as Dream and Reality* (Cambridge: MIT Press, 1997); and Stephanie Schwam, ed., *The Making of* 2001: A Space Odyssey (New York: Modern Library, 2000).

2. Roger Ebert, *Roger Ebert's Movie Home Companion*, 1st ed. (Kansas City, Mo.: Andrews, McMeel & Parker, 1984), 390–91.

3. Ibid., 390.

4. Roger Ebert, "2001: A Space Odyssey" (website movie review), www.suntimes.com/ Ebert/old_movies/space_odyssey.html, p. 3.

5. Roger Ebert, ed., *Roger Ebert's Book of Film* (New York: W. W. Norton, 1997), 779–80.

6. Rita Kempley, "American Film Institute's Pick of the Flicks," *Washington Post*, 17 June 1998, D1 and D8; Russell Watson and Corie Brown, "The 100 Best of 100 Years," *Newsweek Extra: 2000*, June 1998, 17–20.

7. Joe Blades and the Editors of Consumer Reports Books, *Guide to Movies on Video Cassette* (Mount Vernon, NY: Consumers Union, 1986), 255.

8. Bizony, *Filming the Future*, 18.

9. Pauline Kael, *For Keeps* (New York: Dutton, 1994), 222–23.

10. Geduld, *Filmguide to* 2001, 30.

11. New Movies, "2001: A Space Odyssey," *Time*, 19 April 1968, 91–93.

12. Glenn Man, *Radical Visions: American Film Renaissance, 1967–1976* (Westport, CT: Greenwood Press, 1994), 53, 56, 54 (my italics). Man supports his position by quoting a statement by Kubrick that "ambiguity . . . was inevitable" in *2001* (54). But since *ambiguous* merely means that something is subject to more than one interpretation, Kubrick's statement cannot be viewed as denying that *2001* has definitive answers to "the figurative associations strung out over the entire film text" (53). Allegory and its figurative (metaphorical) elements, by their very nature, have more than one meaning—the surface story meaning and the figurative meaning. Some of the metaphorical symbols in *2001* have four meanings, three of them figurative. The material is ambiguous, yes, but definitive interpretations—meanings intended by Kubrick—exist, at least where the allegorical meanings are concerned and in large measure for the surface story as well.

13. Friedrich Nietzsche, *Thus Spake Zarathustra*, trans. Thomas Common, rev. with introduction and notes by H. James Birx (Buffalo: Prometheus, 1993), 35.

14. Clarke, *Lost Worlds,* 38.

15. Geduld, *Filmguide to* 2001*,* 68.

16. For maps and illustrations showing the location and layout of Troy, see Caroline Alexander, "Echoes of the Heroic Age," *National Geographic* 196, no. 6 (December 1999), 54–78.

17. Arthur C. Clarke, *2001: A Space Odyssey* (New York: Signet, 1968), 147.

18. Ibid., 173–74.

19. Nietzsche, *Zarathustra*, 180.

20. Ibid., 301, 341.

21. Ibid., 56.

22. Ibid., 35, 36.

23. Theodore M. Bernstein, *The Careful Writer: A Modern Guide to English Usage* (New York: Atheneum, 1985), 393.

24. Norman Friedman, "Allegory," in *Princeton Encyclopedia of Poetry and Poetics*, ed. Alex Preminger, Frank J. Warnke, and O. B. Hardison, Jr. (Princeton, N J.: Princeton University Press, 1974), 12.

25. John Allen, untitled 1968 review of *2001*, in Agel, ed., *Making* 2001, 229–34; Joseph Gelmis, untitled 1969 re-review of *2001*, in Agel, ed., *Making* 2001, 269; David G. Hoch, "Mythic Patterns in *2001: A Space Odyssey*," *Journal of Popular Culture* 4, no. 4 (Spring 1971), 961; and H. James Birx, introduction to Nietzsche, *Zarathustra*, 23.

26. Joseph Morgenstern, "Kubrick's Cosmos" (review), *Newsweek*, 15 April 1968, 97; Joseph Gelmis, untitled 1968 review of *2001*, in Agel, ed., *Making* 2001, 264–65; Geduld, *Filmguide to* 2001, 44; Roger Ebert, *Movie Companion* (1984), 390; and Bizony, *Filming the Future*, 16.

27. Geduld, *Filmguide to* 2001, 48.

28. Agel, ed., *Making* 2001, 155.

Chapter 2

The Surface Story

The surface story is what is in plain sight, the story you see on the screen. It can be taken literally as a story in its own right, except that in *2001*'s case the literalism is tempered with surrealism and symbolism in the last part, where even the surface story is told symbolically. Because *2001* is an allegory—really three allegories in one—the surface story must also be given figurative or metaphorical interpretations. The surface story contains a continuing series of symbols—characters, things, events, names, and so on—that collectively tell an entirely different story, hidden below the surface. In a well-done allegory, the surface story should be entertaining—emotionally, intellectually, visually, or otherwise—but don't forget that the real point of the allegory is the hidden story (or, in *2001*'s case, stories). The surface story is secondary.

Secondary, but not unimportant. With *2001*, people don't even know the allegory is there. So most of the discussion and controversy *2001* has generated concerns the surface story. People don't understand it. They don't know what the four monoliths are or how they fit into the story. Neither are they sure whether alien beings—extraterrestrials—are operating behind the scenes or, alternatively, supernatural entities are at work. Most of all, people are baffled by the scenes that take place beyond Jupiter—the tunnel of lights, the cosmic art gallery, the strange planet in a faraway part of the universe, the bizarre hotel room where unexplained and impossible things happen, and the earth-sized star-child gazing at the earth (or is it the aliens' planet?) in the final scene.

This chapter has two purposes. One is to clarify the surface story. You are going to learn what the monoliths are, who put them there, what is going on in the last part, and what happens to the hero, Dave Bowman. The second purpose is to provide context for the symbols that will be explained in the following chapters. Memories need to be refreshed. The symbols and what they represent will be more easily understood if their places in the surface story are recalled. In the chapters dealing with the three allegories, some of this surface story material will necessarily be repeated, generally in more detail. But this chapter's start-to-finish review and interpretation of the surface story remain necessary for seeing the later material in perspective.

THE BASIC NARRATIVE

The surface story tells of

(1) a tall, domino-shaped black monolith's mysteriously appearing in Africa 4 million years ago,

(2) ape's evolution into man after physical contact with this monolith,

(3) man's discovery in our time of another monolith, buried under the surface of the moon crater Tycho,

(4) space program official Heywood Floyd's trip from earth to the moon to inspect the monolith, which he touches,

(5) the monolith's beaming a powerful signal toward Jupiter during the inspection,

(6) the spaceship Discovery's mission to Jupiter to find the target of that signal,

(7) astronaut Frank Poole's murder by Discovery's humanoid computer, Hal,

(8) mission commander Dave Bowman's desperate but successful battle with Hal in outer space,

(9) Discovery's arrival at Jupiter,

(10) Bowman's sighting of a third black monolith, floating in Jupiter space,

(11) Bowman's taking a one-man utility pod outside in an apparent attempt to reach and inspect the monolith,

(12) Bowman's being pulled into a fantastic tunnel of lights that seems to transport him almost instantly to another part of the universe,

(13) Bowman's seeing all kinds of strange cosmic wonders at the far end of the tunnel and then skimming over the surface of a planet,

(14) Bowman's sudden and unexplained materialization, still in his pod, within a cagelike hotel room, seemingly provided by the aliens responsible for the monoliths,

(15) Bowman's rapid aging in the hotel room and then his rebirth as or metamorphosis into a radiantly illuminated baby, encased in a

transparent globe and apparently the first member of a new humanoid race, and

(16) the star-child's return to earth, where as an earth-sized object he shines on and gazes at the planet, whose lone moon (cratered and recognizable from the movie's opening scene) identifies the planet as earth.

Kubrick presents this story in three titled parts: (1) "The Dawn of Man," (2) "Jupiter Mission: 18 Months Later," and (3) "Jupiter and Beyond the Infinite." Part 1 consists of two episodes: (*a*) the title episode, in which ape evolves into man, and (*b*) the moon monolith episode, in which Heywood R. Floyd travels from earth to the moon, inspects the newly discovered monolith, and experiences its signal to Jupiter. The two episodes are substantively independent and could have been separately titled. The obvious reason Kubrick left Floyd's trip under the "Dawn of Man" title is this: flashing a title on the screen before the second episode would have interrupted an artistically and symbolically important transition—the transition of a primitive weapon into a space-age weapon, an orbiting nuclear bomb. Part 2 begins with the start of the Jupiter mission and ends with the arrival of the spaceship at Jupiter. Part 3 covers the rest of the movie, beginning with Bowman's encounter with the third monolith near Jupiter.

The Dawn of Man and Dr. Floyd's Trip to the Moon

Part 1 begins with the morning sun peeking over the African horizon, clearly symbolizing part 1's title, "The Dawn of Man." Kubrick then portrays the plight of the prehuman apes. They squabble with other animals over food, get killed by lions, huddle together in fear at night, and engage in intergroup fights over a waterhole. Then one day that baffling black monolith appears on the desert. It is standing upright, with its longest dimension running vertically up and down. The clan leader, named Moonwatcher in Clarke's novel but nameless in the film, approaches and touches the monolith. The other apes follow suit.

Shortly thereafter Moonwatcher is inspired to pick up a leg bone of a dead-and-devoured animal and use it experimentally to smash the other bones of the animal's skeleton; the skull gets crushed last—with an extra-powerful blow. Kubrick cuts to the monolith and then back to Moonwatcher to establish a connection. Realizing that the bone can be used as a club—a tool!—Moonwatcher becomes a tool-user. (Tool use was long regarded as a definitive characteristic of man.) He leads his clan, now armed with bone-clubs, back to the waterhole for another confrontation with the rival clan. In the film's first postmonolith battle, the

Battle at the Waterhole, Moonwatcher clubs to death the rival clan's leader. The tool-users, no longer apes but men, win. Moonwatcher triumphantly flings his bone-club—his *primitive* weapon—high into the blue sky, where it . . .

. . . becomes a *modern* weapon, a nuclear bomb, orbiting high above the earth. To be honest, I had thought that the space vehicle the club becomes was a spaceship. But Frederick Ordway, a technical consultant on the film, writes that "we cut to the orbiting bombs."[1] By way of confirmation, Walker writes that "an early draft of the film script intended to make the point, via [a] narrator, that a nuclear stalemate had been reached between the United States and the Soviet Union, each of whom has a nuclear bomb orbiting the globe which can be triggered by remote control."[2] He notes that Russian and American markings can still be seen on the first two bombs. Bizony, who interviewed Clarke and Ordway, also says the objects are bombs, "weapons of thermonuclear destruction."[3] And in Clarke's novel, nuclear bombs orbit the earth.

Kubrick next cuts to a long, narrow, winged, self-propelled space shuttle, the *Orion*, representing an evolutionary step beyond the orbiting (non-self-propelled) bombs. On board the *Orion* as its only passenger is Dr. Heywood R. Floyd, a high official with the National Council of Astronautics. Floyd is chairman of the Council in Clarke's novel but seems to be subordinate to an offstage Dr. Howell (chairman?) in the movie. But Floyd does later speak for the Council and, still later, he briefs Bowman (the Jupiter recording); he seems to be at least a Council member.

The *Orion* is heading from earth to an orbiting space station. The space station is a combination hotel (Hilton, no less) and transfer point for travelers going to the moon. (The winged shuttle can't land on the moon, which has no atmosphere.) Consisting of two 4-spoke wheels connected by a short axle, the station rotates slowly to provide artificial gravity through centrifugal force. Its axle has a sexually symbolic slot for the shuttle to enter.

The *Orion* docks. (Here Kubrick keeps things subtle: we see the approach, but we don't actually see *Orion* penetrate the axle.) Dr. Floyd exits, rides up a spoke in a circular elevator, and steps off into the space station's interior—in the rim of one of the two wheels. After meeting a man named Miller and passing through security (voiceprint identification), he phones his daughter "Squirt" back on earth—while a symbolic optical illusion makes the earth seem to move in a circle outside the phone booth window. Then he encounters a group of four Russian scientists. He knows one of them, Elena; she mentions that her husband is off in the Baltic. (Two more symbols just flew past you.) One Russian, Andrey Smyslov, queries

Floyd about rumors of an epidemic at Clavius, the American base on the moon. After being evasive and then getting pressed, Floyd finally replies, "I'm sorry, Dr. Smyslov, but, uh, I'm really not at liberty to discuss this." He then excuses himself.

The next shot shows the moon lander on its way from the space station to the moon. The lander is a sphere with four rocket clusters on the underside that give it an invisible *tail* (symbolism) of exhaust gas; viewed from almost any angle it has two lit-up windows that look like eyes and suggest life. (Any resemblance to a sperm cell is purely intentional.) Floyd is aboard, again as the only passenger. As the lander descends to the moon, it heads for a relatively flat dome, the closed circular entrance to an underground hangar. Eight pie-wedge-shaped teeth—the hangar doors—pull back from the center of the circle into the entrance's outer rim; the lander settles into the hangar. Now the lander is inside the spherical moon. (Think about that: If the lander is a sperm cell, what does the moon—a sphere, bigger than the sperm—symbolize?)

The next scene is a briefing attended by Floyd and eleven others. Floyd has come from earth to learn more about something—we aren't told what—that has been found on the moon. Before being briefed, Floyd says a few words. He first relays Dr. Howell's "congratulations on your discovery, which may well prove to be the most significant in the history of science." He then asserts "the need for complete security in this matter." Why? The reason seems half-baked and gobbledygookish: "You're all aware of the extremely grave potential for cultural shock and social disorientation contained in this present situation, if the facts were prematurely and suddenly made public without adequate preparation and conditioning." Floyd then states the purpose of his visit: to gather facts and opinions for incorporation into a report to the Council "recommending when and how the news should eventually be announced."

That's all we learn from the briefing scene. We don't hear the real briefing that follows. (Actually we do learn one more thing: the meeting sets a world's record for the most sentences beginning with "Well.")

(The bureaucratese, banal talk, and near gibberish in the briefing scene suggest that its surface story content is relatively unimportant. What counts is that a briefing is being symbolized. Pause a few moments and see if you can guess what character in one of the three allegorized narratives is being symbolically briefed on what subject having nothing to do with moons and monoliths.)

After the briefing, Floyd takes a low-altitude rocket vehicle, the moon bus, from the base at Clavius, a huge crater, to the smaller crater Tycho, north of Clavius. (These are real places on the moon.) Two colleagues—

Halvorsen and Michaels—accompany him. Michaels brings out some charts, including one marked TMA-1. TMA stands for Tycho Magnetic Anomaly. (It also stands for that "wooden horse" anagram mentioned in chapter 1.) It seems that an intense magnetic field, too intense to come from even a big nickel-iron meteorite, has been found at Tycho. The Americans have excavated and have found something. Halvorsen elaborates: "The evidence seems completely conclusive that it hasn't been covered up by natural erosion or other forces. It seems to have been deliberately buried." They have no idea what it is. But they have determined its age: 4 million years. (Clarke changes this to 3 million years in the novel.)

The moon bus lands. We next see a shot of the TMA-1 excavation. It is night; the excavation is illuminated with floodlights. Six men wearing space suits come in from the right and descend a ramp leading into the hole. Kubrick now gives us a close-up of the TMA object, which was fairly distant in the first shot. TMA-1 is another upright black monolith, just like the one the apes found in Africa! Dr. Floyd, like Moonwatcher before him, touches the monolith.

The faces aren't visible under the helmets, so how do we know it is Floyd? The fact has to be deduced from the context. Floyd came to the moon alone. The other five people are moon personnel and presumably have already examined the monolith. If you're still not convinced, you have the word of Bizony. He had access to the script and writes that it is Floyd who touches the monolith.[4] (From the standpoint of the Zarathustra allegory, this fact is critically important. The character symbolized by Floyd is symbolically absorbing whatever the monolith symbolically represents. And what he absorbs will inspire him to create Hal-Discovery, who symbolizes God.)

Five members of the group line up in front of the monolith for a picture; the sixth person has the camera. Suddenly the monolith emits a piercing, high-pitched signal that (we learn much later) is beamed at Jupiter. Heard through speakers inside the space helmets, the signal inflicts severe distress on the members of the inspection team. They retreat in apparent pain and try unsuccessfully to cover their helmeted ears.

Then we see an upward-angled shot of the sun beginning to rise over the top of the monolith. The long lunar night is over. The sun's rays are striking the now-uncovered monolith for the first time in 4 million years. Whether through light or through heat, the sun has triggered an internal sensor that tells the monolith it has finally been unburied. And the monolith has relayed the news to an unknown destination. Somewhere out there aliens have learned that the apes and their civilization have evolved to the point where they can travel to the moon and detect underground magnetic objects. End of part 1.

The Jupiter Mission

Part 2 begins with its title, "Jupiter Mission: 18 Months Later." The title is projected onto the screen over a shot of a dark, star-filled universe. Then a spaceship—the Discovery—slowly emerges into view from the left, head-first. (You can take the word "head" literally: Discovery has a big spherical head, which is mounted on the end of a segmented spine and which has three mouths; the mouths are situated beneath eyes that are hidden behind wide-band mod sunglasses.) We are witnessing the birth of Hal-Discovery; he is entering the universe from an offscreen womb. Hal is the brain and central nervous system—a conscious, sentient, thinking, talking computer—and Discovery is the body, the spaceship. Hal-Discovery's birth is taking place 18 months after the spermlike moon lander entered (fertilized) the ovumlike moon; the gestation period was 18 months. (Part 2's subtitle, "18 Months Later," is a symbol—a symbol referring to gestation and birth.)

This fertilization-gestation-birth symbolism was previewed in chapter 1 and will be looked at again in its allegorical contexts in chapters 4 and 5. But right now we need to see the symbolism in its chronological context so it can be fully understood and appreciated. The sexual reproduction imagery isn't just a Kubrick joke. It is fundamentally important to both the man-machine symbiosis allegory and the Zarathustra allegory. In the sym-biosis allegory, it is the single most important piece of symbolism signify-ing that the new humanoid machine species symbolized by Hal-Discovery really is living and humanoid. And in the Zarathustra allegory, it is the sin-gle most important piece of symbolism signifying that Nietzsche's God (Hal-Discovery) is the image of man—created by man *in his own image*. Make no mistake, this machine is *humanoid*. And there is more: concep-tion, gestation, and birth are three links in a chain of causation that leads to a hilarious yet marvelously disguised joke.

Kubrick next presents a series of spaceship interior scenes. In the first, Dr. Frank Poole, second in command, is jogging along inside the rim of a wheel-like exercise centrifuge. Poole and Dr. David Bowman, mission commander, then sit down to eat machine-dispensed meals—after Bowman burns his fingers while "looting" the food-dispensing machine. While eat-ing, they watch a BBC telecast. BBC is carrying an interview with Bow-man and Poole, recorded earlier through long-distance television. (Bow-man and Poole watch themselves on their individual screens.) We learn that the spaceship has a crew of five men plus Hal, the HAL-9000 computer, identified as "the sixth member of the crew." Three crewmen, "the survey team," were put aboard in hibernation to conserve, in Bowman's words, "our life support capability—basically food and air." (That explanation is an allegorical ploy. The three men were really put into hibernation so they could symbolize the three members of Odysseus's crew—an earlier survey team—who became disabled when they ate lotus.)

The BBC announcer proceeds to describe and then interview Hal, the extremely anthropomorphic-anthropopathic onboard computer. Hal mentions *proudly* that he is "foolproof and incapable of error." He says he *enjoys* working with people, and he refers to himself as "a *conscious* entity." (That's three human mental characteristics.) Asked if Hal has emotions, Bowman replies, "Well, he acts like he has *genuine emotions*."

The next three scenes provide more evidence that Hal is essentially human: he is a valet, a chess player, an art critic, and a clinical psychologist. We first see Poole relaxing under a sunlamp. Hal informs him that a birthday transmission is coming in from his parents. At Poole's request, Hal moves the lounge in closer to the TV screen. In the next scene, Hal beats Poole in a game of chess. Bowman's scene arrives. Hal asks to see—he has a big red eye that sees—some sketches Bowman has made of the hibernating astronauts. "That's a very nice rendering, Dave. I think you've improved a great deal." Hal then begins asking questions about the mission's secrecy and about "rumors about something being dug up on the moon." Bowman isn't fooled: "You're working up your crew psychology report."

Hal sheepishly admits this, then abruptly changes the subject: "Just a moment. Just a moment. I've just picked up a fault in the AE-35 unit. It's going to fail within 72 hours." The AE-35 unit is a component of the external antenna system. Mission control (on earth) okays a plan to replace the defective unit with a spare. We next see Bowman, now wearing a space suit, go to the pod bay, a room where three small, spherical utility pods repose. The pods are for outside work. Each sits in front of its own circular door—one of the three anthropomorphic mouths in Discovery's circular face. While Poole watches at a monitoring station, Bowman climbs into the center pod.

Kubrick interrupts the action with an external shot of the spaceship. From out of nowhere, two meteoroids come hurtling past. Near misses. (This is symbolism depicting an event from the Odyssey. If you check the list of Odyssey events in chapter 1, you should be able to figure out which one it is. Kubrick is working this event in at a spot where it harmonizes reasonably well with other events.) The rock storm creates apprehension when Bowman goes outside, although no more meteoroids appear.

Bowman's pod bay door opens, a pod-launching ramp slides forward with the pod at its tip, and the pod rises over the top of Hal-Discovery's head. (Kubrick joke: You have just seen Hal stick out his tongue and blow a bubble. The joke has a point: Hal is playful, just like a human.) Positioning the pod near the antenna, Bowman opens the pod door, spacewalks over to the antenna, and replaces the AE-35 unit.

Back inside the spaceship, the two astronauts run exhaustive tests on the "defective" unit. It seems to be in perfect condition. Hal suggests that they put the unit back in operation and let it fail. "It should then be a simple matter to track down the cause." Mission control approves the idea but, at the same time, delivers some ominous news. All data have been analyzed by a twin HAL-9000 computer back on earth, and "our preliminary findings indicate that your on-board Niner Triple-Zero computer is in error predicting the fault." Hal greets the news with skepticism: "This sort of thing has cropped up before, and it has always been due to human error." (Notice Hal's human personality: blame the other guy.)

Bowman contrives an excuse to go inside one of the pods with Poole for a private discussion, where Hal can't hear. They talk about shutting down Hal if it turns out that Hal was mistaken—that is, if the original unit doesn't fail within 72 hours. Looking in through the pod window with his red eye, Hal reads the lips of Bowman and Pool. He now knows their innermost thoughts.

And he acts on them. When Poole gets in a pod and goes outside to put the original AE-35 unit back in place, Hal waits until the astronaut leaves his pod and begins his spacewalk. Then, by remote control, Hal brings the pod up behind Poole and severs Poole's air hose with the pod's mechanical hands.

At the monitoring station inside the spaceship, Bowman realizes something has gone wrong. Already wearing a space suit but without a helmet, he rushes to the pod bay and orders Hal to prepare another pod. Before getting in, he asks Hal what happened. Hal lies: "I'm sorry, Dave. I don't have enough information." Bowman takes his rescue pod outside and manages to gather Poole's drifting body into the pod's mechanical arms.

The scene switches to the three hibernating astronauts. As Hal's red eye watches, an electric warning sign goes on: "Life Functions Critical." Then the six vital-signs graph lines of each hibernator's life-support system monitor go flat. The sign changes: "Life Functions Terminated." Hal has murdered three more astronauts. Only Bowman is left.

Meanwhile, Bowman has maneuvered his rescue pod back to its closed pod bay door. "Open the pod bay doors, please, Hal." No response. Bowman tries several other channels but still gets no answer. Finally, Hal does acknowledge that he hears. Hal's reply: "I'm sorry, Dave. I'm afraid I can't do that." Further conversation reveals that Hal knows about the plan to disconnect him. He isn't going to let Bowman back inside.

Bowman sees an alternative: "All right, Hal. I'll go in through the emergency airlock."

Hal taunts him: "Without your space helmet, Dave, you're going to find that rather difficult." (Holding his breath long enough for a slow spacewalk from the pod to the airlock could by itself be a fatal problem. But the bigger problem is staying alive in a vacuum. According to Clarke, research with chimpanzees suggests that a man could survive in a vacuum for about ten seconds.[5])

Bowman conceives a plan. It involves the pod's emergency-eject system. He releases Poole's body and moves his pod to a position outside the emergency airlock. The pod won't fit into the airlock, but maybe he can get in. After opening the airlock's door with the pod's arms and hands, Bowman turns the pod around so its door (in back) faces the airlock opening. He then activates the pod's eject system and blasts himself into the airlock. Luckily, while bouncing around inside the airlock, he is able to grasp the "emergency hatch close" lever. The hatch closes, and air floods the airlock. No more vacuum. He can breathe again.

Now Bowman has the upper hand. He moves resolutely to the chamber holding Hal's brain. From a compartment outside the chamber door, he grabs an elongated service key, somewhat like an Allen wrench. (Think about it and you will see a resemblance between this key and the stake Odysseus used to disable the cyclops monster.) Once inside the brain chamber, Bowman repeatedly *plunges* the key into slots beside Hal's higher-brain-function modules, giving the key a *twist* (just as Odysseus did to the cyclops with the stake). Hal begs Bowman to stop, but Bowman knows better. As Hal winds down, he begins to sing "Daisy, Daisy," which he learned during his infancy.[6] (One more human characteristic: senility.)

Hal's voice gradually gets lower and slower, and then his higher brain functions go dead. (Nietzsche's most famous quotation has just been dramatized.) Almost immediately, a prerecorded message from Heywood Floyd cuts in. Floyd declares, "Now that you are in Jupiter space, and the entire crew is revived, it can be told to you." He then tells his assumed audience — actually just Bowman — about the discovery of the moon monolith, the signal it beamed toward Jupiter, and the purpose of the mission. We don't hear the details of that purpose, but we can easily guess. Discovery's crew was supposed to investigate whatever they could find near Jupiter that was the target of the monolith's transmission. End of part 2.

Jupiter and Beyond

Part 3, the last part, is "Jupiter and Beyond the Infinite." ("Infinite" sounds so abstract as to be devoid of any real meaning. But it is really a symbol, derived from theology, for God, whom Hal-Discovery represents in the Zarathustra allegory.) In the opening shot we see another black monolith. The first two monoliths were stationary and upright, but this one is moving and horizontal. It floats slowly in front of Jupiter as the spaceship approaches the planet. Jupiter's five moons also come into view. (Jupiter actually has sixteen moons, but five were apparently all Kubrick could readily handle and were all that he needed for symbolic purposes.[7]) Several more glorious shots of Jupiter, its moons, the monolith, and the spaceship follow. Bowman seems to see the monolith passing in front of him. Deciding to investigate—that's what he's here for—he departs from the spaceship in the remaining pod.

Somehow, Jupiter's moons have come into vertical alignment, with Jupiter sitting at the bottom of the stack. The monolith moves toward the moons; Bowman apparently is in pursuit. As Bowman watches, the monolith disappears in the distance among the moons. He shifts his gaze upward to a point well above the highest moon. Suddenly, multicolored lights burst from that point, streaking toward the camera—Bowman's eyes—and past it on both peripheries. We sense that Bowman has been drawn into what has come to be called the tunnel of lights.[8] The pod is no longer under his control. He is being transported somewhere at fantastic speed.

Finally, Bowman emerges from the tunnel into a surrealistic cosmos. Celestial wonders—exploding stars, galaxies, comets, ethereal membranes—are everywhere. Soon he is skimming over the surface of a planet. Its features glow in all sorts of changing two-tone color combinations. Intermittently, but with increasing frequency, we see close-ups of one of Bowman's eyes, blinking, and again in those changing two-tone combinations. And then, without visible explanation, the pod is resting on the floor inside *2001*'s famous hotel room. (The room itself refuses to disclose whether it is a hotel room or just an ornate bedroom, perhaps in some mansion, but a subsequent scene shows Bowman dining at a hotel room-service cart; two of its four legs have wheels.)

Our first view of the room is through the pod window. Next we see several shots of the room from outside the pod, with Bowman still inside. The floor is glass, divided into rectangles; all illumination comes from below. The walls display expensive-looking paintings with strangely arched tops; statuettes stand in wall recesses, again arched. Period furniture is everywhere. A large bed projects from one of the two longer walls. The wall to the bed's left (head-to-foot perspective) has a bathroom door. The pod stands in the corner formed by the wall opposite the bed and the wall opposite the bathroom door.

Bowman looks out the pod window again, and this time he *sees himself*, standing in the room in his *orange* space suit. A close-up of the orange Bowman's face, seen through his helmet visor, shows he has aged: his hair is gray, and his skin is wrinkled. A shot from behind the second Bowman shows him looking at the pod's corner of the room. The pod has vanished. The new (older) Bowman explores the room and then checks out the bathroom, which has an interesting privy-style toilet bench. Hearing a clicking sound, the second Bowman returns to the main room and sees a third Bowman eating dinner at a not-there-before table in the corner where the pod had been.

This latest Bowman is older still—he has white hair—and is dressed entirely in *black*. He hears something, looks toward the bathroom, sees nothing—the second Bowman has vanished—and turns back to his dinner. But he has second thoughts. He gets up, walks to the bathroom, inspects it, finds nothing, and returns to the dinner table. After taking another bite of his food, he reaches for a sauce dish (béarnaise sauce?) and accidentally knocks his wine glass to the floor. It breaks. Bowman stares at the broken glass and then slowly shifts his attention to the bed. (Symbolism: his gaze shifts from cause to effect.)

Lying in bed is a fourth Bowman, even older—bald, shriveled, and seemingly near death. This Bowman is wearing *white* pajamas. The camera switches to a side view of the new Bowman. Slowly, feebly, he extends his right arm toward the foot of the bed, lifting his head to see as he does so. And then a shot from behind the head of the bed shows what he is trying to reach—a fourth black monolith. It is upright, like the first two, and is standing on the floor at the foot of the bed. An angled shot from beyond the foot of the bed shows the monolith and the bed, with Bowman still in it. This shot is followed by a from-the-headboard perspective showing just the monolith.

The next shot shows the bed, viewed from the monolith. The old man is gone. In his place, as though put there by some miracle, is a baby, encased in a glowing transparent globe and surrounded by light. The implication—just about everyone has grasped this—is that Bowman has been (or is about to be) reborn as, or has metamorphosed into, the first member of a new, higher race.

The baby has come to be known as the star-child, the name Arthur Clarke gives him in the novel. (Clarke spells it Star-Child.) The camera, in birth symbolism parallel to that which began part 2, glides from the bed into the blackness of the monolith; the screen becomes black. And then we see the cratered moon against a starry black sky. The camera slowly moves right, and the earth with its swirling cloud cover comes into view. To the left of the screen is a glow, such as might come from the sun. As the camera shifts left the star-child, still encased in a transparent globe but now bigger than the earth, becomes visible. He is gazing at and shining sunlike on the earth. Bowman has returned. A final shot shows the face of the star-child, looking into the camera (= shining on the audience). End of movie.

FUZZY AREAS OF THE NARRATIVE

Reviewers, other analysts, and the public have been troubled by four main questions:

1. Are aliens operating behind the scenes?
2. What are the four black monoliths?
3. Why did Hal decide to kill the astronauts?
4. What is going on in part 3, especially at the end?

These questions can be answered by combining straightforward inference with information from Clarke's novel, which is based on the movie. By way of reservation, the novel is not a reliable source on all matters. It differs from the film in many areas, including the hotel-room sequence at the end. The novel also loses most of Kubrick's symbolism, and not just because so much of the symbolism is visual. Clarke apparently was not privy to most of Kubrick's symbols, although the truth may be that Clarke either wasn't interested in the allegorical part of the story or was respecting Kubrick's secrets.

Whatever the reason, Clarke *acts* as though he were only superficially familiar with Kubrick's symbolism. Take the broken wine glass. We shall see that it truly symbolizes a decapitated serpent used metaphorically in a parable in *Thus Spake Zarathustra*. But in an interview with Agel, Clarke suggests a different—and vague—explanation: "I think . . . breaking the wine glass was a cinematic gimmick. Stanley was listening to his inner demons at the time and they may have been telling him, 'What's a nice Jewish boy like you doing in a place like this.'" Agel goes on to explain that, in Judaism, glasses are broken to symbolize the destruction of the temple at Jerusalem in A.D. 70.[9]

Two of the many plot changes in the novel further illustrate Clarke's unreliability. Clarke concocts the myth that Hal had a "breakdown."[10] Hal supposedly became neurotic; he supposedly was torn between his impulse to be truthful and his instructions to keep the mission's purpose a secret from Bowman and Poole. But Kubrick has an entirely different slant, a symbolic one. Far from having a breakdown, Hal simply made *a mistake*. And the reason he made it was that Kubrick wanted to symbolize a common aphorism—I'll identify it later—that reveals Hal's humanity. It's part of the process of making Hal the image of man.

In another plot change, Hal tries to kill Bowman indoors—inside the spaceship—rather than outdoors. Bowman does not take a second pod and try to rescue Poole after Hal attacks Poole. But Kubrick had a symbolic reason for Bowman's going after Poole, a reason Clarke seems not to know. (Or is Clarke deliberately getting rid of the allegorical material?) When Bowman picks up Poole's body in Bowman's pod's arms, Kubrick is analogically symbolizing something Zarathustra did—something that identifies Bowman as Zarathustra and Poole as the rope dancer.

So, Clarke is not entirely reliable. But he is sometimes useful and can be consulted when his version, or his additional detail, is consistent with the movie. With that understanding in mind, we can turn to the four questions posed in the opening paragraph under this heading.

Aliens and Monoliths

The first two questions can be answered together, because aliens are definitely behind the four black monoliths. Here is some evidence:

- Clarke's short story "The Sentinel," on which *2001* is loosely based, makes it quite clear that the moon monolith was placed on the moon by aliens. Its purpose in both the short story and the movie is to allow aliens to monitor human progress.
- Clarke's novel has various direct and indirect references to the aliens. In the hotel room, for example, Bowman learns that "his hosts [the aliens] had based their ideas of terrestrial living upon TV programs."[11]
- Clarke's book *The Lost Worlds of* 2001, which is about ideas for the movie that weren't used, presents (from his "log") this idea: "Suddenly realized how the novel *should* end, with Bowman standing beside the alien ship."[12] also joked about the aliens: "One hilarious idea we *won't* use. Seventeen aliens—featureless black pyramids—riding in open cars down Fifth Avenue, surrounded by Irish cops."[13]
- David Stork, who interviewed insiders for his book *Hal's Legacy*, identifies the glittering octahedra Bowman encounters when he approaches the alien planet as "Kubrick and Clarke's extraterrestrials."[14]

As for the monoliths, they are devices built for various uses by the aliens, who are from another galaxy. We know their home is not in our galaxy because Bowman streaks past other galaxies on his way to the aliens' planet. Each monolith has a different use, although the first and fourth do much the same thing on different levels.

The First Monolith

The first monolith was planted by the aliens in Africa 4 million years ago. The timing can be deduced from information given to Heywood Floyd on the moon bus and later repeated in the prerecorded Jupiter message. Floyd says the moon monolith's age has been established as 4 million years. The African monolith must have been planted on the same alien visit to our solar system. We can deduce this from knowledge that the moon monolith's purpose is to notify the aliens of the outcome of their African monolith's work.

And what was that work? Kubrick leaves no doubt about the association between the first monolith and the apes' becoming tool-users. There is some sort of cause-and-effect linkage between the apes' finding and touching the monolith and their acquisition of intelligence—that is, their learning how to use tools. To avoid any possible doubt on this point, Kubrick went back and inserted a quick flashback to the monolith in the middle of the scene where Moonwatcher experimentally uses a bone as a club.[15]

Clarke provides additional detail. He says the African monolith is a device for probing minds, mapping bodies, evaluating potentials, and— most important—boosting intelligence.[16] Ape gets a shot of intelligence, figures out how to use tools (starting with the bone-club), and thereby evolves into man. The dawn of man was arranged by aliens.

The Second Monolith

The second monolith, found on the moon, imitates the one in Clarke's short story "The Sentinel." Both are monitoring and signaling devices. The second monolith was buried on the moon by the aliens at the same time they installed the first monolith in Africa. The aliens wanted to know if and when human civilization progressed to the point where men could travel to the moon and detect a magnetic object buried below the moon's surface. The monolith was designed to beam a signal to the aliens (indirectly, via the Jupiter relay station) when man unburied the device. Unburying the monolith would allow the sun to strike it, thereby activating the signal beam.

Frederick Ordway, who held the position of scientific adviser for the film, elaborates. Kubrick originally intended to have narration at certain points in the film. The narration for the third monolith alluded to the signal it received from the second: "For four million years, it had circled Jupiter, awaiting a moment of destiny that might never come. Now, the long wait was ending. On yet another world intelligence had been born and was escaping from its planetary cradle. An ancient experiment was about to reach its climax."[17] Although there is no direct reference to the aliens, it is clear that aliens are monitoring developments on earth.

The Third Monolith

The third monolith is the one orbiting Jupiter. The movie allows uncertainty about whether the monolith is in orbit, but it would probably have to be in order to remain in the same general location for eons. If the monolith weren't orbiting Jupiter, its tendency would be to either (*a*) surrender to gravity and crash into the sun or into Jupiter or (*b*) fly out of the solar system because of excess inertia or (*c*) be away from Jupiter most of the time in an elliptical orbit around both the sun and Jupiter. We also have Clarke's word. He says the monolith is in planetary orbit, although he has it circling Saturn rather than Jupiter (another difference between the movie and the novel).[18]

I said the monolith would *probably* have to be in orbit because another possibility exists. In theory, the monolith could be flying or hovering, using solar energy for power. And in fact it does fly off toward the Star Gate when it lures Bowman in that direction. Whether this maneuver is a temporary deviation from orbit or a sign that the device never was in orbit, we don't know.

Anyhow, the Jupiter monolith has two functions. First, it is a relay station for retransmitting to the aliens' planet the moon sentinel's signal, if and when that signal is transmitted. Second, it is the keeper of the Star Gate, a metaphorical door to an opening in space—a "wormhole" in Star Trek terminology.[19] That opening takes you to another part of the universe almost instantly, without being bothered by old-fashioned laws that forbid going faster than the speed of light. As gatekeeper, the monolith has super-high-tech capabilities that allow it to yank Bowman's pod into the opening and through the intergallactic corridor, the tunnel of lights.

The term Star Gate, by the way, comes from Clarke's novel.[20] It is not in the movie. To repeat, the gate is metaphorical, figurative. It is just an opening that leads to a corridor where different and unusual physical laws apply. The laws are necessary for faster-than-light science fiction space travel.

The Fourth Monolith

The fourth and last monolith is the one in the hotel room on the home planet of the aliens. This monolith is much like the first, but more powerful. The extra power has inspired a facetious comment by Geduld: "Apparently, better monoliths have been developing over the eons, too, and this one accomplishes its work with more finesse and speed than the original one on Earth."[21]

The hotel-room monolith, in short, is another device for boosting intelligence and accelerating—or maybe causing—evolution. At least that is a first approximation. Other evolutionary details besides intelligence might or might not be involved. Significant physical changes and powers might be involved too. In Clarke's novel, the last scene has the star-child detonating the nuclear bombs orbiting the earth. That's something you and I can't do, at least not by figuratively snapping our fingers.

But the exact nature of the evolutionary changes the monolith effects is ultimately irrelevant. Even Kubrick doesn't know exactly what the star-child is in the surface story; to him it is primarily a symbol, and its surface story details don't matter. All we have to understand is that the star-child is an evolutionary step beyond humans. It is something better than man.

Hoch's Interpretation

Before we leave the monoliths, a few words must be said about Hoch's interpretation of them. He says the monolith (the four viewed as one) "resembles" and is "like" a mythical (supernatural) entity, such as Paul Tillich's God above the God of theism.[22] But Hoch is wrong. To begin with, Tillich's God above God is a figurative God, humanity, rather than a supernatural entity.[23]

Even if we interpret Hoch as referring to a metaphysical or other supernatural entity, his interpretation is badly flawed. *2001* is science fiction, not fantasy; Arthur Clarke doesn't formulate supernaturalistic plots. *2001* is based on Clarke's short story "The Sentinel." In that story the title object is incontrovertibly a scientific device placed on the moon by aliens. In *2001*'s surface story, all four monoliths are likewise scientific, or at any rate science-based, devices created by scientifically advanced aliens. Clarke makes it plain in his novel that the first monolith, for example, is a device for (among other things) expanding and developing intelligence and that it was placed on earth by aliens. In chapter 3, I will show where the aliens actually appear in one scene in the surface story.

The monoliths, of course, are also *symbols*. But, except for the Odyssean Sirens, none of the things they symbolize is supernatural. As mentioned in chapter 1, the moon monolith symbolizes the Trojan Horse in the Odysseus allegory. In the man-machine symbiosis allegory, all of the monoliths symbolize milestones along the road of humanoid evolution. (The third monolith, which is not upright, is a *toppled* milestone, representing an evolutionary advance that led to a dead end.)

Why Did Hal Decide to Kill the Astronauts?

To judge by comments posted on several *2001* websites, many viewers are unsure why Hal decided to kill the astronauts. And some people think Hal deliberately lied when he said the AE-35 unit was going to fail—lied to lure the astronauts outside the spaceship where he could kill them. But Hal's subsequent actions refute the theory that he deliberately lied. At first, Hal really thought the AE-35 unit was going to fail. If he had been lying, he would have begun killing astronauts at the first opportunity, namely, when Bowman took the first space walk to replace the supposedly defective unit with a spare.

Only when the "defective" AE-35 unit was tested and found to be in perfect working order did Hal realize he had made a mistake. (As will be explained in chapter 3, Kubrick portrays Hal as a mistake maker because being a mistake maker has symbolic value in the last two allegories.) Later, Hal read Bowman's and Poole's lips and learned of the astronauts' plan to shut him down—in effect, kill him—if the original AE-35 unit did not fail after being put back in place. Now it was kill or be killed, because at this point Hal knew that the AE-35 unit was not defective and would not fail. So Hal decided to kill the astronauts. Hal's decision to kill was, in short, a matter of survival.

Can we be sure that, before killing Poole and the three hibernating astronauts, Hal recognized he was mistaken about the AE-35 unit? Absolutely. If Hal had still believed that the unit was going to fail (i.e., if he had still believed he was "foolproof and incapable of error"), he would have had no reason to kill the astronauts. Bowman and Poole weren't going to shut him down if his prediction proved to be correct—that is, if the AE-35 unit actually did fail. And if they weren't going to shut him down, he had no reason to kill them.

What Is Going on in Part 3?

Two things are responsible for most of the confusion in the final part of *2001*. One is the substitution of surrealism for realism. The other is the use of symbols to tell not just the allegorical stories, which are *supposed* to be hidden, but the surface story, which is not supposed to be hidden.

The Problem in More Detail

The *American Heritage College Dictionary* says that surrealism is "characterized by fantastic imagery and incongruous juxtapositions of subject matter." What Bowman sees, along with the colors he sees, on the way to the alien planet is certainly fantastic; so is what happens in the hotel room. What we see is obviously not reality but something abstracted from reality. Although some of the cosmic objects Bowman sees are recognizable—the spiralish galaxy comes to mind—most are so abstract and fanciful, so unreal, that only by studying their allegorical antecedents can you even tentatively guess what they are.

"Incongruous juxtapositions" are another part of surrealism. If you're looking for incongruous juxtaposition, try looking at a person who is in two places at once and is older in one of those places than in the other. Or try looking at the clash between (*a*) the geometrically patterned art deco glass floor, with its beneath-the-floor illumination, and (*b*) the ornate period furniture and statuettes above the floor. You *know* that what you're looking at isn't a literal representation of the true action and true setting.

The surrealism is by itself confusing enough. But when its negative effect on comprehension is compounded by that of symbolism, confusion becomes something close to chaos. The final sequence is overflowing with symbols—the glass floor, the underfloor lighting, the Palladian arches, missing features in the walls, the pod in the corner, the pod's vanishing, Bowman inside the pod, Bowman outside the pod in his orange spacesuit, Bowman's seeing his next self (three times), Bowman's hearing something in the bathroom, Bowman's black clothing at the dinner table, Bowman's white clothing in bed, Bowman's eating his last meal, Bowman's breaking the wine glass, Bowman's staring at the broken glass and then at the bed, Bowman's aging, the monolith, the star-child, the light surrounding the star child, the star-child's return to earth, the transparent globe enclosing the star-child, and the star-child's shining down on earth. *Every one of these features is a symbol.* With symbols flying in from so many directions, how is the viewer supposed to discern reality?

Having to deal with all these symbols but not knowing what they mean is only part of the problem. All of the symbols relate to at least one of the three allegories, but some—and only some—also relate to the surface story. (The glass floor, the underfloor lighting, the black clothing and the white, and some other things have no relevance to the surface story.) But which symbols do you have to concentrate on and interpret to understand the surface story?

The Answers

Fortunately, Kubrick has provided enough information to allow us to strip away the surrealism and the symbolism and get down to reality. The hotel room is a sort of combination laboratory and cage. Benevolent aliens have put Bowman there to change him into something better. As they did once before, back in Africa, the aliens are helping the highest earth creature— previously the ape, this time man—to evolve.

The real laboratory is unlikely to look like the surrealistic hotel room we see, because the aliens are unlikely to have enough information about earth architecture and interior decorating to produce what we see in the movie. In Clarke's novel, the aliens have based their ideas about earth design and decorating on TV programs monitored from space. Slightly plausible, but not terribly convincing. What TV programs or old movies could the aliens have watched to find a hotel room like the one in *2001*? (Well, okay, maybe they watched *2001*.) Another problem with Clarke's they-saw-it-on-TV explanation is that it conflicts with what we know about the moon monolith's purpose. If the aliens had been monitoring earth TV, they would have known about the technological revolution on earth and about the moon bases: there would have been no need to wait for the moon monolith to signal that the earthlings were ready for another boost in their evolution. Besides, with millions if not billions of civilizations in countless galaxies to monitor, the aliens could hardly invest the time required for the intensive sort of monitoring that the TV thesis implies. So recognize that the surrealism of the hotel room is symbolism, not reality. Just assume that Bowman is in a nice comfortable room that might, but probably doesn't, look like the one in the movie.

In the room, Bowman certainly doesn't see himself, except in the mirror. Bowman's seeing his next self is surrealism and symbolism, not something to be taken literally. (Clarke wisely eliminates the two-Bowmans-in-one-scene material from his novel. It is purely symbolic—appropriate for the movie but not for the novel, whose text is literal rather than symbolic.) Bowman's aging is also symbolism. It depicts the maturing (a form of aging) of the fetus, which is itself another symbol—a symbol for evolutionary metamorphosis or mutation.

So does Bowman grow older? For the surface story to make sense, it really doesn't matter whether he does or doesn't. All that matters is that he undergoes change under alien auspices. For what it's worth, Clarke's Bowman does *not* grow older. He simply spends part of a day in a hotel suite (not just one room) and then goes to sleep "for the last time [as a human]."[24]

But Clarke has dispensed with allegory, whereas Kubrick is deeply into allegory. In allegory, the surface story is taken literally and the deeper story is interpreted symbolically. At least that was true until Kubrick's part 3 came along. Even in part 3, however, there is some room for literalism. And, going by the rules of allegory, we should take Kubrick's surface story as literally as the details permit. Realism does not forbid that Bowman grow older, so we should assume that he does.

But realism does forbid that Bowman grow as much older as he does in the movie. In the movie he starts out at about age 35, which is also Bowman's age in the novel.[25] The next three hotel-room Bowmans (beyond Bowman in the pod) seem to represent twenty-year intervals: their ages are about 55 (gray hair), 75 (white hair), and 95 (bald, bedridden). But taking 95 literally requires taking Bowman's rebirth as a baby literally too, whereas both age 95 and the baby are symbols: 95 symbolizes the mature fetus—as old (as well developed) as it can get before birth—and the baby symbolizes both a newly evolved race (surface story and second allegory) and Nietzsche's overman (third allegory).

The baby symbolism requires elaboration, and elaboration requires anticipating some material that will be developed further when we examine the Zarathustra allegory. A child is one of three main symbols Nietzsche uses for the overman; the symbol comes from Nietzsche's "three metamorphoses of the spirit" metaphor, wherein "the spirit becomes a camel [lower man], the camel a lion [higher man], and the lion at last a child [overman]."[26] (Nietzsche's other two symbols are a "light-surrounded being" and the "great noontime" sun.)[27] The virtue of using a child—a baby in this case—as a symbol for a new species is that a child represents a new beginning.

But a symbol is just a symbol. It would make no sense for Bowman to go back to earth as a baby, especially as an earth-sized baby. Even as a normal-sized baby, he couldn't care for himself and might well die. And as an earth-sized baby he literally wouldn't fit. Bowman has to go back to earth as an able-bodied adult; only that concept makes sense. The only sensible interpretation is that Bowman metamorphoses from an able-bodied human into an able-bodied post-human, the first member of a new species.

Look at it this way: Kubrick is developing a parallel between (*a*) Moonwatcher's transformation from ape into man and (*b*) Bowman's transformation from man into whatever comes next. Just as Moonwatcher went from an *able-bodied* member of the old species to an *able-bodied* member of the new species, so does Bowman. And why shouldn't this be the case? After all, both transformations are the result of exposure to a monolith, and both monoliths work essentially the same way: they boost intelligence.

So, even though realism allows Bowman to grow older, he cannot reach 95; he must, like Moonwatcher, remain able-bodied. But if 95 is off-limits, how much older does Bowman get? I like to think that Bowman zaps those orbiting nuclear weapons when he gets back to earth, as he does in Clarke's novel and in Kubrick's originally planned ending of *2001*. To get at those bombs before they blow up the earth, he should get back within, say, ten years. That figure isn't entirely arbitrary. It is the length of time it takes Odysseus to get back from Troy. I have a hunch that if Kubrick had been creating just one allegory, the Odysseus allegory, he would have had Bowman spend ten years in the hotel room before coming back to earth. Since Kubrick is allowing us to flesh out the details of the surface story's ending, I suggest that we have Bowman spend ten years in the hotel room.

With the hotel room out of the way, how do we interpret the final scene, where Bowman comes back to earth? The image of an earth-sized baby encased in a transparent globe and radiating light is obviously surrealistic and symbolic. It can't be reality. It therefore should not be taken literally. In case you doubt that I'm right, consider some additional information. Kubrick is taking the above-mentioned noontime sun symbolism from *Zarathustra*. This symbolism applies to the Zarathustra allegory. The idea, taken straight from Nietzsche, is that the overman is a *metaphorical* sun illuminating the earth with Nietzschean wisdom and morality. Nietzsche's overman isn't literally a sun, and neither is he a child. The sun and the child are *both* metaphors—symbols, if you will. So don't take either the sun metaphor (the globe shining on the earth) or the child metaphor literally.

And don't take the star-child's location high above the earth literally either. That's part of the "great noontime" metaphor. As we have already deduced, Bowman goes back to earth as an able-bodied adult. He is not encased in a transparent globe (the globe is there to make Bowman spherical, like the noontime sun). And neither does he hang in the sky. Like Odysseus, he goes back to where he came from. He didn't come from the sky. He came from earth. In the surface story, the last scene symbolizes Bowman's return to earth. "Earth" means terra firma—solid ground.

Let's recapitulate. What really happens in *2001*'s ending is that the last monolith, an alien machine for bringing about evolution, changes Bowman into a higher humanoid being. The best assumption is that the process takes about ten years, though how long it takes doesn't matter. When their laboratory work is done, the aliens transport Bowman back to earth. How they do this again doesn't matter, but we can assume they use the tunnel of lights (the wormhole to our galaxy and solar system) and then, for the final leg between Jupiter and earth, a fast spaceship. The spaceship assumption agrees with Clarke's discarded idea, mentioned earlier, of having Bowman standing beside the alien ship at the end.

What happens after Bowman gets back to earth we don't know. The story ends when he gets back to earth. But for Bowman to be truly the first of a whole new species, not just another evolutionary dead end, he must reproduce. (We must assume that Bowman isn't an entirely new species. He can still interbreed with humans, just as wolves can interbreed with dogs.) So be romantic. Pretend Bowman finds himself a brilliant and lovely woman, marries her, has ten boys and ten girls and a hundred grandchildren, and lives happily ever after—spreading wisdom and good deeds across the planet. Or, if a no-nonsense approach is better suited to your literary tastes, pretend that Bowman makes a few thousand—or a few million—clones of himself and uses them to establish the new race.

Oh, yes, I almost forgot. He somehow finds a way to get rid of those orbiting nuclear bombs before they destroy civilization. Maybe the aliens have given him long-range telekinetic zapping power. That's what the starchild has—and uses—in Clarke's novel.

NOTES

1. Frederick Ordway, "Perhaps I'm Just Projecting My Own Concern About It," in Jerome Agel, ed., *The Making of Kubrick's* 2001 (New York: New American Library, 1970), 196.

2. Alexander Walker, *Stanley Kubrick Directs* (New York: Harcourt Brace Jovanovich, 1971), 247.

3. Piers Bizony, 2001: *Filming the Future* (London: Aurum Press, 1994), 27.

4. Ibid., 36.

5. Victor Cohn, "Idea for New Space Movie Came from a Fertile Mind" (interview with Arthur C. Clarke), *Washington Post*, 31 March 1968, G2.

6. Hal makes a second mistake when he tells Bowman that the title of the song he is about to sing is "Daisy." "Daisy" is not among the song's three correct titles: "Daisy, Daisy," "Daisy Bell," and "Bicycle Built for Two."

7. Kevin Conod, "Astronomical Gaffes," *Science News* 152, no. 14 (4 October 1997), 211. For a list of Jupiter's sixteen moons, accompanied by an illustration showing their relative sizes, see "Shoot the Moon," *Newsweek*, 26 July 1999, 66.

8. The word *tunnel* comes from Clarke, who uses it in the novel: "He was emerging from the tunnel." Arthur C. Clark, *2001: A Space Odyssey* (New York: Signet, 1968), 197.

9. Agel, ed., *Making* 2001, 155.

10. Clarke, *Space Odyssey*, 148–49, 159.

11. Ibid., 214.

12. Arthur C. Clarke, *The Lost Worlds of* 2001 (Boston: Gregg Press, 1979), 38.

13. Ibid., 33.

14. David G. Stork, *HAL's Legacy:* 2001*'s Computer as Dream and Reality* (Cambridge: MIT Press, 1997), 343.

15. Bizony, *Filming the Future*, 16.

16. Clarke, *Space Odyssey*, 21–23.

17. Ordway, "My Own Concern," 198.

18. Clarke, *Space Odyssey*, 184.

19. In the novel, Clarke anticipates—and perhaps inspires—Star Trek's use of "wormhole." Discussing hypothetical shortcuts across the universe, he resurrects "an expressive phrase coined by a Princeton mathematician of the last century: 'Wormholes in space.'" (Ibid., 172).

20. Ibid., 184.

21. Carolyn Geduld, *Filmguide to* 2001: A Space Odyssey (Bloomington: Indiana University Press, 1973), 62–63.

22. David G. Hoch, "Mythic Patterns in *2001: A Space Odyssey*," *Journal of Popular Culture* 4, no. 4 (Spring 1971), 961.

23. Leonard F. Wheat, *Paul Tillich's Dialectical Humanism: Unmasking the God above God* (Baltimore: The Johns Hopkins Press, 1970), 29–21, 78, 99–146, 220.

24. Clarke, *Space Odyssey*, 215.

25. Ibid., 95.

26. Friedrich Nietzsche, *Thus Spake Zarathustra*, trans. Thomas Common, rev. with introduction and notes by H. James Birx (Buffalo: Prometheus, 1993), 51.

27. Ibid., 181, 301, 341.

Chapter 3

The Odysseus Allegory

Many *2001* fans know that the film's subtitle, "A Space Odyssey," alludes to the return voyage from Troy of Homer's Greek hero Odysseus. They also know that Dave Bowman represents Odysseus. And some people are aware of three other parallels: the hero's safe return, the death of all crewmen, the battle with the cyclops. A few other symbolic analogies connecting *2001* to *The Odyssey* have surely been observed without getting into print. I'd be amazed if I were the first to have noticed the symbolism in Dave Bowman's name.[1] But isolated symbolic references to a work don't constitute allegory; they show allegorical *tendency*. Allegory, you will recall, requires more or less *continuous* reference to the events and ideas of the narrative being symbolized. So far, nobody has suggested that *2001* is a full-fledged allegory.

An allegorical retelling of *The Odyssey* is, nevertheless, what *2001* is (in part): Kubrick has provided the continuous symbolism needed to make his film an allegory. In this chapter, I will reveal and explain Kubrick's *Odyssey* symbols, taking them largely in their proper narrative order. But I will start with Dave Bowman's name, discussing it out of order. There are two reasons for doing so. First, Bowman is the hero of the movie and deserves priority. Second, the material that explains Bowman's last name provides a foundation for explaining the symbolism in the African monolith, the symbol or symbolized event that comes first in chronological order in both *2001* and *The Odyssey*.

DAVE BOWMAN'S NAME

Dave Bowman. An ordinary sounding name. But when you examine it carefully, it divulges unexpected meaning. It tells us that Dave Bowman is Odysseus—and that he is metaphorically related to a character from the Bible.

Chapter 21 in *The Odyssey* is titled "The Great Bow."[2] It tells of the incurved bow given to Odysseus by his friend Iphitus. Left behind by Odysseus when he sailed for Troy, the bow is so strong that ordinary men cannot bend it to string it. In the climactic scene in the great hall of Odysseus's home, Penelope, Odysseus's wife, challenges the suitors who have occupied her home and turned her life into hell. She will wed the man who can string the bow and shoot an arrow through twelve axes lined up in a row, the way Odysseus used to do. All fail. Then Odysseus, secretly back home and disguised as a beggar, effortlessly strings the bow, inserts an arrow, and shoots it through all twelve axes. Inserting another arrow, he sends it through the neck of the most obnoxious suitor. One by one Odysseus slays the rest of the suitors, first with the remaining arrows, then (helped by his son and two loyal servants) with spears and swords.

Odysseus was a bowman. And so is Dave—with a capital B.

Bowman's first name was originally going to be Alex.[3] Alex, short for Alexander, apparently referred to Alexander the Great: like Odysseus, he was both a Greek and a warrior. Kubrick later changed Alex to David. David almost certainly comes from another warrior, the Hebrew David who slew the giant Goliath by embedding a rock in his forehead. Don't overlook the analogy: Odysseus "slew" (disabled) the *giant* cyclops by *embedding* a huge stake in the eye in its *forehead*, then twisting the stake. What a remarkable model for Bowman. He too slays a one-eyed *giant* (Hal-Discovery) by *embedding* an elongated key, symbolizing the *stake*, in slots in the interior of the giant's *forehead*, then *twisting* the key.

THE AFRICAN MONOLITH

Is the first monolith, the one the apes find in Africa, a symbol in the Odysseus allegory? Several considerations, taken together, leave little doubt that it is. Without the monolith as a symbol, the Odysseus allegory would be without a single symbol from the Dawn of Man episode. When you see how thick and fast this allegory's symbols fly in the three remaining episodes, you may agree that the monolith fills what would otherwise be a significant gap in the symbolism.

Since the monolith shows up near the beginning of *2001*, it would have to symbolize something that happens very early among the events surrounding *The Odyssey* (including pre-*Odyssey* events). It would also have to symbolize an event that occurs before the next two *Odyssey* events that Kubrick symbolizes—the beauty contest among three goddesses and

Paris's seduction of Helen. Kubrick symbolizes these events, described under the next three headings, in the Heywood Floyd (earth-to-moon) episode. The monolith comes before the Heywood Floyd episode, so it symbolizes (assuming it is a symbol) something before the beauty contest and the hanky-panky.

The only earlier incident for which the first monolith would be an appropriate symbol is Iphitus's giving the Great Bow to Odysseus as a gift. The monolith thus seems to symbolize (in this allegory) the Great Bow and, more broadly, the occasion of the gift's being given.

Four arguments support this interpretation. First, as just observed, the chronology fits. Odysseus's receiving the Great Bow is the earliest event mentioned in *The Odyssey* that involves Odysseus; it even precedes the events (not mentioned in *The Odyssey*) that precipitated the Trojan War. Since the first monolith arrives early in the movie, before we see any other symbol based on *The Odyssey*, the timing is perfect. Second, a good analogy exists between the Great Bow and the monolith: both are gifts. The Great Bow was a gift to Odysseus, and the monolith can be viewed as a gift of intelligence to the apes from the aliens. Third, consistency in the pattern of monolith symbolism demands that the first monolith represent *something* in *The Odyssey*. Each of the other three monoliths has three symbolic meanings, one for each allegory. If the first monolith does not symbolize the Great Bow in the first allegory, then it is a symbol only in the second and third allegories. That leaves a gap in the structure of the monolith symbolism, a gap Kubrick is unlikely to have left.

Fourth, the idea that the first monolith symbolizes the Great Bow ties in beautifully with a forthcoming interpretation of the fourth monolith, the one in the hotel room. To anticipate, that monolith also symbolizes the Great Bow. It was left behind when Odysseus sailed for Troy, so he had to get it back before he could slay the suitors. The timing of the fourth monolith is, as we shall see, exactly right for it to symbolize Odysseus's regaining of the Great Bow: he regains it just before he is reunited with Penelope.

In chapter 2 we saw that, in the surface story, the first and last monoliths have essentially the same function: both are devices used by the aliens to enhance intelligence and accelerate evolution. If both monoliths are essentially the same thing, why shouldn't they symbolize the same thing (at least in this allegory)?

There is one problem. If the first monolith is the Great Bow, this fact suggests that Moonwatcher is Odysseus. That is certainly a flaw in the symbolism, but not a fatal one. When we get to the Zarathustra allegory, we shall see that two *2001* characters symbolize Zarathustra. One symbolizes

the young Zarathustra (who creates God); the other symbolizes the older
Zarathustra (who declares that God is dead). If two characters can symbol-
ize Zarathustra, why can't two characters separately symbolize the young
Odysseus and the Odysseus of twenty-some years later?

THE JUDGMENT OF PARIS

The events of *The Odyssey* take place after the Trojan War—after Troy falls
to Greek attackers. But the events symbolized in *2001* cover a broader
period that includes events leading up to the fall of Troy. These earlier
events, compiled from several ancient sources, are chronicled in Edith
Hamilton's *Mythology: Timeless Tales of Gods and Heroes*.[4] To understand
the allegory—and Kubrick's symbols—we need to review them.

Paris, a son of the king of Troy (hence a prince), has been sent by his
father to the countryside to tend sheep. His father doesn't want him around
because the king has been warned that Paris will some day bring ruin to
Troy. Meanwhile, a squabble develops among three goddesses—Aphrodite,
Hera, and Athene—over who is the most beautiful. They are competing for
a golden apple marked "For the Fairest" that Eris, the goddess of Discord,
has put up for grabs. The three goddesses ask Zeus to judge, but he wisely
passes the buck to Paris, who is reputed to be a keen judge of beauty. The
goddesses go before Paris. Each offers him a gift—really a bribe—on the
condition that he choose her. Aphrodite offers him the fairest woman in the
world. Naturally, Paris gives Aphrodite the golden apple. This event has
become known as The Judgment of Paris.

The fairest woman in the world happens to be Helen, daughter of Zeus
and Leda (a mortal). Helen is married to Menelaus, king of Sparta.
Menelaus was one of many aristocratic suitors who wanted Helen's hand.
Her reputed father, a king, had to choose the groom but was afraid to do so:
he feared the others would be angered and would rise against him. So the
king made all the suitors promise to come to the chosen suitor's aid if anyone tried to take Helen away. The king then chose Menelaus and made him
king of Sparta.

Aphrodite brings Paris to Sparta, where he becomes the guest of
Menelaus and Helen. Menelaus, a trusting soul, then takes a trip to Crete—
he goes off to the *Mediterranean*—leaving Paris with Helen. Paris
promptly *seduces* Helen and takes her to Troy. When Menelaus returns, he
is *briefed* on the situation. Holding the other former suitors to their oaths of
support, Menelaus raises a huge army. He also puts together a fleet of *a*

thousand ships. He then puts the army on the ships and embarks for Troy. Helen becomes known as "the face that launched a thousand ships." (The italicized elements are symbolized by Kubrick.)

The second episode of *2001* begins when the bone-club, tossed high into the air at the end of the first episode, metamorphoses into an orbiting nuclear bomb. Kubrick next cuts to a second bomb and then a third. Although the artistry of the presentation might lead you to believe otherwise, Kubrick didn't put those bombs up there just for decoration. They are there to symbolize Aphrodite, Hera, and Athene, and they are floating in the sky because that's where gods and goddesses spend a lot of their time. (According to Zeus himself, the Greek deities are "the immortals who live in heaven.")[5] The bombs are a sort of prelude to the entry of Paris, who shows up disguised as Heywood Floyd a few cuts later. Paris, we shall see, is on his way to meet Helen—in a very sexual way.

In the originally planned ending of *2001*, the orbiting bombs were also going to symbolize, at the movie's end, the suitors harassing Odysseus's wife, Penelope. The exploding bombs would be the dying suitors. But that symbolism wouldn't have prevented the bombs from symbolizing something else, the three goddesses, earlier in the film.

Interpolated between the second and third bombs is a shot of the brilliant golden sun. It is emerging from behind the earth, whose visible side is dark (unlit)—evidence that the orb is the sun rather than the moon. The golden sun is the golden apple, tossed out among the three goddesses.

After showing the first three orbiting bombs, Kubrick brings out a fourth. But this one looks different. The first three have something in common: they all have a structure that resembles a warship's gun turret mounted on top. Each turret has a horizontal stem antenna running parallel to the central axis of the bomb; the antenna seems to represent a gun sticking out of the turret. The turret-and-gun abstractions presumably serve as hints that these first three space vehicles are weapons. The fourth bomb is of radically different design. For one thing, it has a dozen solar panels arranged in two arrays.[6] For another, it uses a different weaponry abstraction, suggesting that it belongs to a different class. This bomb has external rodlike longitudinal ribs that could be abstracted arrows, packed in a quiver. Two pods at one end have what look like the head ends of smaller arrows sticking out; weaponry symbolism is again suggested.

I could be misinterpreting the weaponry symbolism, but the point remains that the fourth bomb is different. Why is it different? Because the first three are females—the three goddesses—whereas the fourth is a male, Zeus. Zeus is present to symbolize his being asked by the three goddesses

to decide which one deserves the golden apple. But he's no dope: he hands
the job to Paris, who makes his debut in the next scene.

HEYWOOD R. FLOYD'S NAME

We learn Heywood R. Floyd's name—his full name, including middle initial—when he goes through voiceprint identification at the space station;
the point of that scene is revealing Floyd's full name. The name bears close
inspection. Dave Bowman, Frank Poole (his name is discussed in chapter
1), and the computer Hal (whose name we'll analyze later) are not the only
characters in *2001* whose names have hidden meanings. All four major
characters, including Floyd, have names with hidden meanings. So does a
minor character, the Russian scientist Elena. And so does the monolith
dubbed TMA-1 (ostensibly an abbreviation for Tycho Magnetic Anomaly
but in truth something else).

Look closely at the boldface particles in **He**ywood R. Fl**oy**d. They seem
to blink on and off like neon signs. **He** suggests Helen—Helen of Troy.
Wood suggests wooden horse—the Trojan Horse. And **oy** suggests Troy.
The other letters also have meanings. But to understand how Helen, the
Trojan Horse, Troy, and the other meanings fit together, we need to learn
about the Trojan Horse.

The siege of Troy lasts ten years. The Greeks finally conquer Troy
through a ruse conceived by Odysseus. Pretending to depart, they leave
behind outside Troy's gates an enormous wooden horse. It is hollow;
Greeks are hidden inside. The Greeks also leave behind a mock defector.
He tells a clever tale designed to trick the Trojans into hauling the horse
into the city. The scheme works. The Trojans drag the horse through the
gates. Later, in the middle of the night, the hidden Greeks slip out through
a secret door and open Troy's gates for their army, which has silently
returned. Troy falls. Helen returns to Menelaus.

Against this background, it is indeed plausible that HEYWOOD R.
FLOYD encodes Helen as **HE**, wooden horse as **WOOD**, and Troy as
OY. But what about that **Y** between **HE** and **WOOD**. And what about the
R, **F**, **L**, and **D**?

Consider these answers. **Y** is Spanish for *and*. **R**, **F**, and **L**, in turn, are
in *ReFLect*. And **D** could stand for *downfall*, *demise*, *death*, *doom*, or
destruction, of which the first—*downfall*—best fits "the fall of Troy."
When you put all the pieces together, Heywood R. Floyd inflates to Helen
and Wooden Horse Reflect Troy's Downfall.

HEYWOOD FLOYD AS PARIS

The message in Heywood Floyd's name is a clue to Floyd's allegorical identity. Or, as it turns out, his allegorical *identities*. Floyd symbolizes both Paris (at first) and Menelaus (later).

The first clue that Heywood Floyd is Paris can be found in Floyd's first scene. After showing the orbiting bombs, Kubrick cuts to the earth shuttle *Orion*. It is heading for the rotating space station, and Floyd is on board as the only passenger. He is asleep. The stewardess enters the cabin, spies a pen floating above the aisle (there is no gravity to make it fall), plucks it from the air, and gently tucks it in Floyd's suit-coat pocket. The pen is a phallic symbol, and its being "given" to Floyd symbolizes Aphrodite's giving her gift-bribe to Paris. Symbolically, Paris is being given the right to possess the fairest woman in the world, Helen.

Let's recognize something: Aphrodite's gift of Helen means the gift of *sex* with Helen. We can be sure that the goddess of love, bidding for the golden apple, has promised Paris more than animated conversation with and a friendly hug from Helen. Helen is going to be, in Edith Hamilton's words, "a faithless woman" while her husband is away.[7] A phallic symbol—the pen—as the gift-of-sex symbol is therefore fitting for the allegorical context.

And there is a second reason for interpreting the pen as Aphrodite's gift to Paris: the sequential context is perfect. The floating pen scene comes (*a*) right *after* the shots of the four orbiting bombs, which symbolize Zeus's saying no to the three goddesses who have asked him to decide who deserves the golden apple, and (*b*) right *before* the widely recognized space machine copulation scene, in which the elongated, phallic *Orion* penetrates the rotating space station. The copulation scene symbolizes Paris's union with Helen: Paris (Floyd) is inside the *Orion* as its symbolic essence, and Helen (we shall see) is inside the space station as its essence. Note that Kubrick is using phallic symbols on two levels—the human level (pen) and the machine level (*Orion*).

All told, eight considerations point to Floyd's being Paris. For completeness, the list that follows repeats in less detail the things just discussed. The eight considerations:

1. The sequential context is right. The three goddesses (first three bombs) turn to Zeus (fourth bomb), who turns the job of judging the beauty contest over to Paris (Heywood Floyd). Floyd arrives right after the Zeus-bomb.

2. Floyd is the one who receives the "gift" of a phallic pen, which represents Aphrodite's gift-bribe, given to Paris, of the fairest woman in the world (Helen).

3. While at the space station on his way to the moon, Floyd meets the Russian woman named Elena. The name Elena is the Russian version of Helen. Interpreted in the context of all the other symbolism and evidence, this encounter must be regarded as symbolizing the encounter between Paris and Helen. Floyd again fits the Paris model.

4. Elena mentions that her husband is doing research in the Baltic. What a coincidence! Helen's husband is in the Mediterranean (on Crete) when she is seduced by Paris. The Baltic Sea symbolizes the Mediterranean Sea.

5. Elena's husband's name is Grego (first mention) or Gregori (second mention). Gregori is again the Russian equivalent of a Greek name: Gregory of Nyssa was a Greek theologian.

6. Floyd's encounter with Elena occurs in the broader context of strong sexual symbolism, symbolism that has been recognized by several reviewers (hence is known by many *2001* fans). Ebert, for example, refers to "the sexually charged moment when the ship penetrates the space station."[8] This symbolism relates primarily to the second and third allegories and will be developed more fully under the second. In brief, Floyd's phallic space shuttle, the *Orion*, copulates with the symbolically female space station containing Elena. A symbolized sperm cell (the spherical *Aries* Lunar Transfer Vehicle) then travels from the space station to a symbolized ovum (the spherical moon, larger by far than *Aries*). *Aries* enters the moon, symbolizing fertilization. The sexual symbolism is on two levels:

    a. *Machine Level.* In one sense, the *Orion*, with Floyd inside, is Paris, and the space station, with Elena inside, is Helen. The mating of the male-and-female shaped machines symbolizes Helen's being untrue to Menelaus.

    b. *Human Level.* In another sense, Heywood Floyd is Paris and Elena is Helen. Their meeting inside the space station symbolizes Helen's seduction by Paris.

7. The originally identified particles of Floyd's name relate him to Helen, the Trojan Horse, and Troy. Paris is connected with all three.

8. Floyd is a symbolic Trojan, one of several who are symbolically slain by symbolic warriors coming from a symbolic wooden horse at a symbolic Troy. This symbolism is developed under the second heading after this one. For the moment, simply recall that Paris too was a Trojan.

HEYWOOD FLOYD AS MENELAUS

Heywood Floyd plays *two* roles in the Odysseus allegory. In addition to playing the part of Paris, he plays the part of Menelaus, Helen's husband. I found this hard to believe. And yet, studying Floyd's first two scenes on the moon (briefing scene and moon bus scene), I came to realize that no other reasonable interpretation is possible. The symbolic meanings in question are so obvious, once you catch on to the symbolism and consider the sequence, that there is no getting around the fact: in *these* scenes, Heywood Floyd is Menelaus.

Floyd arrives at Clavius, the American base on the moon. There he attends a briefing. After being introduced, Floyd says a few words. He emphasizes "the need for complete security in this matter" and the related need for the "cover story" about an epidemic at the base. But Floyd's remarks aren't the briefing. When Floyd finishes, Dr. Halvorsen, the presiding official, says, "And as there seems [*sic*] to be no more questions, I think we oughta get on with the briefing." Floyd, who came alone from earth, is the principal briefee.

We don't hear the actual briefing. But in the context of the allegory and of the preceding and following scenes, which establish the chronology, we can infer that the briefing went as follows: "Menelaus, Paris has seduced your wife and carried her off to Troy!" Floyd's literal briefing symbolizes the figurative briefing Menelaus received when he returned home from Crete.

Do you remember what Menelaus did when he heard the news? He raised an army, launched a thousand ships, and headed for Troy.

In a hauntingly beautiful scene after the briefing, the moon bus glides along above the barren moonscape, bound for Tycho. The bus has two huge front windows that glow with red light from inside; viewed head-on, they give the bus a bug-eyed appearance. On each side, sticking out at the bottom, are two rows of landing feet. Kubrick has had the moon bus designed to look like an abstracted millipede, a "thousand-footed" crawler (*mil* = thousand, *ped* = foot). The millipede's figurative thousand feet, in turn, symbolize the thousand ships in Menelaus's fleet. So the moon bus indirectly symbolizes what Helen's face launched. And inside the bus, as the chief passenger, is Heywood Floyd. The conclusion that he is Menelaus in this scene and in the briefing scene is unavoidable. Menelaus is headed for Troy.

The moon bus scene has some additional symbolism. Because Kubrick loves to create names with hidden meanings—Dave Bowman, Frank Poole, Heywood R. Floyd, Elena, and Hal—I couldn't help wondering about the label given the moon monolith. On the bus Floyd is shown charts of the newly discovered monolith. It is labeled TMA-1, which in the surface story stands for Tycho Magnetic Anomaly. Mightn't that label stand for something else in the Odysseus allegory?

In the next scene, the moon monolith scene, it becomes evident that TMA-1 symbolizes the wooden Trojan Horse; hence, we are looking for a hidden meaning that refers or alludes to the Trojan Horse. And that meaning can be found in TMA-1. Spell out the figure "1" and you get TMA-ONE. Those letters, like the last nine in Frank Poole (see chapter 1), can be rearranged to form an anagram. In this case the anagram is "No Meat." A wooden horse has no meat on its skeletal framework.

Could this anagram be a coincidence, the result of there being only six letters to rearrange? Hardly. Three counterarguments rebut the coincidence argument:

1. Although "No Meat" conceivably could come up accidentally, its being a fitting description of a wooden horse cannot be a coincidence. And the next scene, the moon monolith scene, leaves no doubt that the monolith (TMA-1) *is* the wooden horse.
2. Just before the TMA-1 charts are brought out, Floyd and Halvorsen are offered sandwiches. Halvorsen asks, "Got any ham?" Michaels, who holds the sandwich cooler, paws through the sandwiches saying, "Ham, ham, ham, ham." Isn't that dialogue intended to direct our thoughts toward meat (as in "No Meat")? If it isn't, Kubrick wasted time on pointless conversation in a movie that was already very long (two and one-third hours). When Kubrick cut nineteen minutes from the film after the first showing, why didn't he cut the "Ham, ham, ham, ham" dialogue? Answer: Because it supported his "No Meat" symbolism.
3. Why did Kubrick give the TMA object a number? Only one "magnetic anomaly" was found at Tycho. So why wasn't it simply labeled TMA instead of TMA-1? Why have a number 1 when there is no number 2? To me, this is the clincher. You can't rationalize the figure "1" in terms of the surface story. Kubrick added the number because he needed the letters of ONE for the "No Meat" anagram. And he wanted the anagram as a symbol that the monolith was the meatless (wooden) horse.

THE TROJAN HORSE AND THE FALL OF TROY

The moon bus lands at Tycho. There another monolith has been found, buried under the crater. The monolith sits in an excavation with shored-up walls. Tycho symbolizes Troy: their spellings share three letters, and both have surrounding walls. Troy's walls could be symbolized by either the natural walls of the crater or the shored-up walls of the excavation; but since the crater's walls are unseen and nonvertical whereas the shoring is visible and vertical, Kubrick must have intended that the *excavation's* walls represent those of Troy.

Tycho seems to have been adapted as another partial anagram. The three boldface letters are three of the four letters of *Troy*. Even the initial letter is the same. Kubrick evidently searched the list of moon crater names until he found one with symbolic value.

At Tycho, Floyd and five other space-suited persons descend into the excavation to inspect the monolith. Floyd examines it with apparent curiosity. Then, as the men line up for a picture, the monolith emits that piercing signal. Vainly trying to cover their helmeted ears to avert the pain, the men stagger back.

The monolith is the Trojan horse. The curious people viewing it are the Trojans, who have just brought the Trojan Horse inside Troy's walls. The signal coming from the monolith is the Greeks sneaking out through the wooden horse's secret door in the middle of the night. And the pain experienced by the people in the excavation (Troy) is the pain of the dying Trojans. This scene's timing is perfect: immediately *after* the moon bus (Menelaus's fleet) arrives, immediately *before* the space voyage. The Trojan War is over; let The Odyssey begin.

THE CITY OF ISMARUS AND LOTUS LAND

The very first thing Odysseus does after leaving Troy is attack and then sack the city of Ismarus, where the Cicones live. Unfortunately, Odysseus's men refuse to leave when the job is done; they choose to drink, eat, and revel, availing themselves of the plentiful wine, sheep, and cattle in the city—and the women. During the revelry, surviving Cicones run to neighboring up-country Cicones for help. The other Cicones are better fighters, and at dawn they attack. An all-day battle ensues. Odysseus loses six men from each of his twelve ships before escaping. Figuratively speaking, he gets *burned*.

Note that the Ismarus episode has three main elements: attacking, sacking, and getting burned in a counterattack. After the moon monolith scene (the fall of Troy), the space voyage begins. The first action on the voyage symbolizes the attack on Ismarus. Frank Poole, who symbolizes the active crew of Odysseus (mission commander Dave Bowman), jogs around the exercise centrifuge, shadowboxing as he goes. Odysseus's crew is running (the jogging) through the streets of Ismarus, attacking (the shadowboxing) the residents. Dave Bowman then comes on stage. He immediately sacks the food-dispensing machine. But in piling the food (loot) onto his tray, he literally gets *burned*: he shakes his burned fingers in pain.

If this interpretation strikes you as forced, reflect carefully on the timing and sequence. First, Troy symbolically falls, and the space voyage begins. Second, Poole runs around and engages in simulated combat. Third, the very first time Bowman appears on camera, he helps himself to the contents of the food-dispensing machine. Fourth, he gets burned. Fifth, immediately after this, we see and hear the symbols describing what happens next to Odyssseus after he flees from Ismarus.

And what is it that happens next? Odysseus gets pushed by a gale to the country of the Lotus-eaters. He sends three men inland to check things out—to *survey* the countryside, so to speak. The scouts encounter the Lotus-eaters, eat lotus, and lose all desire to return home. Odysseus and some of his other men have to go after them, forcibly bring them back to the ships, and keep them in irons thereafter—unable to perform their duties.

Dave Bowman's crew on the spaceship Discovery likewise has three incapacitated crewmen. They are in hibernation. We learn about them on a delayed-broadcast TV interview received on the ship; the interview comes on right after Bowman burns his fingers. According to Bowman, who is being interviewed, the three hibernators "represent the *survey* team." And they are hibernating "in order to achieve the maximum conservation of our life-support capabilities—basically, food and air." But we know better. Bowman's explanation holds only for the surface story. The true reason Kubrick has the three crewmen in hibernation is that he wants to symbolize the three crewmen of Odysseus who ate lotus and had to be put in irons, unable to perform their duties.

THE CYCLOPS MONSTER

Odysseus next sails to the land of the Cyclopes. They are fierce, giant, man-eating creatures of incredible strength; they have only one eye. Homer does not say the eye is in the forehead, but that is where tradition puts it.[9] Taking twelve of his best men, Odysseus enters the cave of the cyclops (one of the Cyclopes race). The cyclops returns home with his sheep, brings the sheep inside, seals the cave's entrance with a boulder, spies the intruders, and devours two of the men. The next morning he gobbles down two more men before taking his sheep out to graze. When he leaves, he effortlessly rolls the boulder aside and quickly replaces it.

Things are going badly. But Odysseus comes up with a plan of escape. While the cyclops monster is out, he and his men sharpen a pole (the monster's staff) they find in the cave. Their product is a huge stake. That evening, after the cyclops returns and eats yet another two men, Odysseus tricks him into a wine-induced sleep. Odysseus then slips the point of the stake into the coals of the monster's dinner fire. When the point is red-hot, four of his men *plunge* the stake into the cyclops's eye while Odysseus *twists* the stake. The cyclops wakes up screaming but cannot see the men to exact revenge. In the morning the men escape by clinging to the bellies of sheep when the cyclops rolls aside the boulder and sends the animals out to graze. The monster takes the precaution of feeling each sheep as it exits, but he doesn't feel the men on the bottom.

Bowman too has a one-eyed adversary. He is Hal, the malevolent computer who reads the lips of Bowman and Poole with his sinister red eye. Hal is the cyclops. His red eye is the eye of the cyclops, and his gigantic body—the spaceship Discovery—makes him a giant, like the cyclops. Also like the cyclops, he is a killer of crewmen: he kills Frank Poole and the three hibernating astronauts. As Odysseus did, Bowman fights back. Again as Odysseus did, he attacks his adversary's forehead, although this time from the inside (in the brain chamber behind Discovery's forehead). Once more as Odysseus did, Bowman uses as a weapon an elongated object, a key, which symbolizes the stake used by Odysseus. And yet again as Odysseus did, he *plunges* his weapon into his adversary and *twists* it. As the cyclops did, Hal screams (figuratively) in anguish: "I can feel it! I can feel it!" But Bowman doesn't stop. When the battle is over, Hal-Discovery is brain-dead, out of commission. (Kubrick really pays attention to details. I count ten parallels: eye, giant, killer, battle, forehead, key-stake, plunge, twist, scream, and out of commission. Take those as ten symbols.)

THE LAESTRYGONIAN ROCK ATTACK

After fleeing from the cyclops, Odysseus sails to the floating island of Aeolia, home of the lesser god Aeolus, king of the winds. Odysseus stays for a month, at the end of which Aeolus gives him a gift—a leather bag containing the energy of winds. Ten days later Odysseus sees his homeland, the island of Ithaca, in the distance. But while he sleeps, his greedy men, thinking the leather bag holds gold and silver, open it. The winds rush out, and the fleet is blown far from home.

Eventually, Odysseus reaches the land of the Laestrygonians. Eleven of his twelve ships anchor in a well-sheltered harbor, which is ringed by steep cliffs that leave just a narrow entrance. Odysseus ties up his own ship just outside the harbor. The Laestrygonians aren't friendly. Standing on cliffs above the ships, they throw down huge rocks. The splintering of timbers and the groans of dying men mark the end of the ships in the harbor, and of the men. Only Odysseus's ship escapes, barely missed by a hail of rocks.

The Odyssey has far too many episodes for Kubrick to symbolize them all. He skips Aeolus and the bag of winds. But he does honor the Laestrygonians. Do you remember the scene in *2001* where Bowman is about to go out to replace the supposedly defective AE-35 unit? Kubrick splices in an exterior shot of the spaceship. Two meteoroids come roaring past the front of the ship and in toward the camera. Those symbolize the rocks hurled by the Laestrygonians at Odysseus's ships. We are watching Odysseus escape from the Laestrygonians.

Admittedly, this particular episode is out of Odyssean sequence. At this point in the movie, Bowman hasn't yet fought Hal: Odysseus hasn't yet fought the cyclops. Yet in *The Odyssey*, the rock attack comes *after* the cyclops episode. Still, the rock storm symbolism is so nearly literal that Kubrick's symbolic intent is undeniable. I suspect Kubrick decided to wink at sequence in this case because he didn't want the meteoroids to intrude on the outdoor performance of Jupiter and its moons, after Bowman's battle with Hal.

THE SIRENS

Odysseus sails on to the island home of the sorceress Circe, who temporarily turns most of his men into pigs. Outwitting and then befriending Circe, he regains his men and departs. He takes a side trip to the kingdom of the dead, ruled by Hades; revisits Circe; and then, guided by advice from Circe, prepares to sail past the bewitching Sirens. These evil twins use their seductive song to lure sailors to their doom. Warned by Circe, Odysseus avoids the Sirens by plugging his men's ears with beeswax and having the men lash him to the mast; he will be able to enjoy the Sirens' voices without jumping overboard under the Sirens' spell. The trip past the Sirens' island proves to be a harrowing experience: Odysseus struggles to free himself but remains bound safely to the mast.

The Sirens are among the better-known characters from *The Odyssey*, so Kubrick isn't about to overlook them. In fact, he reserves for them one of the most prominent symbols in *2001*: the Jupiter monolith. Just as the Sirens *lure* sailors to their island shore, this monolith *lures* Bowman through the Star Gate and into the tunnel of lights. The symbolism is not only visual but auditory. While Bowman is being lured to the Star Gate, we hear an eerie chorus of feminine voices—the call of the Sirens. The voices continue as Bowman careers along the tunnel. They are Kubrick's helpful translation of what Bowman only *sees* in the surface story, multicolored lights flashing past. The beauty of the lights symbolizes the beauty and seductiveness of the Sirens' voices. During his ride through the tunnel, Bowman trembles and displays facial contortion: Odysseus is under the Sirens' spell and is struggling to get loose and jump overboard.

THE SURF, CHARYBDIS, AND SCYLLA

Beyond the Sirens, Odysseus immediately sees raging surf and a cloud of smoke. With great effort his crew rows through the turbulent water and up a strait on the far side. Ahead lies a dilemma Circe has told him he will face. On one side is the deadly whirlpool Charybdis, which pulls ships into its hungry vortex and swallows them. On the other side is a high cave in which the horrible monster Scylla lives. Scylla has six long necks, each with a grisly head. The necks swoop down so the heads can snatch up passing sailors on ships that avoid Charybdis. Odysseus steers his ship past Charybdis, but as he does so Scylla's six heads attack. Odysseus loses six men.

Although Kubrick's next symbolism (if such it is) is highly ambiguous, it seems to fit the above three episodes. The interpretations that follow gain strength from (*a*) Kubrick's now-clear intent to create an allegory representing *The Odyssey* and (*b*) correct sequence among the next three symbols and between them collectively and the Sirens. As Bowman emerges from the tunnel of lights (just beyond the Sirens), he sees what Agel identifies (from interviews with the production staff) as an exploding galaxy.[10] Two grayish streaks rise from it. A booming sound from the sound track (audio symbolism) suggests that the exploding galaxy symbolizes surf exploding on rocks. The gray streaks would be the smoke.

Bowman next passes a flat, spiralish galaxy. That should symbolize the whirlpool Charybdis, although the vagueness of the spiral permits skepticism. (A shot of the glorious spiral galaxy Andromeda might have served better.) A brilliant star follows. It has distinct narrow rays—the long necks of Scylla?—radiating out. Moving out along the "necks" are white spots that might symbolize the heads of Scylla. The very next scene shows an expanding red orb that, in the surface story, is probably a red giant star in its death throes. Does it symbolize the red blood of the six crewmen being eaten by Scylla?

HYPERION AND ZEUS

Sailing on, Odysseus reaches the Island of the Sun, home of the sun god Hyperion and his cattle. Circe has warned him not to harm the cattle. For a month unfavorable winds keep the men landbound; their food runs out. Though the men have promised Odysseus to leave the cattle untouched, their hunger overpowers their loyalty. When Odysseus goes inland to pray to the gods for help, the men round up, slaughter, and eat the best cows. Odysseus rebukes his men, but it is too late. Hyperion is furious and asks Zeus for assistance. When the weather improves—Hyperion arranges this—Odysseus and his men sail off. But Zeus calls up a dark cloud above the ship. He then destroys the ship with a lightning bolt, killing all but Odysseus.

Back to Bowman. The cosmic images after the red giant star remain ambiguous but, interpreted in chronological context, seem to provide a good fit with *The Odyssey*. Bowman first sees waves of light. They probably symbolize the ocean waves Odysseus sails on going to the Island of the Sun. Next, a gnarled, multishaded, golden yellow blob, apparently a sun, provides a suitable symbol for the sun god Hyperion or his island, probably both. Nothing resembling cattle comes along, but an ominous dark form appears and expands across the screen. That suggests the cloud sent by Zeus or the shadow it casts on the ship. Finally, we get an angry-looking red image with two eyes—the one on the left is quite distinct—and a snout and a black mouth. It looks something like the head of a porpoise. The mouth opens and moves forward as though to bite. Could that be Zeus, and is the bite his lightning bolt?

SEVEN YEARS WITH CALYPSO

When his ship is destroyed by Zeus, Odysseus grabs the floating keel, has another encounter with Charybdis (the whirlpool), and then drifts for nine days. Finally he reaches Ogygia, the island of the nymph-goddess Calypso. He does not share her passion but, marooned and unable to go on without her help, he remains in her clutches for seven years. Although "the Nymph [has] long since ceased to please," he is forced to sleep with her, "cold lover with an ardent dame."[11] But by day he is filled with heartache; he yearns for his beloved wife, Penelope. The goddess Athene takes pity on him and intervenes with Zeus. Zeus sends his messenger, Hermes, to tell Calypso to send Odysseus on his way. She helps him build a small boat, and he rewards her with a genuine "night of love."[12] Then off he sails.

Bowman's next scene after the angry-Zeus one is hard to interpret but seems to suggest Calypso. We see some filmy, gossamer, diaphanous, gently flowing folds of space, studded with stars. Perhaps this is Kubrick's idea of a seductive gown that might be worn by the nymph. Or, what amounts to the same thing, we may be seeing the nymph herself. The latter interpretation is suggested by a U-shaped string of nine stars in the upper left of the screen; the first one on the right is extra-bright, and the last two on the left are faint. The nine stars could represent a string of pearls worn by Calypso. Could they simultaneously represent the nine days spent adrift? Think about it. The first day (brightest star) held the most hope for survival; the last two days (two faint stars) were when hope was almost gone.

The Calypso interpretation agrees with the next one, which has hardly any ambiguity: it can be interpreted both visually and from context. What looks like a comet (for surface story purposes) arcs through the cosmos. But it is like no comet you have ever seen. A comet has an ever-widening tail, whereas this "comet" is a round white object with a long, narrow tail like that of a sperm cell; the resemblance is strong. The comet symbolizes, I suspect, Odysseus's sleeping with Calypso. In the scene after the comet-sperm, we see a very bright star with a much smaller star shooting out rapidly from it. The big fellow could be Zeus, chief of the gods. If so, the little tyke is his messenger, Hermes, on his way to tell Calypso to release Odysseus. Another possibility is that the big star is Calypso's island and the small star shooting out is Odysseus, departing from the island in his newly built boat. Or, to look ahead, the big star could be the boat and the small one Odysseus swimming for shore.

These interpretations gain credence when we realize that they mesh perfectly with the scene that immediately follows. That scene has absolutely no ambiguity; insiders have provided the information needed to interpret it accurately. It symbolizes the Phaeacians.

PHAEACIAN HOSPITALITY

Poseidon, the one god who really hates Odysseus, attacks Odysseus's boat with a violent storm. The boat is smashed but, helped by Athene and the minor goddess Leucothoe, Odysseus struggles to shore in a heroic three-day swim. He has reached the Phaeacians' country. Athene again intervenes. She arranges for Odysseus to be found by Nausicaa, daughter of the Phaeacian king. Nausicaa directs him to the palace of her hospitable father, where Odysseus relates his adventures. Deeply moved by his plight, the Phaeacians put him on one of their ships and provide a crew. Odysseus thanks his hosts: "I have secured your *escort*."[13] The Phaeacians escort him home to Ithaca, put him safely on land, and *depart*.

Bowman, in the scene after the one with the big star and the small one, sees seven glittering octahedra (eight-faceted geometric solids) cruising in V-formation in front of him. I had no idea what those things were. But in his book *Hal's Legacy*, Stork identifies them, apparently on the basis of interviews with Clarke and others who worked on the film. (Stork, by the way, is unaware that the aliens symbolize anything.) The octahedra are the aliens. This information is revealed in Stork's interview with Stephen Wolfram:

> *Wolfram*: Kubrick added some flashing octahedra just to make it clear that the whole thing [the cosmic wonders sequence] wasn't supposed to be completely natural—unless perhaps those octahedra were crystals, or something.
>
> *Stork*: Actually, the octahedra were Kubrick and Clarke's extraterrestrials—sort of *escorts* bringing Dave through the stargate.
>
> *Wolfram*: Gosh! And there I was thinking that the octahedra were just supposed to be simple beacons, flashing like lighthouses or something.[14]

It seems that Kubrick wanted to get the aliens onstage, perhaps to clarify their existence and influence, but didn't want to use Hollywood-style extraterrestrials. He settled for abstract representations, essentially symbols for the aliens. But I digress. The crucial point here is that Stork refers to the aliens as *escorts*. Here we have the plural of the very word Homer put in Odysseus's mouth when Odysseus said to the Phaeacians, "I have secured your *escort*."

That cinches it: the octahedra-aliens symbolize the Phaeacians who are escorting Odysseus back to Ithaca.

The aliens deposit Bowman in the replicated hotel room on their planet. We see the pod inside the room, but then it disappears. The pod represents, at various stages of its journey, the boats that Odysseus is traveling in. In the hotel room, symbolizing Ithaca, the pod is the Phaeacian ship that carried Odysseus back to Ithaca. Its disappearance symbolizes (in this allegory) the *departure* of the Phaeacians after they put Odysseus safely on land at Ithaca.

PALLAS ATHENE

Meanwhile, let's not forget Athene. She has been helping Odysseus—first by intervening with Zeus in the Calypso episode and then by helping Odysseus escape Poseidon's wrath. And she will help again as Odysseus restores order in Ithaca. Doesn't Athene deserve to be symbolized?

She certainly does. And I think she gets her symbol—really symbol*s*. In the hotel room, the paintings have strange, unorthodox shapes and frames: they are arched at the top. The wall recesses in which the statuettes stand also have arches. And the bathroom door frame is arched at the top. These arches are called Palladian arches; the name comes from the Renaissance architect Palladio. But *Palladian* also has a second meaning. It means relating to Pallas Athene, better known simply as Athene. Athene seems to be lurking in and on the walls, ready to assist.

PENELOPE, HER SUITORS, AND THE GREAT BOW

Odysseus's faithful wife, Penelope, is having a hard time of it. She sobs in anguish—anguish over being besieged by the suitors, who are behaving badly; anguish over the probable death of Odysseus, who has been gone for twenty years; and anguish over an ambush of her son, which she learns the suitors have planned. (The ambush fails.) But her anguish is soon to end. Odysseus arrives and disguises himself as a beggar. He reveals his identity only to his son, two loyal servants, and his childhood nurse. Influenced by Athene, Penelope arranges a bow-and-arrow contest intended to frustrate the suitors. She pledges to wed the suitor who proves handiest at stringing the Great Bow and shooting an arrow through twelve axes lined up in a row, the way Odysseus used to do. Odysseus, brought before Penelope but unrecognized in his disguise, encourages her to hold the contest as soon as possible. The time arrives. All suitors fail in their efforts to string the bow. One of the loyal servants then picks up the bow and delivers it to Odysseus, still in disguise. Finally, the Great Bow is back in his hands.

Kubrick provides symbols for both Penelope's cry of anguish and Odysseus's regaining the Great Bow. In the hotel room on the alien planet, Bowman explores his new environment. He enters the bathroom. Weird, indistinct voices come from the sound track. Then, as Bowman's gaze shifts to the bathtub, an anguished woman's voice can be heard. Though badly distorted, it seems to be crying, "Help me! Help me!" Unless I am mistaken, it is Penelope crying out for help. What other woman could possibly be calling for help?

And where in *2001* does Odysseus regain the Great Bow? The aged Bowman, lying in bed, reaches out with his arm toward the last monolith, which stands at the foot of the bed. It somehow comes into his grasp, and we see him transformed. He is now in control; he is ready to deal with the suitors. The hotel-room monolith—the last monolith—is the Great Bow.

Earlier, I suggested that the first monolith is also the Great Bow. The harmony between the two monoliths can now be seen clearly. In discussing the first monolith, I pointed out that both it and the last monolith have essentially the same surface story function, namely, enhancing intelligence and accelerating evolution. If they are essentially the same thing, they can both symbolize the same thing—the Great Bow. The African setting represents the occasion where Odysseus receives the Great Bow as a gift. The hotel-room setting represents the occasion where Odysseus regains the Great Bow after it has been out of his hands for twenty years.

SLAYING THE SUITORS

When I explained the derivation of Bowman's name at the beginning of this chapter, I revealed the fate of those nasty suitors. In case you've forgotten, Odysseus begins by passing Penelope's test, the test that the suitors have all failed to pass: he effortlessly strings the Great Bow and shoots an arrow through the twelve axes lined up in a row. Then he starts shooting arrows into the suitors, starting with the worst of the lot. When the arrows run out, he, his son, and the two loyal servants—plus Athene, who is invisibly deflecting enemy spears—finish off the rest of the pack, using spears and then swords.

Kubrick does not *directly* symbolize the slaying of the suitors. He originally intended to but changed his mind. In the final scene the star-child (Odysseus) would detonate (kill) the nuclear bombs (suitors) orbiting the earth (Penelope). The concept was superb—and is still there in spirit—but artistic problems got in the way. Agel, in a tersely worded picture caption in his book, explains what happened:

> [The] only ending that went to shooting-script stage, and was eliminated, was having [the] star-child detonate nuclear weapons orbiting the Earth, as in [Clarke's] book version. Consensus: [The] ending would have been too similar to [the] ending of [a] previous Kubrick film, *Dr. Strangelove*.[15]

There was probably more to the decision than duplication of *Dr. Strangelove*. Having the star-child detonate the nuclear weapons orbiting the earth would have thoroughly messed up the "great noontime" symbolism in

2001's final scene. That symbolism will be explained when we get to the Zarathustra allegory. For the moment, suffice it to say that the great noontime is a beatific metaphor that has no room in it for exploding nuclear bombs.

It seems fair to conclude that Kubrick would have liked to have the star-child explode the bombs but was constrained by artistic, rather than plot, considerations. I suspect he decided that the monolith could serve his purpose: regaining the Great Bow *implies* the death of the suitors. Meanwhile, Clarke felt no artistic constraint, although he certainly had no intention of symbolizing the death of the suitors. Clarke had the star-child explode the bombs after arriving back at earth. I'd say we have to go with Clarke on this one. Carrying the Odysseus allegory to its climax requires that the star-child explode the bombs. Kubrick knows it happened; he just couldn't show it. As far as I'm concerned, it happened.

REUNION WITH PENELOPE

Though forced to forgo symbolizing the climactic battle in the great hall, Kubrick does provide the denouement. When we see the star-child gazing at the earth in the final scene, we are seeing Odysseus gazing at Penelope. The earth symbolizes Penelope. *2001* ends with the reunion of Odysseus and Penelope.

NOTES

1. With this book almost ready for press, I have learned that at least one other person has indeed independently deciphered the symbolism in Dave Bowman's name. Barry Krusch precisely identifies the antecedents of both David and Bowman on his "Kubrick on the Web" website, http://www.krusch.com/kubrick/Q14.html, page 5.

2. Homer, *The Odyssey*, trans. E. V. Rieu (Baltimore: Penguin, 1946), 316–27.

3. Arthur C. Clarke, *The Lost Worlds of* 2001 (Boston: Gregg Press, 1979), 33.

4. Edith Hamilton, *Mythology: Timeless Tales of Gods and Heroes* (New York: New American Library, 1953), 178–201.

5. Homer, *The Odyssey*, 27. Another god, Proteus, the Old Man of the Sea, refers to his celestial cousins as "the everlasting gods who live in the broad sky" (Ibid, 77).

6. The fourth bomb's solar panels seem to be comic symbols. The eight on the front end are shaped and mounted like windmill blades; they seem to represent either (1a) a misconceived (because of the vacuum) propeller for propelling the bomb or (2a) a decorative spinner that operates when the bomb falls. The four panels on the rear end are arranged to symbolize either (1b) a secondary propulsion sys-

tem, namely a comically mismanaged paddle wheel, mounted sideways, or (2b) fins to guide the bomb when it falls.

7. Hamilton, *Mythology*, 181. Helen herself admits that Hamilton is right, saying "shameless creature that I was" (Homer, *The Odyssey*, 68). But she blames her "infatuation" with Paris on Aphrodite, who "lured me to Troy from my own dear country and made me forsake my daughter, my bridal chamber, and a husband who had all one could wish for in the way of brains and good looks" (Ibid., 71).

8. Roger Ebert, *Roger Ebert's Movie Home Companion*, 1st ed. (Kansas City, Mo.: Andrews, McMeel & Parker, 1984), 390.

9. See the illustration in Tim Severin, "The Quest for Ulysses [Latin for Odysseus]," *National Geographic* 170, no. 2 (August 1986), 201.

10. Jerome Agel, ed., *The Making of Kubrick's* 2001 (New York: New American Library, 1970), 146.

11. Homer, *The Odyssey*, 92.

12. Ibid., 94.

13. Ibid., 203 (my italics).

14. David G. Stork, ed., *HAL's Legacy:* 2001*'s Computer as Dream and Reality* (Cambridge: MIT Press, 1997), 343 (my italics).

15. Agel, ed., *Making* 2001, 164.

Chapter 4

The Man-Machine Symbiosis Allegory

Kubrick's second allegory uses the same surface story, Dave Bowman's journey (plus its preamble, "The Dawn of Man"), to symbolize a journey far different from that of Odysseus. This journey is essentially philosophical, although the philosophy is whimsical in many aspects. The allegory depicts humanoid (not just human) evolution as a trip along an evolutionary road leading from (1) prehuman apes to (2) humans to (3) a wrong-fork evolutionary dead end, malevolent humanoid machines, and finally back to the right fork and on to (4) a nobler, benevolent humanoid. Each of the three evolutionary movements (e.g., ape to man) is marked by a prominent milestone—a tall, *upright*, domino-shaped black monolith that actually looks like a milestone. And there is a toppled milestone; it marks a return to the road fork where evolution went astray.

OVERVIEW OF THE ALLEGORY

The story centers on that evolutionary dead end, humanoid machines, where we find a message. Taken literally, the message is that humanity will not degenerate into a race of humanoid machines. This message is a playful poke at Arthur Clarke's theory about man's eventually becoming indistinguishable from machine. (The theory is not at all ridiculous in a science-fiction context. Humanoid robots have a long history in science fiction. Robby the Robot, from the 1956 film *Forbidden Planet*, is the best example. The theme is further developed in a 1984 film, *The Terminator*, where a future race of humanoid machines wages war against the remnants of humanity.) Taken metaphorically, the message says that humanity will not get worse. This message complements another found at the end of the main road, where man evolves into the benign, innocent star-child: Man will overcome his deficiencies and evolve into a nobler, more benevolent being.

To grasp the second allegory, you must see the parallel between the Battle at the Waterhole and the Battle in Outer Space. Seeing the parallel requires recognizing that (a) each battle follows the appearance of a monolith, (b) Hal-Discovery in the second battle, like man in the first, symbolizes a newly evolved humanoid race, (c) each battle is fought between two symbolized *races*, contrasted with the surface story individuals, and (d) each battle is a battle for *racial* survival.

Recognizing that Hal-Discovery represents a new humanoid race is the key to understanding the allegory. And finding this key requires that you perceive how thoroughly manlike Hal-Discovery is, not just in Hal's psyche but in Discovery's physique and in Hal-Discovery's being a tool-weapon user. Contrary to what Wallich has written, Hal's anthropomorphisms are not just "throwaway detail[s]."[1] They are the very essence of the allegory. Hal tells lies, for example, because humans tell lies and Hal is human, or at least humanoid.

The idea of a race of humanoid machines is, once again, a caricature of Clarke's idea of man-machine symbiosis. Bizony summarizes this idea: "Clarke has long propounded his theory that humans and computers will one day become all but indistinguishable, as our ever-advancing technology supersedes natural evolution and comes up with some kind of symbiotic breed. In the far future, 'we will not travel in spaceships. We will *be* spaceships.'"[2] Now some words directly from Clarke: "The tool we have invented *is* our successor. Biological evolution has given way to a far more rapid process—technical evolution. The machine is going to take over."[3] Kubrick takes this idea and runs with it. A humanoid machine becomes "our [would-be] successor," a "symbiotic breed" that is both human and machine.

The humanoid evolution allegory has five main aspects: (1) the evolution of man, (2) the evolution of humanoid machines, (3) the strongly humanoid nature of those machines, (4) the defeat of the humanoid machines by man, and (5) the evolution of a genuinely higher humanoid being. This chapter examines each of these five topics. In the process, it elucidates Kubrick's sexual symbolism, including some new material in the movie's last part ("Jupiter and Beyond the Infinite") that was not relevant to the Odysseus allegory. Geduld has extrapolated wildly from the sexual symbolism in coming up with her Freudian-Jungian interpretation of *2001*. The last section of this chapter explains why the Freudian-Jungian interpretation should not be taken seriously.

THE DAWN OF MAN

Everyone understands that the "Dawn of Man" episode that begins *2001* depicts the evolution of man from an earlier apelike being. I have called the earlier being *Australopithecus*, the humanoid species that came before the *Homo* series (*Homo habilis*, *Homo erectus*, *Homo sapiens*). People also understand that the ape who picks up a bone and realizes he can use it as a club—a weapon, a *tool*—is the first human. And they understand that he isn't just a character; he is a *symbol*, a symbol of *Homo sapiens*. (Technically, *Homo habilis* follows *Australopithecus*, but to simplify and to accommodate Nietzsche in the next allegory, Kubrick jumps directly to man.)

What people don't recognize, however, is that these symbols are just the beginning of a long and continuous stream of symbols. Hal-Discovery, for example, is also more than just a character. Like the tool-user ape (i.e., the first man), he is a *symbol* for a new species.

The black monolith is another poorly understood aspect of the Dawn of Man. We saw in chapter 2 that, in the surface story, the monolith is an alien-planted device for boosting intelligence and thereby accelerating evolution. In the Odysseus allegory, the monolith is the Great Bow, being given as a gift to Odysseus. But in the symbiosis allegory it is something else. The monolith symbolizes the very thing it resembles: a milestone, the first milestone along the road of humanoid evolution. At this milestone, ape becomes man. At the next milestone, on the moon, man will "evolve" into (by creating) a humanoid machine that will become an evolutionary dead end. The Jupiter monolith, which is lying flat rather than standing upright, symbolizes a toppled milestone: it is where humanoid life returns from the dead end and gets back on the main road. The last milestone, in the hotel room on the alien planet, marks the point on the road of evolution where man evolves into a genuinely better humanoid species.

Viewed as a milestone, the monolith is a clue that two things are about to happen. If you observe these two things happening after the first upright monolith appears, you can look for and find them happening again after the second monolith—the one on the moon—appears. First, a new humanoid species arrives. Second, shortly after the new species arrives, it turns on the older species and tries to kill it. In the battle that follows the coming of the first monolith—the Battle at the Waterhole—the new species wins, defeating the old one. But the next new species, humanoid machines, won't be so successful: it will be the loser in the Battle in Outer Space.

One other comment: Kubrick is technically incorrect in depicting man as the only tool user, but he is justified both by artistic considerations and by tradition. For many years tool use was viewed as a distinguishing characteristic of human beings. But in the mid-1960s Jane Goodall found that chimpanzees probe termite mounds with twigs. And chimps aren't the only nonhuman tool users. Sea otters use stones to crack mollusk shells. Fifteen species of birds use tools.[4] For example, crows on the islands of New Caledonia bite twigs to create hooks, which they use to drag prey out of holes.[5] Even some insects use tools.[6] Still, Kubrick is fully justified in exercising allegoric license by adopting the traditional view for symbolic purposes. Kubrick's work is art, not science.

THE EVOLUTION OF HUMANOID MACHINES

The next species (after man) to evolve is humanoid machines, symbolized by Hal-Discovery. Hal, you will recall, is the spaceship's brain and central nervous system, a remarkably humanoid computer; Discovery is the suspiciously skeletal spaceship in whose skull-like head Hal is ensconced. Kubrick's brilliantly imaginative eight-stage evolution of Hal-Discovery, *Homo machinus*, is an artistic feat that for too long has gone unrecognized and unappreciated. Take a look at what Kubrick has done:

Stage 1: Critics have applauded the artistry of the transformation whereby the bone tossed in the air by victorious man becomes a space vehicle. Hirsch, for example, calls this transformation "the most majestic match cut in the history of movies."[7] And most have perceived that the bone and the space vehicle are both tools—a good start. But did you know that this transition is the second stage of an eight-stage sequence in the evolution of *Homo machinus*? The sequence begins with the transition of an animal bone into a primitive tool-weapon, a club. *Homo machinus* is going to evolve from the bone of a dead animal.

Stage 2: After using the club to vanquish *Australopithecus* (and thereby become *Homo sapiens*), man triumphantly flings the club high into the air. The air becomes outer space, and the primitive weapon evolves into a high-tech weapon, an orbiting nuclear bomb.

Stages 3 and 4: Following a preliminary shot of the rotating, two-wheeled space station, the orbiting (non-self-propelled) bombs evolve into (3) a self-propelled phallic spaceship. It is the Pan-American shuttle *Orion*, and it is en route from earth to the space station. The sexual symbolism becomes evident when the shuttle (4) copulates with the space station.

Stages 5 and 6: After the male shuttle and the female space station mate, (5) a spherical moon lander, symbolizing a sperm cell, travels to the moon, a larger sphere symbolizing an ovum (which is much larger than a sperm cell). (6) The surface of the moon opens up and accepts the lander, then closes again. The sperm is inside the egg; fertilization has occurred.

Shortly after fertilization, the second upright monolith appears. The monoliths, remember, are milestones along the road of humanoid evolution. When you see a milestone—an *upright* one—you know a new humanoid species is about to emerge. The first milestone marked the evolution of ape into man. The second milestone signifies that man is about to evolve into a new species of humanoid machines.

At both milestones, the metaphorical dawn of the new species is accompanied by a literal dawn, pregnant with symbolism. The Dawn of Man episode begins with the sun peeking over the horizon on the African desert. Correspondingly, the Dawn of *Homo machinus* begins with a lunar dawn: the sun peeks over the top of the moon monolith. Kubrick is presenting the message in two different ways: milestone and dawn. So be alert. Look for the next humanoid, the one announced by the milestone and the dawn.

Stages 7 and 8: Immediately after the monolith scene at Tycho, the words "JUPITER MISSION: 18 MONTHS LATER" flash on the screen against a black, star-studded universe. Then Hal-Discovery, the symbol of a new humanoid race, drifts into view—slowly, horizontally, headfirst, like an emerging baby, from off the side of the screen. After (7) a gestation period of eighteen months, which began when the moon was fertilized, (8) a new humanoid race has been born. Note the length of that gestation period. Eighteen months is exactly twice the length of the nine-month gestation period of humans. Kubrick seems to be implying that the new humanoids are twice as smart as humans.

An intriguing series of engineering coincidences, which might be more than coincidences, raises the question of whether Kubrick has provided a general symbol pointing to the presence of *eight* stages. During the earth-to-moon trip you can find no less than six pieces of space equipment that display what might be described loosely as eight-part circles:

1. The second orbiting nuclear bomb has an approximately cylindrical shape, but instead of being perfectly round it has eight flat facets running lengthwise. They resemble boards and form octagonal cross sections at the ends of the "cylinder."
2. The fourth orbiting bomb (Zeus) has eight blades on that circular propeller or spinner formed by the eight solar panels in front.

3. The space station has two circular wheels, each of which has four spokes. If the two wheels are viewed as one circular space station, the circular station has eight spokes.
4. The elevator leading up a spoke from the space station's shuttle bay (axle) to the station's lobby-restaurant-hotel area (rim area) has a semicircular bench—the circle is broken by the door—that has eight evenly spaced, padded dividers. (You can't see all the dividers, but you can judge the positions of the unseen ones from the positions of those you can see.)
5. The moon lander, viewed from the bottom, has a circular shape that is broken into eight equal sectors by four rocket clusters plus a landing leg located between each cluster (four legs in all)—a total of eight components spaced evenly around the circle.
6. The moon lander's hangar has a dome-shaped, upward-pointing circular entrance divided into eight "pie slices," pointed doors that meet in the middle and pull back into the rim. The slices divide the entrance into eight approximately triangular (slightly curved on the outside edge) sectors.

The most suspicious aspect of these "coincidences" is that they all occur within the series of events that symbolize the eight stages of evolution. Maybe all the eight-part circles really are coincidences or, at any rate, just a design idiosyncrasy of someone on the special-effects team. But you can't help wondering whether Kubrick didn't inject all those eights as a way of symbolizing or hinting at the presence of the eight-stage evolutionary process. He did something similar when he injected the "Ham, ham, ham, ham" dialogue into the moon bus scene as a hint that TMA-ONE (being discussed) was an anagram involving meat.

HAL-DISCOVERY AS A GENUINE HUMANOID

The man-machine symbiosis allegory is predicated on Hal-Discovery's being a genuine humanoid. Without this quality, he could not symbolize a would-be successor to man: *Homo machinus* would not be the evolutionary offspring of *Homo sapiens*. True, Hal-Discovery does not organically evolve from man, but any demand for organic evolution misses the artistic spirit of the movie. Hal-Discovery is created by man, is also the product of symbolized sexual conception, and has a strong physical and mental resemblance to man. In these senses he is man's offspring and is humanoid.

Because Hal-Discovery's essential humanity is so critical to the allegory, Kubrick goes to great lengths to symbolize it. The sexual reproduction symbolism is just the beginning. We find all sorts of other anthropomorphic and anthropopathic traits, both mental and physical, in the humanoid machine. To drive home the point, Kubrick even gives Hal a symbolic name, a name that says, in effect, "I am a synthesis of man and machine." In order to appreciate what Kubrick has done to make Hal-Discovery a humanoid, we need to take a closer look at (1) his mental traits, many of which have been recognized by others, (2) his physical traits, which have been largely overlooked, and (3) the name Hal, a shortened form of "HAL-9000 computer."

Mental Traits

For the most part (but not entirely), the anthropomorphic-anthropopathic mentality of Hal is well understood, but some details—including some extremely important ones—have been overlooked. Hal's human mental traits include the following:

1. *Consciousness:* Hal refers to himself in the BBC interview as "a conscious entity."
2. *Cognition:* Hal plainly can think.
3. *Confidence:* Hal says, "No 9000 computer has ever made a mistake."
4. *Enjoyment:* Hal says, "I enjoy working with people."
5. *Enthusiasm:* Hal says, "I've still got the greatest enthusiasm."
6. *Pride:* The BBC interviewer says, "I sensed a certain pride in his answer."
7. *Secretiveness:* While working up his crew psychology report on Bowman, Hal pretends to know nothing beyond rumor about the moon monolith. Yet in the prerecorded briefing Bowman hears after killing Hal, we learn that Hal was fully informed about the monolith and the mission's purpose.
8. *Puzzlement:* Hal says, "Yes, it's puzzling."
9. *Blaming:* After seeming to be caught making a mistake, Hal says, "It [the appearance of a mistake] can only be attributable to human error."
10. *Treachery:* While pretending to support Bowman and Poole, Hal kills Poole and tries to kill Bowman.
11. *Fear:* Hal says, "I'm afraid, Dave."

12. *Panic:* Hal pleads: "Dave, stop! Stop, will you? Stop, Dave! Will you stop, Dave? Stop, Dave!"
13. *Lying:* After Hal kills Poole, Dave asks Hal if he knows what happened. Hal replies: "I'm sorry, Dave. I don't have enough information."
14. *Senility:* When Bowman lobotomizes Hal, cutting off his higher brain functions, Hal regresses to his childhood mentality, singing "Daisy, Daisy," a song he learned during his infancy at a laboratory.

Hal also has human talents. He plays chess—and wins. In complimenting Bowman on some sketches of the hibernating crew members, Hal acts as an art critic. In working up his crew psychology report, he becomes a clinical psychologist. And—here is the most symbolically important human characteristic of all—he is a tool-user. When Hal kills Frank Poole, he uses Poole's vacated utility pod as a weapon, cutting Poole's air hose.

Physical Traits

Discovery's anatomy is much less understood. Let's start with that big round head. When the movie was released in 1968, an amusing still of Discovery opening one of his three mouths (circular pod bay doors), sticking out his tongue (pod launching ramp), and blowing a bubble (launching a spherical pod) was seen by the public. Here Kubrick's obvious sense of humor alerts us to look for other humorous physical traits. We don't have to look far. Right above those three mouths, Discovery is wearing some jaunty, wide-band, mod sunglasses. How's that for human? And, of course, Hal speaks, hears, and—with that red eye—sees.

Behind Discovery's head is his neck, and running back from the neck is a segmented spine with the usual elongated sacrum (tailbone) at the end. Hardly any imagination is needed to recognize this as an abstracted human spine. (When Bizony describes Discovery's skeletal structure as being similar to that of a "dinosaur skeleton," he completely misses the point of what Kubrick is doing.[8])

Now we come to the rear end and to some scatological humor. Lest there be doubt that Kubrick's humor sometimes *is* scatological, recall Colonel Bat Guano from *Dr. Strangelove*. At the rear of the spaceship are six rocket nozzles, used by Hal-Discovery to excrete his wastes. The nozzles are arranged in three pairs, each of which is enclosed in a hexagon. Why three pairs? Go back to the head. Three mouths. We can infer that each mouth has its own alimentary tract. So each mouth is supported by the normal number of excretory orifices, two.

But why the hexagons? Why not circles or squares or nothing? When I was growing up in the 1930s, which is the same time Kubrick was grow-ing up, most reasonably modern houses had white tile bathroom floors. The tiles, in vogue from the turn of the century through World War II, were hexagons, one inch across (measured edge-to-edge) and fitted together in a honeycomb pattern. The rear-end hexagons are bathroom tiles! They symbolize bathrooms. Hal-Discovery has three bathrooms, one for each mouth. And what is the only being that uses bathrooms to answer the call of nature? *Homo sapiens*. Once more we see that the intel-ligent spaceship is a humanoid.

Hal-Discovery is also a telephone-user—yet another human trait. About halfway down his spine is a telephone-shaped array of three dish (circular) antennas. A big dish is flanked by two smaller ones connected by a curved handle. Viewed from a certain angle, the configuration looks like an abstract version of a standard 1960s dial telephone. I hadn't noticed the resemblance when watching the movie, but a still in Bizony's book brings out the symbolism.[9] You can see that the big dish is the telephone's base, on which the handle rests; the two small dishes at either end of the handle are the mouthpiece and the receiver.

Hal's Name

The name Hal is widely, and I think accurately, believed to be derived from IBM—International Business Machines. If you take each letter of IBM and retreat it one notch back down the alphabet (I to *H*, B to *A*, M to *L*), you get HAL. The name Hal is thus a perfect symbol for a humanoid machine that is a synthesis or symbiosis of *man* (Hal, a man's name) and *machine* (IBM, a firm that makes machines). What makes the symbolism truly perfect is that IBM does not stand for just any old machines; it stands for *computers*, machines of the very class Hal belongs to.

Arthur Clarke swears that this supposed derivation is just a coincidence and that HAL is derived, as he says in his novel, from *H*euristically pro-grammed *AL*gorithmic computer. The IBM story is an "annoying and per-sistent myth."[10] But I wonder if *Kubrick* didn't choose the name Hal and if Clarke didn't later work out the acronym, with or without encouragement from Kubrick. (Without seems more likely: the meaning of Clarke's acronym isn't mentioned in the movie and has no symbolic value for any of the three allegories.)

There is good evidence that Kubrick chose the important names at the very least. The symbolic names are obviously Kubrick's work. Both Kubrick and Clarke tend to ignore the other party's names. The hero of Clarke's short story "The Sentinel," on which *2001* is loosely based, is named Wilson, and his assistant is Louis Garnett. Neither name is used by Kubrick. One symbolic name from the movie, Elena, isn't even in Clarke's novel. In the movie, the inquisitive Russian scientist at the space station is Andrey Smyslov;[11] in Clarke's novel, he is Dimitri Moisevitch. In the movie, the three hibernating crewmen are named Hunter, *Kimball*, and Kaminski; in the novel they are Hunter, *Whitehead*, and Kaminski. The mutual independence of Kubrick and Clarke when it comes to names (and plot) is grounds for doubt that Clarke came up with Hal's name.

I'm sure Clarke is sincere in denying that Hal is derived from IBM. He remembers inventing the parent name: there is no reason to doubt that "heuristically programmed algorithmic computer" came from Clarke. But Clarke could have forgotten that the name he converted to an acronym, Hal, came from Kubrick.

Six compelling considerations, taken collectively, make it almost inconceivable that the IBM connection is just an accident:

1. Kubrick undeniably uses names as symbols. And not just occasionally where *2001* is concerned. *2001* has four major characters: Dave Bowman, Heywood R. Floyd, Frank Poole, and Hal. We have already seen that the names Dave Bowman (chapter 3), Heywood R. Floyd (chapter 3), and Frank Poole (chapter 1) embody symbolic meanings. Even a minor character's name, Elena, has a symbolic meaning. The name of the moon monolith, TMA-1, also has a hidden meaning. And the crater name Tycho has a hidden meaning. Why would Kubrick sneak hidden meanings into the names of three of his four major characters, not to mention Elena and TMA-1 and Tycho, but decide not to play games with the fourth major character's name?

2. Hal's full (and formal) name is HAL 9000. The 9000 is definitely symbolic. Its symbolism will be explained in detail in chapter 5, which concerns the Zarathustra allegory. Why would Kubrick make 9000 but not HAL symbolic? That would be like including ONE but not TMA in the TMA-1 symbolism.

3. Kubrick would hardly have abandoned a previously chosen symbolic name, Athena, in favor of Hal if Hal were not also symbolic. Clarke himself mentions that the computer was originally christened Socrates and later renamed Athena.[12] Socrates is mildly sym-

bolic: it gives the computer a Greek identity that harmonizes with *The Odyssey*, and it also suggests intelligence. Athena is much better. As the name of a Greek goddess who plays a prominent role in *The Odyssey*, Athena gives the filmgoer another hint that Homer's work is being depicted. And in the Zarathustra allegory, Athena has even more symbolic value. There the computer (combined with the spaceship) symbolizes God. Giving the computer the name of a deity—letting one deity symbolize another—provides Kubrick with an excellent symbolic name. Athena also embodies a good joke: God is a woman. Why would Kubrick have abandoned such a versatile symbolic name if he hadn't come up with an even better symbolic name? Hal, symbolizing a synthesis of man (Hal) and machine (IBM) *is* better.

4. The fact that IBM—International Business Machines—represents just what Kubrick needs it to represent, machines (and, more specifically, computers), is too much of a coincidence. If IBM meant International Bread Makers, Clarke's contention that the HAL-IBM connection is a coincidence would be somewhat plausible. In that case IBM would have no symbolic value (Hal does not secretly represent a loaf of bread); the connection would amount to nothing more than a limp joke. But IBM represents *computers*—not just any old machines but the very class that Hal belongs to. How can this be a coincidence?

5. Viewed as an acronym for Heuristically Programmed Algorithmic Computer, HAL fails to meet the tests of an acronym. And this failure strongly implies that Clarke was working backwards from HAL, struggling unsuccessfully to produce a phrase from which HAL could be derived as an acronym. An acronym is a pronounceable word (not just a set of letters) formed from the initial letters and sometimes additional letters of a name or series of words: NOW stands for National Organization for Women. Letters representing articles (*a*, *an*, and *the*) and prepositions (*for*, *by*, *in*, and so on) can be omitted, but all major words must be represented. HAL not only fails to represent two of the four major words, it snubs the single most important word, Computer. How can Clarke assert that HAL is an acronym when both the only noun and an additional major word (Programmed) from the parent name are omitted? The logical acronym for Heuristically Programmed Algorithmic Computer is HEPAC. (The E, taken from the first word, is needed because HPAC is not a pronounceable word.) The omission of P and C from HAL is compelling evidence that HAL was chosen (by Kubrick) *before* Clarke came up with his supposed parent phrase. Indeed, if all Clarke (or

Kubrick) wanted had been a nonsymbolic name that was a computer acronym, he would surely have used a true acronym such as ALEC (ALgorithmic Empathic Computer), CHARLES (Computer for Heuristic Algorithms and Rationally Logical Empathic Symbiosis), MAC (Machine for Algorithmic Computation), or MURPH (Machine for Undertaking Rationally Processed Heuristics). He could even have kept SOCRATES (SOphisticated Computer for RATional Empathic Symbiosis).

6. The mathematical odds against coincidence are overpowering, no matter which of three possible assumptions you use to compute those odds:

a. Clarke assumes that, because the letters of IBM actually are one alphabetic notch *above* the letters of HAL, *above* is the only possibility to be factored in. He therefore computes the odds as $1/26 \times 1/26 \times 1/26 = 1/17{,}576$, or 17,576 to 1 against coincidence.[13] (One chance in 26 is the odds that a specific letter of IBM will be exactly one notch above the corresponding letter of HAL, given that the alphabet has 26 letters. Multiplying the three probabilities gives the odds that *all three* letters of IBM will beat the 1/26 odds.)

b. The HAL-IBM connection would be just as strong and meaningful if all letters of IBM were one alphabetic notch *below* the letters of HAL. So a fairer assumption (fairer to Clarke) is that coincidence permits the letters of IBM to be *either* one notch above *or* one notch below those of HAL, provided that all letters shift in the same direction. The odds that each letter of IBM will be (*a*) adjacent to *and* (*b*) on the same side of the corresponding letter of HAL are $2/26 \times 1/26 \times 1/26 = 1/8{,}788$, or 1 chance in 8,788. (The first letter can be either advanced *or* retreated one notch—2 chances in 26—but the other two letters must be on the same side of HAL as the first. The second and third letters thus have only 1 chance in 26 of coming out right by chance.)

c. At the price of weakening the association between IBM and HAL, we could also assume that all letters of IBM merely need to be advanced or retreated the *same* number of notches—any number from 1 to 25. (Here we use a circular alphabet in which A follows Z when letters are advanced.) Now the odds against coincidence are $25/26 \times 1/26 \times 1/26 = 1/703$, or 1 chance in 703. (For the first letter, the odds of getting a letter other than H by chance are 25 chances in 26; the last two letters have only 1 chance in 26 of being advanced or retreated the same number of notches as the first.)

No matter which assumption we make, the odds against coincidence are formidable. I'd say the middle assumption is the most reasonable: the odds against coincidence are 8,788 to 1.

The six arguments presented above leave almost no room for doubt that Kubrick did base the name Hal on IBM and that Hal is therefore symbolic: it symbolizes a synthesis of man and machine. Kubrick thus symbolizes that Hal-Discovery represents man-machine symbiosis in three ways: (1) through Hal's human personality traits, (2) through Discovery's human physical characteristics, and (3) through the name Hal—a synthesis of man (Hal) and machine (IBM).

THE DEATH OF *HOMO MACHINUS*

To reiterate, each of the three upright monoliths represents a milestone in humanoid evolution. Each milestone marks the emergence of a new species—first, *Homo sapiens*; second, *Homo machinus*; third, *Homo futurus*. And that's not all that follows the milestones. The first monolith is also followed by a deadly battle between the new species and the old one from which it evolved: *Homo sapiens* kills *Australopithecus*, the apelike species from which man sprang.

The second monolith is likewise followed by a deadly battle between the new species and the old. Hal-Discovery symbolizes the new species that comes after the *second* milestone, just as Moonwatcher (the first man) symbolizes the new species that comes after the *first* milestone. Do you remember what Moonwatcher did? He used a bone to club to death the leader of a rival group in the Battle at the Waterhole. Hal imitates Moonwatcher. He turns on his human crew, killing Frank Poole and the three hibernating astronauts. Only Dave Bowman is left to fight back.

And fight back he does. Locked outside the spaceship and apparently doomed, he battles his way back in through the emergency airlock, advances grimly to the brain chamber, and lobotomizes Hal with a special brain-module shutoff key. The Battle in Outer Space, analog of the Battle at the Waterhole, is over. For all practical purposes, and certainly for symbolic purposes, *Homo machinus* is dead. This time the *older* species has won the postmonolith battle. Humanoid life, which had started down the wrong fork in the road of evolution, can retrace its steps and proceed down the right fork. Clarke's vision of a symbiotic breed of spaceships will not be realized.

This interpretation raises an obvious question. Immediately after the Battle in Outer Space, the spaceship arrives at Jupiter. There an orbiting third monolith greets it. This monolith is one that received and relayed the second monolith's beamed signal from the moon. It is also the operator of the Star Gate. Now the question: If the monoliths mark the emergence of new humanoid species, why isn't this third monolith followed by the appearance of a new species? The answer: Only the three *upright* monoliths (Africa, moon, and hotel room), the ones that *look* like milestones, symbolize evolutionary milestones.

Nevertheless, the Jupiter monolith *is* a milestone of sorts. It is a toppled milestone. At least it can be visualized as such; I'm not sure Kubrick had that vision in mind. When man slays the dead-end species of humanoid machines, the *Homo machinus* milestone topples. And when man retraces his steps back to the fork where evolution temporarily went astray, he finds the second milestone knocked over, lying horizontal. He must go quite a bit farther — down the right fork — to get to another solidly planted, upright milestone.

THE EVOLUTION OF *HOMO FUTURUS*

At Jupiter, Bowman leaves the spaceship in a pod to investigate the monolith he sees. The monolith yanks him into the tunnel of lights, where he is whooshed along lickety-split to another part of the universe.

What a Strange Room

When Bowman emerges from the tunnel, he sees all sorts of celestial wonders and then skims over the surface of the alien planet. All of a sudden he is inside that mysterious hotel room or bedroom. Its decor — period furniture, oil paintings, statuettes displayed in windowlike Palladian wall recesses, pedestal art — has been described as Louis XVI,[14] French high baroque,[15] and Regency.[16]

But apart from the decor, writers have used the words "movingly conventional,"[17] "very worldly,"[18] and "ordinariness"[19] to describe the room. Conventional? Worldly? Ordinary? The room has no external door (just the bathroom door), no windows, no carpet, no lamps or light fixtures, and no bathroom-sink shaving mirror. The toilet seat is built-in, mounted on a wall-to-wall bench, as in a privy. The floors — bathroom and bedroom — are translucent glass; all illumination comes from below.

Much of this is just there to distract us and to create a surrealistic effect by establishing incongruity between the room's ornate period furnishings and the stark art deco floor of geometrically patterned glass. What is essential is (1) the absence of a door and windows, (2) the translucent glass floor, and (3) the below-the-floor lighting. Kubrick lets us see the full length of all four walls. No door. No windows. He also shows us the three nonabutting walls of the bathroom. (Two-thirds of the toilet-seat wall is slyly shown indirectly—in a mirror on the opposite wall, over the bathtub.) Still no door or windows.

What's going on here? When is the last time you saw a hotel room (or a bedroom, for that matter) with no door or windows, let alone one that also had a glass floor through which all illumination came? What's going on is fetal development. Bowman, with help from the unseen aliens, is evolving into a higher humanoid being, the first of a new race. Kubrick is using growth—aging—in a fetus to symbolize evolution. The windowless, doorless hotel room symbolizes the amnion, or fetal sac; it has no openings. And the translucent glass floor that admits light from below represents both the translucency of the amnionic membrane and the light coming in through the birth canal (allow some artistic license here): in humans the birth canal is *below* the fetus (when the mother is standing) and leads to the outside world of light.

How the Fetus Was Conceived

Before examining Kubrick's fetal development symbolism in more detail, we need to back up to some earlier symbolism involving the pod's trip (with Bowman inside) from the spaceship to the hotel room. I temporarily skipped this earlier symbolism because its interpretation might have seemed dubious in the absence of foreknowledge that fertilization and fetal development were coming up. Recall that the birth of Hal-Discovery after that eighteen-month gestation period was preceded by sexual symbolism. The phallic space shuttle *Orion* penetrated a slot in the revolving space station. Then a spherical moon lander, symbolizing a sperm cell, traveled from the space station to the moon, a much larger sphere symbolizing the ovum (larger than the sperm). The moon opened to take the smaller sphere inside—eighteen months before the birth of Hal-Discovery, *who symbolized a new race.*

For the final stage of evolution, Kubrick is using more or less the same symbolism—the details differ—all over again. The spherical pod, like the spherical moon lander before it, symbolizes a sperm cell; Bowman, seated inside, is the chromosomes of humanity. In a distant shot of the elongated spaceship (analog of the elongated earth shuttle from the earlier sequence), we see the pod emerge from Discovery's tip: ejaculation. This action means that Discovery, which (along with Hal) originally symbolized a new race of humanoid machines, has been reconceptualized as a phallus.

This interpretation is reinforced by a seemingly trivial, but genuinely important, inconsistency in one of the details. Discovery has three pods, each with its own circular pod bay door (representing one of Hal-Discovery's three mouths). Poole takes the *center* pod on his ill-fated repair mission; this pod, the weapon used to kill Poole, drifts off into space. Bowman, in his foredoomed effort to rescue his already dead colleague, takes the pod behind Hal-Discovery's right mouth. When Bowman uses the pod's eject system to blast his way back into the spaceship through the emergency airlock, this right-side pod too is abandoned in space. Only the pod in Discovery's *left* cheek remains. And yet, when Bowman uses the last pod to investigate the Jupiter monolith, we see it exiting from the *center* bay.

Did Kubrick get careless? Hardly. Kubrick was keeping track of pods. The interior scene where Bowman prepares to go after Poole clearly shows that only the right and left pods remain. Kubrick knew this. But to symbolize ejaculation, he had to have the sperm coming out of an opening in the *center* of the phallus's tip. So he did what his symbolism required and, I suppose, hoped nobody would notice the inconsistency.

Almost immediately after exiting from Discovery, the pod enters and zips along the tunnel of lights. Major symbolism. The tunnel of lights is a cosmic fallopian tube! (How much better this is than the invisible fallopian tube the moon sperm used.) Eventually the pod reaches the spherical planet of the aliens. Like the spherical moon-ovum before it, it is larger than the sperm — as an ovum should be. The aliens bring the pod inside their planet: the sperm fertilizes the egg. Just as the birth of the humanoid machine was preceded by fertilization, so is the birth of the star-child preceded by fertilization.

In humans and other animals, when fertilization occurs the chromosomes of the sperm merge with the chromosomes of the egg; the sperm cell dissolves and disappears. This happens symbolically in the hotel room. We first see the room from inside the pod, through Bowman's eyes, which look out through the pod window. Three external shots follow, showing the pod inside the room from various angles: the sperm cell is inside the egg. Fertilization has occurred.

Once more Bowman peers out the pod window. This time he sees *himself* in his orange space suit, standing outside in the room. Now there are two Bowmans: *the first cell has divided.* A close-up of the second Bowman's face shows it has become wrinkled: the fetus has grown older, hence symbolically larger. The new, older Bowman looks across the room toward the corner where the pod had been. The pod is no longer there: the sperm has dissolved, becoming one with the egg. (Notice how the pod's disappearance symbolizes different things in different allegories. In the

Odysseus allegory, it symbolized the departure of the Phaeacian ship after the Phaeacians put Odysseus ashore at Ithaca.)

Fetal Growth and the Star-Child's Birth

This doubling of Bowmans—one Bowman seeing his next self, older than before—is the first of three such doublings. In the second, the space-suited Bowman sees a white-haired Bowman, who is dressed in black and seated at a dining cart, eating dinner. This Bowman, in turn, sees a bald, aged, seemingly moribund Bowman, dressed in white and lying in bed. These doublings symbolize the repeated doubling or dividing of fetal cells as the fetus grows and matures. Kubrick has condensed into three the billions of cell splittings that actually occur during fetal growth. And Bowman's aging augments the cell-splitting symbolism by depicting the aging, hence growth, of the fetus. The fetus is maturing. The first member of a new race is about to be born. It will have evolved from the chromosomes of the old race, humanity.

The aged, bedridden Bowman does not see another Bowman, because *this* Bowman represents the fully developed fetus. What this Bowman does see is the final monolith, which has suddenly materialized within the room and is standing upright at the foot of the bed. This monolith, like the first two *upright* monoliths, symbolizes a milestone along the road of humanoid evolution. Each such milestone signifies that a new humanoid race is about to emerge. The first milestone thus marks the evolution of man from ape; the second marks the evolution of humanoid machine from man.

Bowman reaches out toward the monolith, repeating the action that pre-ceded the emergence of the two previous new races. And with that he is transfigured into a radiantly glowing baby, the star-child. We first see the not-yet-born infant when it is still enclosed in the amnion (the hotel room), inside the womb. Kubrick symbolizes the star-child's birth—its emergence from the womb into the universe—by having the camera lens move slowly toward and then into the blackness of the monolith, blackness that becomes the outside universe. With the star-child's birth, humanity evolves into a new, better species.

How do we know it is better?

There are three clues. First, the usual postmonolith battle between the new race and the old one is not repeated. Both of the two previous upright monoliths were followed by battles to the death. Both new races attacked and killed or tried to kill the preceding race; both new races were malevo-lent. But the last new race, *Homo futurus*, is different: it does not try to kill the old race. Indeed, in the film's originally planned ending (which remains in Clarke's novel), *Homo futurus* returns to earth and destroys the orbiting nuclear bombs that threaten mankind. The new race is protective and benevolent.

The second clue that the new race is better is the new race's symbol—an innocent, harmless infant. The third clue, not fully differentiated from the second, is the combination of angelic countenance and beatifying radiance with which the star-child is endowed.

Though Kubrick is sometimes accused of pessimism, the three clues deliver an optimistic message: humanity will not take the wrong fork in the road. It will evolve into something better.

WHAT ABOUT FREUD AND JUNG?

Geduld recognizes some (not all) of the sexual reproduction symbolism in *2001*'s earth-to-moon sequence.[20] She also perceives the star-child as "a fetus *in utero*"—not quite right but close enough.[21] (Bowman in bed is the last fetus; the star-child is a baby. The hotel room, not the globe around the baby, is the amnion. The globe is a Zarathustran symbol representing the sun, a sphere.) To her further credit, Geduld recognizes that *2001* is a rich stew of symbols. And she looks for a unifying theme.

Unfortunately, instead of finding that theme in allegory, she finds it in Freudianism. By Freudianism I mean a tendency to be preoccupied with sexual explanations. Geduld is led astray by her two correct or semicorrect interpretations. She begins to see, tentatively at least (her text has several question marks), uteruses and wombs and other fetal and sexual symbols in every corner of the movie. She also sees Jungian (often called neo-Freudian) refrains in Kubrick's supposed fascination with the number four.[22] She even provides a Jungian interpretation of Kubrick's symbolization of the cyclops.[23]

Geduld's implied hypothesis that Freud and Jung—fetuses and fours—are unifying themes in *2001*'s symbolism is false and needs to be put to rest. (The Jung part has already been picked up and repeated by at least one analyst.[24]) Kubrick's sexual reproduction symbolism is neither sex for the sake of sex nor a preoccupation. And it is not in every corner of the movie. His sexual symbolism is narrowly focused and purposeful, used to advance his allegories. It ties in splendidly with the evolution themes of the second and third allegories; it also provides the context for the Odysseus allegory's encounter between Paris and Helen, an encounter that *did* involve sex. And

Kubrick's earth-to-moon sexual symbolism is part of the structure of a hilarious joke that, by the way, has nothing to do with sex. (We'll get to this intricate joke in the next chapter.) As for the number four (Jung), you can find far more threes and sixes, even eights, than fours in *2001*, not to mention the fact that most of Geduld's fours are contrived.

Imaginary Freudian Elements

Although some of Geduld's interpretations are hesitant, she can fairly be accused of letting her imagination run wild. Below is a list of Freudian symbols (and my comments on them) that she imagines Kubrick put in *2001*:

- In *2001*'s opening shot, the sun's rising over the moon to shine on the earth is "abstract eroticism of the slow-moving globes in the sky to the aggressive thrust of [Richard Strauss's] music"(35). (Was I watching the same movie? Did I mistake erotically moving globes for Nietzsche's climbing-sun metaphor, which symbolizes the climb from ape to overman? And did I mistake erotic thrusting in the music for musical representation of man's climb—the ascending notes—from ape to lower man to higher man to overman?[25] Also, was Strauss, who composed the music in 1896, collaborating with Kubrick by providing composed-on-order sexual music?)
- Given that the "arrow shaped" *Orion*'s docking in the slotted axle of the space station provides a "uterine" image, "the entire universe is made to seem an outsized uterus" (44). (The axle is not a uterus. The sperm—the moon lander Geduld mistakes for the "ova" [*sic*]—fertilizes the moon, the real ovum. Whereas an ovum implants in the uterus, the moon is not inside the space station. Could the universe be the uterus? No. Hal-Discovery is born from offscreen *into*, not out of, the starry universe.)
- The rectangular excavation surrounding the moon monolith at Tycho "is yet another uterine-like cavity" (49). (Wrong. The walls are the walls of Troy, and what is inside is a wooden horse, not a fetus. I can't help wondering why anyone anyone would think a chamber that opens at the *top* symbolizes a uterus.)
- The spaceship Discovery "resembles the delicate vertebra of a half-formed fetus" (51). (The spaceship resembles what it's supposed to resemble: the abstracted skeleton of a fully formed adult. The spine extends straight out from the skull; it is not curled in fetal position.)
- The three hibernating astronauts are "encased in their womb-like beds" (51). (They are really encased in coffin-like capsules.)

- "The infant pod is 'born' by way of the pod bay door, a tunnel opening on the underside of the ship" (55). (The door is not the least bit tunnel-like; it is a hole in a wall like any other door. And the door is in front, not on the underside: the pod launching ramp extends straight forward, not downward. The pod launch symbolizes the spaceship's sticking out its tongue and blowing a bubble, which is about as far from childbirth and Freud as you can get.)
- "Heavy breathing on the soundtrack" during the pod launch suggests "the start of childbirth" (55). (Is *that* what childbirth sounds like?)
- The pod "claws" (mechanical fingers) Hal uses to cut Poole's air hose suggest "a forceps birth" (57). (To me, they suggest hands: Kubrick is further humanizing Hal by giving him remotely controlled hands.)
- Bowman's escape from his rescue pod into the ship's emergency airlock is another birth, "the climax of all preceding erotic and fetal imagery," wherein "the astronaut is forced through the tunnel toward a life-sustaining air supply" (58). (Now the previously identified baby—the pod—is giving birth to its *own* baby?)
- The monolith (the four monoliths, viewed collectively) is a "box, a Freudian symbol of the womb" (68). (The monolith resembles a domino, not a box. It is much too thin to be a box. Different monoliths symbolize different things in different allegories, but never a womb.)
- "In a Freudian sense, *2001* concerns a regression to an idea of earliest childhood, when the infant is happily unaware of any difference between the sexes, believing that men somehow produce the babies" (70). (*2001* uses the child symbol not because Kubrick came up with the idea but because Nietzsche uses it metaphorically to describe the birth of a new race, overman. This is not regression, which would require going *backward* to the start of the old race; it is progression, going *forward* to a new race.)
- The question *2001* raises is: "Does evolution represent the wish to evolve out of the individual's adult, sexualized state?" (70) (Answer: No. The evolution depicted by Kubrick is essentially a process, not a wish. The "will to power" that drives evolution in the Zarathustra allegory does resemble a wish, but it is a wish to evolve *into*, not "out of.")

Ironically, Geduld misses all of the real fetal symbolism—the symbolism provided by the first four Bowmans in the hotel-room sequence. She also misses the ejaculatory and fallopian tube and sperm symbolism that precedes it. And she misidentifies the star-child as a fetus, whereas it is really a baby.

Imaginary Jungian Elements

Turning to Jung, Geduld says, "Kubrick seems to be fascinated by the number four" (34). The evidence—I abuse the word—includes (1) the film's four episodes, (2) the supposed fact that *2001* took four years to complete, (3) the four million years the moon monolith lay buried, (4) the four supposed heroes (ape, scientist, machine, astronaut), (5) the four supposed evolutions (man, machine, alien [she apparently means star-child], universe), (6) the four composers whose music was used, and (7) the four-sided rectangular shape of the monoliths.

I apologize for using harsh language, but Geduld's argument is absurd. To begin with, five of the seven items are contrived, requiring manipulation and arbitrary classification to extract the number four. The film may have four episodes, but the first two fall under one title ("The Dawn of Man"); the film has only three titled parts. *2001* took about two and a half years, not four, to film. You have to go back to the first meeting between Kubrick and Clarke—you have to manipulate the starting date—to get four years, and then you have to assume Kubrick arranged for what followed to take four years. One of the four supposed "heroes," the machine (Hal), is really the villain in his episode; only three of the named characters are really heroes. There are only three evolutions; *2001* does not deal with Geduld's fourth evolution, the evolution of the universe. The monolith has six sides, not four; you have to treat the three-dimensional monolith arbitrarily as two-dimensional to get four sides.

Even if Geduld had 7 noncontrived pieces of evidence instead of just 2, her argument would still be absurd. You can watch almost any movie and come up with a list of 7 or more fours—rectangular doors and windows and picture frames, four-door sedans with four wheels, four people in a scene, four *other* people in the scene with the hero, four puppies, four letters in someone's name, four chairs in a room, four engines on a plane, four outlaws in the gang, four flowers in a vase, four shots exchanged, you name it. And you can pick a different number—two, three, five, or six—and again find lots of "evidence" that the director is fascinated by the number.

Let's do some counting for three other numbers from *2001*, the numbers three, six, and eight. We can start with the number three. *2001* has (1) three titled parts, (2) three episode heroes (Moonwatcher, Heywood Floyd, and Dave Bowman), (3) three upright monoliths, (4) three celestial spheres (sun, moon, earth) in the opening scene, (5) three celestial spheres (moon, earth, star-child) in the closing scene, (6) three spheres in space (sun, earth, moon lander) in a third scene, (7) three "female" orbiting bombs, (8) a crew of three (two pilots plus flight attendant) on the *Orion*, (9) three voiceprint examination corridors on the space station, (10) three items of information (destination, nationality, and name) requested by the voiceprint identification machine, (11) three Russian women on the space station, (12) a cockpit scene with three people on the moon lander, (13) three space-suited men waiting on the moon for the moon lander to land, (14) three-sided doors on the moon lander's hangar, (15) three windows in the briefing room on the moon, (16) three photographs taken by the photographer at the briefing, (17) three passengers on the moon bus going to Tycho, (18) three banks of lights facing the men going into the excavation at Tycho, (19–22) a space ship with three mouths, three pairs of exhaust nozzles, three hexagons in back, and three dishes in the antenna array, (23) three utility pods, (24) three men in hibernation, (25) three sections in the lounge Poole uses when sunbathing, (26) three hotel-room scenes in which one Bowman sees the next, (27) three fixtures in the bathroom, (28) three colors of apparel (orange, black, and white) worn by Bowman in the hotel room, (29) three arches on the bathroom-door wall (the door frame and two paintings), and (30) symbolization of Nietzsche's "three metamorphoses" (discussed in chapters 5 and 6). That's 30 threes—more than four times as many as the 7 fours Geduld counted. Does this mean Kubrick is "fascinated" by the number three?

How about the number six? *2001* has (1) black monoliths with six faces, (2) six tapirs in the first "Dawn of Man" animal scene, (3) six species (tapir, lion, leopard, zebra, ape, and man) in the "Dawn of Man" episode, (4) six persons met by Floyd inside the space station (receptionist, Miller, four Russians), (5) six people in the scene the moment Floyd enters the phone booth, (6) six letters in the nickname, "Squirt," of the girl played by Kubrick's daughter, (7) six letters in the label TMA-ONE, (8) six letters in the name Bowman, (9) six persons in the excavation at Tycho, (10) six exhaust nozzles on Discovery, (11) some six-sided hexagons at the rear of the ship, (12) a crew of six (including Hal, identified on BBC as "the sixth member of the crew"), (13) a total of six arms on the three utility pods, (14) six vital-signs lines on the electronic monitor for each hibernator, (15) a large panel with six TV screens at the foot of the ladder outside the pod bay, (16) a six-sided door to the pod bay, (17) six spheres (Jupiter and its five moons) aligned at Jupiter, (18) six unnaturally colored blinking eyes in immediate succession as Bowman enters the hotel room, (19) six sit-down pieces of furniture (five chairs and a bench) in the hotel room, (20) six works of art—four paintings and two statuettes—mounted on or in the hotel room walls, and (21) six food-and-beverage holders (two plates, two glasses, a food server, and a butter server) at the dinner table. That's three times as many sixes as fours—21 versus 7. Does this show that Kubrick is "fascinated" by the number six?

One more comparison: eights. It's generally harder to come up with eights than to come up with fours. Yet earlier in this chapter I noted (1) the eight stages in the evolution of Hal-Discovery and (2–7) six examples of eight-part circles in the earth-to-moon sequence. Just a cursory review of the rest of the movie reveals (8) eight corners (where three edges meet) on each monolith, (9) eight rows of seats on the space shuttle *Orion*, (10) eight liquid food compartments—plus eight straws—in the dinner trays on the moon lander, (11) eight instruments on the post between the cockpit windows on the moon bus, (12) eight Automat-type windows (two stacks of four) on the food-dispensing machine on the spaceship, (13) eight video screens at the station where Hal interviews Bowman, (14) eight switches (plus eight switch lights), arranged in a line, that Bowman shuts off when he and Poole go into the pod for their "private" conversation, (15) eight moving bodies in "Jupiter space"—Jupiter, five moons, Discovery, and the monolith—when Bowman arrives at Jupiter, (16) eight small rectangles within the black band across the back of Bowman's orange helmet in the hotel room, and (17) a hotel room that is eight glass rectangles wide, from the head of the bed to the opposite wall. That is more than twice as many eights as fours—17 versus 7. Is Kubrick "fascinated" by the number eight?

Forget about Freud and Jung. Geduld's Freudian and neo-Freudian unifying-theme hypothesis does not withstand scrutiny. Kubrick's unifying theme is allegory, not Freudianism.

NOTES

1. Paul Wallich, "Remembrance of Future Past" (book review), *Scientific American* 276, no. 1 (January 1997), 114–15.

2. Piers Bizony, 2001: *Filming the Future* (London: Aurum Press, 1994), 77.

3. Arthur C. Clarke, quoted in Jerome Agel, ed., *The Making of Kubrick's* 2001 (New York: New American Library, 1970), 113.

4. David Abrahamson, "Creatures of Invention," *National Wildlife* 23, no. 2 (February–March 1985), 25.

5. Earth Almanac, *National Geographic* 192, no. 1 (July 1997), unpaginated rear matter.

6. Abrahamson, "Creatures," 26.

7. Foster Hirsch, introduction to *The Lost Worlds of* 2001, by Arthur C. Clarke (Boston: Gregg Press, 1979), viii.

8. Bizony, *Filming the Future*, 103.

9. Ibid., 48.

10. Arthur C. Clarke, *The Lost Worlds of* 2001 (Boston: Gregg Press, 1979), 78.

11. The name Andrey Smyslov seems to be a combination of *Andrey* Vishinsky, a prominent Soviet diplomat when *2001* was released in 1968, and Vasily *Smyslov*, the Russian who was world chess champion during 1957–58. (Kubrick is a chess enthusiast. See John Baxter, *Stanley Kubrick: A Biography* [New York: Carroll & Graf, 1997], 6, 20, 32–33.) The Vishinsky-Smyslov combination suggests a synthesis of diplomacy and strategy, which fits the space station character.

12. Clarke, *Lost Worlds*, 78.

13. Ibid.

14. Penelope Gilliatt, "After Man" (*New Yorker* review), in Bizony, ed., *Filming the Future*, 65; Tim Hunter, with Stephen Kaplan and Peter Jasci, untitled 1968 *Harvard Crimson* review of *2001*, in Agel, *Making* 2001, 222; Joseph Morgenstern, "Kubrick's Cosmos," *Newsweek*, 15 April 1968, 100; Carolyn Geduld, *Filmguide to* 2001: A Space Odyssey (Bloomington: Indiana University Press, 1973), 61; and Hirsch, intro. to *Lost Worlds*, ix. So many writers (most of whom probably don't know any more about Louis XVI furnishings than I do) have used the Louis XVI description that I suspect it comes from *2001*'s 1968 press kit, which is no longer available.

15. Harvey R. Greenberg, *The Movies on Your Mind* (New York: Saturday Review Press/E. P. Dutton, 1975), 261.

16. Charles Champlin, untitled 1968 *Los Angeles Times* review of *2001*, in Agel, ed., *Making* 2001, 215, and David G. Hoch, "Mythic Patterns in *2001: A Space Odyssey*," *Journal of Popular Culture* 4, no. 4 (Spring 1971), 964.

17. Gilliatt, "After Man," 65.

18. Geduld, *Filmguide to* 2001, 65.

19. Bizony, *Filming the Future*, 61.

20. Geduld, *Filmguide to* 2001, 44, 48.

21. Ibid., 63.

22. Ibid., 34, 40.

23. Ibid., 68.

24. Hirsch, intro. to *Lost Worlds*, xii.

25. See note 1 of chapter 5.

Chapter 5

The Zarathustra Allegory: Background and Cast

The third allegory depicts the main themes of Nietzsche's best-known work, *Thus Spake Zarathustra*. Kubrick boldly calls attention to the work his first allegory depicts (*The Odyssey*) by giving *2001* the subtitle *A Space Odyssey*. Hence it should be no surprise that he almost as boldly alludes to the work his third allegory is based on. By now, everyone interested in *2001* knows that the stirring music that opens and closes *2001*—three sets of five heraldic notes, punctuated by kettle drums and followed by a crescendo—is the opening fanfare from Richard Strauss's symphonic poem "Thus Spake Zarathustra."[1] This composition was inspired by Nietzsche's book. The music announces, loudly, that Kubrick intends to allegorize *Thus Spake Zarathustra*.

In case we miss the musical clue, Kubrick slips into the film's title a subtler, more esoteric, clue—*2001*. Zarathustra, better known in the West as Zoroaster (a Greek corruption), was a prophet in ancient Persia. Though fictionalized as an atheist by Nietzsche, Zarathustra was actually the founder of the Persian religion Zoroastrianism. Zoroastrian mythology holds that history consists of a 12,000-year struggle between good and evil—between the true god, Ahura Mazdah, and the evil spirit, Angra Mainyu (later called Ahriman). Both exist transcendentally before history begins. History has four 3,000-year periods. In the first, Ahura Mazdah creates angels and other spiritual (nonmaterial) beings. In the second, material creation arises with the appearance on earth of primal man and primal animal. In the third, Angra Mainyu invades the earth, killing primal man and primal animal, but he is thwarted when the first human couple and first cow spring from the seed of their slain prototypes. The last period begins when Ahura Mazdah causes Zoroaster to be conceived to help man resist Angra Mainyu and his demons. Every thousand years thereafter over the last 3,000 years, a new prophet—three more altogether—will be born of a virgin; she will conceive when Zoroaster's seed, preserved in a lake, enters her body as she bathes. The last prophet, or Saoshyant, will resurrect the dead and begin the final struggle that will culminate in the destruction of all evil. As of 1968, when *2001* was released, the next prophet was due (symbolically, at least) in the first year of the next millennium, 2001.[2] Kubrick therefore gave his manned-mission-to-Jupiter film a ridiculously close 2001 setting instead of a more realistic setting of, say, 2051 or 2068. The year 2001 could be interpreted as a symbol for either (*a*) the beginning of the *first* millennium of the final 3,000-year period, 9,000 years (or 3 × 3,000) after the beginning of history, when Zoroaster himself appears, or (*b*) the beginning of the *third* (last) millennium of the final period, when a descendent of Zoroaster appears.

Two considerations suggest that the first interpretation is the correct one. First, the Zarathustra allegory is about Zarathustra (a.k.a Zoroaster), and he comes in 9001, the first year of the tenth millennium. Second, we have another numerical clue (in addition to the film's title, *2001*), a clue that also points to 9001. Where do you think Kubrick got the number 9000 in the computer's full name, HAL-9000? I think he got it by multiplying 3,000 (the number of years in a Zoroastrian 3,000-year period) by 3 (the number of periods that precede the appearance of Zoroaster-Zarathustra). In the movie, Hal (the HAL-9000 computer) and Dave Bowman (Zarathustra) arrive at the same time. What time is that? In terms of Zoroastrian history, it is the year Zoroaster arrives: one year beyond 3 × 3,000 = 9,000 years after the beginning of history. The number 9000 in HAL-9000 tells us that the year 2001 symbolizes 9001 (or 9000 + 1), the year when Zoroaster (Zarathustra) arrives to begin the final struggle.

The Zarathustra allegory is Kubrick's principal allegory and is much more complicated than the first two. My analysis is therefore longer and requires two chapters. This one provides background information and introduces the cast—the monoliths, Frank Poole, Heywood Floyd, Dave Bowman, and the notorious Hal-Discovery. It also carries the plot forward to the point where God has been created. The next chapter describes the main action and its climax: the evolution of man into overman.

NIETZSCHE'S CHARACTERS AND THEMES

We find in *Thus Spake Zarathustra* ten relevant themes and characters: (1) evolution, or the basic theme of advancement from ape to man to overman, (2) the death of God, a theme for which Nietzsche is famous, (3) the will to power, an intense psychological drive that dooms God and shapes evolution, (4) eternal recurrence, or time as a circle, a gratuitous theme that goes beyond the ape-man-overman theme, (5) the rope dancer, the protagonist in a parable that presents an overview of Nietzsche's philosophy, (6) Zarathustra, an atheistic prophet who is Nietzsche's mouthpiece, (7) lower man, who creates God, (8) God, created by man in his (man's) own image, (9) higher man, who kills God and aspires to become overman, and (10) overman (*übermensch*), an evolved superior being—a species—beyond man.

Evolution

Influenced by Darwin, Nietzsche described evolution as a progression from worm to ape to man to overman. Man subdivides into lower man and higher man; the latter is really a series of ever-higher higher men, climbing toward overman. Lower man comes first. Man's evolutionary progress is blocked by God, whom lower man creates in his own image (the opposite of what the Bible says). Nietzsche's remodeled prophet, Zarathustra, puts it this way: "Yes, you brothers, that God whom *I* [man] created was *human work* and human madness, like all the gods! A *man* he was."[3] Man created God, and the God man created was a man—that is, he was the *image* of man.

Zarathustra avers that God stifles man's intellect, controls man with arbitrary values and rules, instills fear, restrains creativity, and humiliates him by peering into him and witnessing his hidden secrets and shame. The Ugliest Man, whom Zarathustra identifies as the murderer of God (actually one of many), summarizes the indictment: "He—*had* to die: he looked with eyes which beheld *everything*—he beheld people's depths and dregs, all [their] hidden ugliness and ignominy."[4] When man (i.e., particular men) can bear this treatment no longer, he rebels, killing God. This act permits Zarathustra to announce, "God is Dead!"[5]—the declaration for which Nietzsche is famous. The death of God also marks the evolution of lower man into higher man (particular men who kill God), who constitutes a tiny minority of the population. The final step of evolution will be overman; he will evolve from higher man.

The Will to Power

The killing of God is a manifestation of "the will to power."[6] This will is a force that drives evolution in all creatures. It pushes life in new directions. In man, it causes life to evolve in the direction of, and eventually to produce, overman. The will to power impels man to transcend himself; to become more intelligent, more creative, and more noble; to triumph over the repressing forces of existence; and to take control of his life.

The will to power is the antithesis of the will of God, which enslaves the populace. "Pious backworldsmen" believe the preachers who declare, "You shall not will!"[7] But this preaching, this call for subjugation to the will of God, "is a sermon for slavery."[8] The will to power, found in those who are "lion-willed" (ready to battle God), frees the human spirit from bondage: "Willing emancipates"—emancipates man from the slavery imposed by God.[9]

The evil will, the black will of God, foolishly seeks to undo the past—an impossible task—through punishment. The will to power, instead of seeking to undo or destroy, looks toward the future. It seeks to create: "The will is a creator."[10] The will to power will create overman. The will's all-consuming goal is power: "power is it, . . . *a ruling thought*."[11]

Power, the thought that rules higher man's mind, is essentially *supremacy*—supremacy not just in a relative sense but in an absolute sense too. Man achieves supremacy when he evolves into overman, when he becomes a figurative god with the same commanding stature as the dead literal God. This happens when man reaches a sufficiently high state of wisdom, creativity (in science, in philosophy, and in the arts), and self-determined morality (contrasted with divinely determined morality based on laws written "beyond the stars"[12]).

Overman and Eternal Recurrence

Zarathustra likens man to a rope stretched across an abyss that separates ape from overman. The crossing is frightening, "a dangerous trembling and halting."[13] But the abyss will be crossed, and man will evolve from a mediocre, religion-oriented being into a superior being, overman. Overman will be as far above ordinary man as man is above the ape. Although *übermensch* is sometimes translated as "superman," which has unfortunate comic-strip connotations, the overman is not a physically superior being. He is mentally and morally superior.

The overman is both the end and a new beginning. Nietzsche believed in "eternal recurrence," the idea that the universe involves a cosmic cycle in which the same series of events, beings, and relationships repeats endlessly. Everything that is has been before and will be again. Everything is reborn repeatedly. Time is a circle.

INTERPRETIVE PROGRESS

Several commentators have noted symbolic parallels between *2001* and *Thus Spake Zarathustra*, but no one has correctly identified more than five of *2001*'s scores of Zarathustran symbols. Birx writes that *2001* "is clearly a visual representation of Nietzsche's philosophy of overcoming" (i.e., overcoming the predicament posed by religion) and of the Nietzscheian theme of "the eternal recurrence."[14] He specifically mentions the Zarathustran theme of "evolution from the apes through human beings to the star-child" and correctly identifies the star-child with "the future overman."[15] Allen, Gelmis, Hoch, and Geduld also refer to Nietzsche's ape-man-overman theme, but none of the four notices anything Zarathustran beyond ape-man-overman.[16] And none of these interpreters spots *2001*'s central Zarathustran symbol: Hal-Discovery, who represents the thoroughly manlike God that man creates in his own image, then loses faith in and kills. In this connection, Allen stumbles badly in guessing that Hal is the overman.

Surprisingly, the most insightful comment comes not from a book or article but from an internet query posted at Phil Vendy's "Underman's 2001" website by one Thomas J. Bogdewic. He theorizes that (1) the space voyage is the tightrope across the abyss, (2) Hal is God, (3) Bowman is mankind, (4) Bowman must "accept" ("achieve" would be more apt) the death of God before becoming overman, and (5) the star-child is overman.[17] I have some quibbles about items 1–3, and the star-child's being overman is old stuff; but Bogdewic nevertheless deserves full credit for a major insight. He is to my knowledge the only person who has recognized that Hal is God. And Hal's representing God is the most important symbolism in the Zarathustra allegory.

(My quibbles, beyond "accept" versus "achieve," are these: The tightrope over the abyss, not to be confused with the rope dancer's tightrope over the marketplace, spans the entire gap between ape and overman; it is not just the space voyage. Bowman is Zarathustra, a higher man, not all mankind. And the Hal-as-God symbolism is far, far more detailed and complicated than the mere fact that Hal symbolizes God. Also, Hal is only part of God; Discovery is the rest. The Zarathustran God is the mental *and physical* image of man—created by man in his own mental and physical image.)

THE MONOLITHS AS HUMAN ATTRIBUTES

The first members of the Zarathustra allegory's cast requiring introduction are the four monoliths. (The apes and Moonwatcher need not be introduced: they play the same role in this allegory that they played in the surface story and in the second allegory.) In all three allegories, each monolith represents something different from what it represents in the other two allegories. Here is how each allegory uses the monoliths:

- *Odysseus Allegory:* The first monolith (Africa) is Odysseus's Great Bow, the second (moon) is the Trojan Horse, the third (Jupiter) is the Sirens, and the fourth (hotel room) is the Great Bow again (regained by Odysseus after a twenty-year absence from Ithaca).
- *Man-Machine Symbiosis Allegory:* The first, second, and fourth monoliths — the upright ones — are milestones marking the emergence of new humanoid species (man, humanoid machine, and future man); the third monolith — the horizontal one — is the second one toppled over, after the humanoid machine species (the man-machine symbiosis) dies out.
- *Zarathustra Allegory:* The monoliths are human attributes that certain characters absorb (acquire) by touching the monoliths. The first monolith symbolizes intelligence (which changes ape into man), the second superstition (which inspires man to create God), the third power (not yet touched, hence not yet attained), and the fourth power again (this time attained, hence able to change man into overman). Power in this context is what man seeks when he exhibits what Nietzsche calls "the will to power." Essentially, it means supremacy, the quality God preempted when alive.

In effect, if not in substance, the Zarathustra allegory's first monolith is pretty much the same thing it is in the surface story and in the symbiosis allegory. In the surface story, the African monolith is an instrument installed by the aliens to inject higher intelligence into the apes. In the symbiosis allegory, the monolith is a milestone marking the place where ape acquires intelligence. Those two things — alien instrument and milestone — are physical objects. But in the Zarathustra allegory, the monolith symbolizes something abstract: intelligence. The ape's touching the monolith represents his acquisition of intelligence.

The moon monolith has no earlier parallels; it is brand new in content. Like the African monolith, it is a symbol for an abstract quality a humanoid — man in this case — acquires when he touches the monolith. And that quality is again one that causes the evolution of a new humanoid being. But this time the quality is a negative one: it is the quality that causes man to create God, who is viewed by Zarathustra (a nonbeliever) as a blight on mankind. Remember, according to Zarathustra (as remodeled by Nietzsche), man created God in his own image: *man came first.*

If intelligence is the attribute that produces man, what is the human attribute that produces God? A believer might say faith or religiosity or spirituality. But neither Nietzsche nor Zarathustra, nor for that matter Kubrick or Clarke, was or is a believer, so we can reject those answers.

No, the attribute that causes man to create gods and goddesses is something else. It is, in the eyes of those who disbelieve in the deities, *superstition*.[18] Superstitions are false beliefs in supernatural things—*beings* (elves, vampires, angels, gods), *places* (heaven, hell, Valhalla), *happenings* (reincarnation, eschatological resurrection of the dead, spirit possession), *cause-and-effect relationships* (bad luck caused by broken mirrors, fates caused by astrological signs or conditions, pain caused by black magic, cures caused by the laying of hands, transmogrification caused by a full moon), and so on. To reiterate, the belief must be false. If ghosts and demons and angels are genuine, beliefs in them are not superstitions. If God exists but does not answer prayers, God is not a superstition but the power of prayer is. Superstition, in other words, creates supernatural things that aren't real.

In the Zarathustra allegory, the moon monolith symbolizes superstition. When man reaches out and touches the monolith, he acquires superstition—just as the ape acquired intelligence when he reached out and touched the first monolith. When man becomes superstitious, he creates God. Hence in the very next scene after man touches the moon monolith, God is born (after that eighteen-month gestation period): Hal-Discovery cruises into the universe, horizontally and headfirst, from the left side of the screen. Compare: In the very next scene after the ape touches the African monolith (thereby acquiring intelligence), Moonwatcher figures out how to use a bone as a weapon, thereby becoming man. Further compare: In the very next scene after bedridden Dave Bowman extends his arm toward the final monolith (thereby acquiring power), he is transformed into overman.

That last comparison anticipates my next point: the third and fourth monoliths symbolize yet another abstract human quality—power. Nietzsche held that what drives man upwards toward his goal of becoming overman is the will to power. In its early phase, the will to power impels man to kill God, who is supreme and thus stands in the way of *man's* becoming supreme. But this early will is not strong enough. The will to power must become all-consuming for man to actually grasp power—supremacy—and become overman.

Bowman exhibits the will to power when he kills Hal (God), but he still has a long way to go before he can grasp power. At Jupiter he sees the third monolith—power—and goes after it. But it is mobile, elusive; it disappears from sight. In the hotel room he again sees power, and this time it is standing still, upright, like the first two monoliths. He reaches out, acquires power, and becomes overman (in the hidden story, not in the surface story).

FRANK POOLE AS THE ROPE DANCER

Nietzsche begins *Thus Spake Zarathustra* with "Zarathustra's Prologue." It centers on the parable of the rope dancer. This parable includes the previously mentioned "rope over an abyss" metaphor, which is a simplified version of the parable. But whereas in the metaphor the *rope* over the abyss between animal and overman is humanity, in the parable a *man* walking on a rope symbolizes humanity. The man is a tightrope walker on a rope stretched between two towers (symbolizing ape and overman) at a town marketplace. He is called "the rope dancer," although he doesn't literally dance.[19]

The rope dancer begins his performance by coming out of a little door in the first tower and going along the rope. Suddenly, the door opens again and out pops "a gaudily-dressed fellow like a buffoon" (42), later called simply "the buffoon" (43). The buffoon goes rapidly after the rope dancer, taunts him, leaps over him with a devilish yell, lands on the rope in front of the rope dancer, and proceeds in triumph; he achieves *supremacy*. Frightened, the rope dancer falls. All onlookers except Zarathustra scatter in terror. Zarathustra, though almost directly beneath the falling man, stands firm. He then kneels and cradles the dying man in his arms and comforts him. Later, he picks up the corpse and disposes of it in a hollow log.

In this parable, the rope dancer's striving to reach the far tower (representing the overman) symbolizes humanity's striving to become a superior being, a supreme being. The buffoon who comes after but overtakes and surpasses man, symbolizes God. Because a creator must exist before that which he creates, the buffoon's coming temporally and spatially *after* the rope dancer symbolizes Nietzsche's idea that man (who comes first) created God (who comes second). In creating God, man dooms his own aspirations: he puts God above (ahead of) himself, making God supreme and thereby making it impossible for himself to become supreme.

The buffoon's leaping over and getting ahead of the rope dancer symbolizes God's coming into the picture, relegating man to inferior status, and achieving supremacy. The rope dancer's death symbolizes the death of any believer's chances of advancing humanity—that is, of progressing toward the far tower. Zarathustra's fearlessness and compassion symbolize the moral superiority of the rare higher man vis-à-vis lower men, symbolized by the crowd in the marketplace. The higher man rejects God and strives to replace God as *the* superior being.

The buffoon actually symbolizes not only God but fear—the rope dancer's fear of falling, which in turn represents fear of God. Fear causes the rope dancer to get jittery and fall. In Nietzsche's eyes, fear of God is foolish, because there is no God. So God is characterized as a buffoon, someone a person shouldn't be afraid of.

In *2001*, Frank Poole symbolizes the rope dancer, who would more aptly be called a rope *walker*. Poole, remember, is Dave Bowman's colleague, the second active (nonhibernating) human member of the spaceship's crew. The name Frank Poole is our first clue to the symbolism. Given that Kubrick plays symbol games with the names Dave Bowman, Heywood R. Floyd, and Hal, not to mention Elena and TMA-1, we should not be surprised that he also plays a name game with Frank Poole. None of *2001*'s four major characters is exempt.

Each symbolic name except TMA-1 employs a different code. Frank Poole embodies what might be called a 90 percent anagram. An anagram, once again, is a word or phrase formed by rearranging the letters of another word or phrase. The last 9 of the 10 letters of

[W]ALK ON ROPE

have been reordered to form the last 9 of the 10 letters of

[F]RANK POOLE.

Why does Kubrick omit the first letter (W) of "walk on rope" from his anagram? Most likely, he was unable to come up with a plausible name—a name that wouldn't attract attention—that used all the letters of "walk on rope," "dance on rope," "rope walker," or "rope dancer." So he did the best he could—quite well, I'd say. He not only put 90 percent of the "walk on rope" letters in Poole's name, he omitted the *initial* letter (W or F) of each phrase from the anagram. (For this extra flourish, I'd be willing to credit Kubrick with a 95 percent anagram.)

Four parallels between the parable of the rope dancer and Poole's scenes from *2001* reinforce the clue from Poole's name in revealing that Frank Poole allegorically depicts the rope dancer:

1. Poole metaphorically dances on rope when, in his first scene, he jogs along the exercise centrifuge, shadowboxing as he goes. The centrifuge is the rope, and the hands-and-feet blend of shadowboxing and jogging symbolizes dancing. One flaw in the symbolism is that the symbolized rope dancing and Poole's death are in separate scenes; the separation weakens the symbolic analogy. Is it possible, then, that the analogical rope walk is Poole's space walk from his parked space pod

toward the spaceship's antenna, the walk during which Hal kills him? Yes, it is possible. But it is unlikely. Besides lacking a visible analogical rope (compare the centrifuge, which *is* visible), the walk to the antenna was taken previously, in both directions, by Dave Bowman: Bowman replaced the AE-35 unit before Poole went out to put the original unit back in place. Bowman would therefore have first claim to the title "rope dancer" under the space-walk metaphor.

2. Just as Nietzsche's rope dancer is killed by a malicious character, the buffoon, who symbolizes God, so is Poole killed by a malicious character, Hal, who symbolizes God. Poole's immediate killer, the space pod, symbolizes the buffoon.

3. Just as the killer approaches his victim from behind in the parable of the rope dancer, so does the killer approach his victim from behind when Hal uses the space pod to sever Poole's air hose. Lest questions be raised about whether Hal (God) is the real killer when the space pod does the dirty work, I'll elaborate. The pod can be viewed as an extension of Hal-Discovery's body. This is analogous to the Holy Spirit's being an extension or agent of God in Christianity. In Christianity, anything the Holy Spirit does is really the work of God. By the same token, anything an unmanned utility pod does is the work of Hal (God). The pod can also be viewed as a tool-weapon. The real killer is the weapon's user, not the weapon itself.

4. Just as Zarathustra picks up the rope dancer's body in Nietzsche's parable, so does Dave Bowman (using his pod's arms) pick up Frank Poole's body in *2001*. And just as Zarathustra later disposes of the body, Bowman symbolically disposes of Poole's body when Bowman releases Poole so he (Bowman) can open the airlock door. Incidentally, Clarke's removal of these two symbolic actions—picking up the body and then disposing of it—from his novel is one of the reasons for doubting that Clarke was in on most of the symbolism. (Again, Clarke could alternatively have been respecting Kubrick's secrets or simply trying to write a nonallegorical novel.)

HEYWOOD FLOYD AS THE YOUNG ZARATHUSTRA

There are two Zarathustras—the young Zarathustra and the older Zarathustra. That is, Zarathustra's life has two stages. The young Zarathustra creates God: he is a believer. The older Zarathustra kills God—ceases to believe—and expounds a philosophy of atheism. Different actors play the two roles.

Heywood Floyd plays the young Zarathustra, who creates God; Dave Bowman plays the older Zarathustra, who kills God. In case you've forgotten these actors, Heywood Floyd was both Paris (who seduced Helen and took her to Troy) and Menelaus (Helen's husband) in the Odysseus allegory, and Dave Bowman was Odysseus.

In chapter 3 of *Thus Spake Zarathustra* we learn that, as a young man, Zarathustra believed in God. Zarathustra tells his story in these words: "Once upon a time, Zarathustra also [like other men] cast his fancy beyond humankind [to supernatural beings], like all backworldsmen [ignorant people]. The work of a suffering and tortured God, did the world then seem to me." It seemed that "the creator wished to look away from himself—thereupon he created the world." But, Zarathustra later realized, this God was not real; he was the creation of Zarathustra's imagination. "That God *whom I created* was *human work* and human madness, like all the gods!" And not just madness: God was the product of Zarathustra's burned-down, barely glowing intellect. "Out of my own ashes and glow it came to me, that phantom [God]." Moreover, the phantom was Zarathustra's own image: "A *man* he was."[20]

When he was thirty, Zarathustra began to doubt. He went off to the mountains to rekindle the flame of his intellect; he lived in a high cave. "I surpassed myself . . . ; I carried my own ashes to the mountain; a brighter flame I contrived for myself. And lo! The phantom *withdrew* from me!" Both "surpassed" (transcended) and "to [up] the mountain" allude to Nietzsche's concept of *higher* man—the man who rejects God and begins the climb to overman. In short, Zarathustra became an atheist, a man for whom "it would now be suffering and torment to believe in such phantoms."[21]

How do these events relate to the surface story of *2001*? They establish, first of all, that there are two Zarathustras: the young believer and the older nonbeliever. And they establish that the young believer creates God. Who is it in *2001* who symbolically creates God? Heywood Floyd. He travels alone from earth to the moon and goes to see the monolith. Five other people accompany Floyd into the excavation to inspect the monolith. But only one, Floyd, touches it. He is the one who acquires superstition. (Recall that the moon monolith symbolizes superstition in the Zarathustra allegory. In this allegory characters acquire traits by touching those traits.)

Since Floyd is the one who acquires superstition, he must be the one who creates God. Do you remember what happens in the very next scene after the moon monolith scene, where Floyd touches the monolith? The next scene is the one where, eighteen months (gestation period) after the moon (ovum) takes the spherical moon lander (sperm) inside and is thereby fertilized, Hal-Discovery is born. The fertilization-gestation-birth process is

not part of the surface story, of course; it is an aspect of the God who is created *in the image of man*. In the surface story, Hal-Discovery is not sexually created. Hal-Discovery is built by Americans; Heywood Floyd, a high-
ranking scientist, directs the project. We don't witness the construction, but
we can deduce that Floyd was in charge from three facts: (1) Floyd was the
one who symbolically acquired superstition (in the allegory), setting himself up to become God's creator, (2) Floyd was the hero of the earth-to-
moon episode, and (3) Floyd was a high official in the space program—
chairman of the National Council of Astronautics in Clarke's novel and
apparently at least a member of the Council in the movie.

Don't overlook the parallel between Moonwatcher and Heywood
Floyd. Moonwatcher figured out how to make and use a tool, the bone-
club, immediately after he touched the African monolith and thereby
absorbed intelligence. Heywood Floyd built a tool for going to Jupiter
immediately after he touched the moon monolith and thereby absorbed
superstition (in the allegory, not in the surface story). In this allegory,
intelligence leads to the creation of man; superstition leads to the creation of God.

As God's creator, Heywood Floyd must be the young Zarathustra. It
was he that the older Zarathustra later referred to when he said: "That
God whom *I created* was human work. . . . A *man* [the image of a man]
he was." True to Zarathustra's statement, the spaceship Heywood Floyd
creates bears powerful physical and mental resemblances to a man. Hal-
Discovery is the physical and mental image of a *man*.

DAVE BOWMAN AS THE
OLDER ZARATHUSTRA AND OVERMAN

It is easy to see that someone else, Dave Bowman, takes over the role of
Zarathustra in *2001*'s last two acts. One piece of evidence we have already
observed. Just as Zarathustra picks up the rope dancer's body and then disposes of it in *Thus Spake Zarathustra*, Bowman uses his pod's arms to
grasp the body of Frank Poole, who symbolizes the rope dancer. Then,
when it becomes necessary for Bowman to save himself, he releases (figuratively disposes of) the body.

Bowman's killing of Hal is even stronger evidence that Bowman is
Zarathustra—the older Zarathustra. In Nietzsche's book, Zarathustra
kills God in his own mind. ("A brighter flame I contrived for myself.
And lo! The phantom withdrew from me!") After ten years of meditating

in the mountains, rekindling the fire of his soul, Zarathustra comes down from the mountain. He will bring "fire into the valleys."[22] Going to the nearest town, where the rope dancer is about to give his performance, Zarathustra announces, "God is Dead!"[23] He then devotes himself (not too successfully) to destroying God in the minds of others. Obviously, the character in *2001* who kills God must represent Zarathustra. God is Hal-Discovery, and the person who kills him is Dave Bowman. Bowman, therefore, is the older Zarathustra.

Another powerful piece of evidence that Bowman is the older Zarathustra comes from the end of the movie. There it is Bowman who is reborn as Nietzsche's overman, the star-child. This event is a close approximation to what happens at the end of *Zarathustra*: Zarathustra becomes the overman in spirit, if not in actual fact. In the third-from-last paragraph of his book, Nietzsche implies that the prophet is about to become the figurative mother of figurative children. The children symbolize members of the anticipated overman race. Zarathustra speaks: "Well! The *lion* has come, my *children* are near, Zarathustra has grown ripe [ready to give birth], *my hour has come.*"[24]

"The lion" and "my children" refer to the opposite end of *Zarathustra*. Chapter 1 is titled "The Three Metamorphoses"—metamorphoses of the spirit.[25] These are

1. spirit into *camel* (the religious person who docilely bears the loads placed on him by his master, God),
2. camel into *lion* (the rebel who struggles with the "dragon"—God—for freedom and supremacy), and
3. lion into *child* (the innocent one who forgets the past and provides a new beginning).

In this triad, the camel is lower man, who obeys God; the lion is higher man, who kills God; and the child is overman, who replaces God as the supreme being. In saying "my children are near," Zarathustra implies that he will be the figurative mother of the new overman race, which is about to emerge. He will not personally metamorphose into overman, but his philosophy and motivation—his will to power—will be embodied in his metaphorical children. Figuratively, Zarathustra becomes overman. And when Bowman metamorphoses into the star-child, Zarathustra becomes overman.

The conclusion is inescapable: Bowman symbolizes Zarathustra in the third allegory. Obviously, he also symbolizes overman—when he is reborn as the star-child.

HAL-DISCOVERY AS GOD

The rope dancer, young Zarathustra (lower man), older Zarathustra (higher man), overman, and God are the main characters in *Zarathustra*. So far, I have identified three actors who play one or another of these roles: Frank Poole, playing the rope dancer; Heywood Floyd, playing young Zarathustra; and Dave Bowman, playing both older Zarathustra and overman. That leaves only one character and one actor. The character is God, and the actor is Hal-Discovery. It becomes a simple matter to deduce that Hal-Discovery plays the role of God. God, incidentally, is born right after the lunar dawn, The Dawn of God.

The Anthropomorphic-Anthropopathic God

Some of the best evidence that Hal-Discovery is God comes from the many anthropomorphic and anthropopathic qualities Kubrick assigns to the humanoid spaceship. Anthropomorphism is the attribution of human characteristics to nonhuman entities; it tends to emphasize (but is not limited to) physical characteristics. Anthropopathism is the attribution of human feelings and emotions to nonhuman entities; it deals with the mental side of resemblance to humans.

My frequent use of the hyphenated Hal-Discovery in place of the usual Hal emphasizes an important fact. Strictly speaking, Hal is just the computer, Discovery's (the spaceship's) brain and central nervous system. But God is symbolized by the *combination* of Hal and Discovery. When Nietzsche suggested that man created God in his own image, the philosopher wasn't speaking only of the mental image of man. He also—indeed, primarily—had the physical image of man in mind. The Bible, which Nietzsche was deliberately turning upside down, says that "God created man in his own image."[26] This was traditionally understood to mean that man was the *physical* image of God; Michelangelo so understood it when he painted God as a husky old man with a white beard. To be turning the biblical verse upside down, Nietzsche had to be implying that God was at least as much the physical image of man as the mental image. And that is why Kubrick has made Discovery the physical image of man while making Hal the mental image of man. Both Hal *and* Discovery symbolize God. They are one being—hence the hyphen.

"In his own image" requires elaboration, because it is the most fundamental and most heavily symbolized idea in Kubrick's Zarathustra allegory. The number of symbols devoted to this one idea is remarkable, as is the imagination and cleverness reflected in some of the symbols. Nietzsche, as I said, was an atheist. He didn't accept the biblical doctrine that man was created by God; much less did he believe that man was the image of God. He thought the reverse was true—that *man* was the creator, that God was a figment of man's imagination, and that the weakness of man's imagination caused him to conceive of God as a manlike being. Hence, in *2001*, Hal-Discovery comes *after* man and is created by man (specifically, by Project Director Heywood Floyd) in man's own image. Arthur Clarke practically comes right out and says this in his production log entry for November 18, 1964:

> Feeling rather stale—went into London and saw Carol Reed's film about Michelangelo, *The Agony and the Ecstasy*. One line particularly struck me—the use of the phrase "God made Man in His own image." This, after all, is the theme of our movie.[27]

Clarke's phrasing of the third allegory's "theme" is a bit careless, or maybe tactful, since Kubrick (an atheist) is really allegorizing the opposite theme: Nietzsche's theme that *man* created *God* in his own image. But the essential point under either phrasing is that God and man share the same image: God is highly anthropomorphic—and male. The Zarathustra allegory accordingly revolves around the birth and death of a highly anthropomorphic, male God. Kubrick intensely symbolizes God's birth, anthropomorphism, and death.

Part of God's anthropomorphism, as symbolized by Kubrick, is the deity's sexual conception and birth. Under the second allegory, I presented a chain of symbols depicting the sexual conception and birth of Hal-Discovery. The earth shuttle and the space station copulate;[28] a sperm cell (the spherical moon lander) swims to the ovum (the spherical moon); the ovum opens up (the dome-shaped hangar door opens) and takes the sperm inside; the gestation period (eighteen months) passes; and then, announced by the symbolic lunar dawn, the humanoid God is born—slowly, horizontally, headfirst, in the usual manner. Granted, sexual reproduction has more to do with being an animal than with being specifically human, but it does move Hal-Discovery away from the machine category and toward the general biological category—animals—to which humans belong. More important, Kubrick is obviously using sexual reproduction as a human characteristic for symbolic purposes.

Another aspect of God's anthropomorphism is a slyly depicted feminine characteristic. The sexual symbolism described under the second allegory is the final stages of a longer eight-link chain of events. Recall, if you will, that the first stage is the transformation of a bone into a primitive tool-weapon, a club. The second stage is the transformation of the primitive weapon, tossed high into the blue, into a high-tech weapon, an orbiting nuclear bomb. And so on until we get to stage eight, the birth of God. God thus starts out as a bone; God is made from a bone. Sound familiar? If it does, you have caught on to Kubrick's biggest and cleverest joke. It again turns a biblical idea upside down. The Bible says God created *woman* from a bone, Adam's rib.[29] But Kubrick says man created *God* from a bone.

These two human characteristics—(1) sexual conception, gestation, and birth and (2) being made from a bone—are just the beginning. Now we come to a supremely important human characteristic. Hirsch mistakenly refers to "Hal's breakdown."[30] He even theorizes that the aliens engineered this breakdown. Similarly, Wallich repeats some revisionist history from Clarke's novel; the novel provides the basis for Wallich's claims that Hal had a breakdown.[31] (This material isn't in the movie.) Clarke attributes Hal's "mental breakdown" to conflicting obligations to his crew (truthfulness) and to Mission Control (secrecy).[32]

But wait a minute. Breakdown? Hal had no mental breakdown. He simply made a mistake. He wrongly predicted the failure of the AE-35 unit. Hal's mistake is counterpoint to his earlier assertion (during the BBC interview) that "no 9000 computer has ever made a *mistake*." Kubrick is making a point, a point about Hal's being *the image of man*. To make his point, Kubrick alludes to a familiar aphorism: "To err is human, to forgive divine."[33] Hal makes an error. Therefore he is human, created in man's own image.

Those are three image-of-man characteristics. Let's look at a fourth. What did the ape (represented by Moonwatcher) do that changed him into a man? Answer: He learned to use tools. As mentioned earlier, tool use was long regarded as a distinguishing characteristic of human beings. Does Hal-Discovery meet the tool-use criterion? You bet he does. He not only uses a tool, he uses the very sort of tool Moonwatcher first used—a *weapon*. Moonwatcher's weapon was a bone-club; Hal-Discovery's is a utility pod. The sinister spaceship uses Frank Poole's empty pod to sneak up behind Poole and cut his air hose.

The four image-of-man characteristics just identified are the most symbolically distinguished, but there are many more. Hal-Discovery has a manlike skeleton, complete with head, neck, vertebrae, and sacrum and overlaid with three mouths, eyes (covered by those mod sunglasses), and three pairs of excretory orifices (one pair for each mouth). He has consciousness, thought, hearing, sight, a human voice, and—here is the anthropopathism—human feelings and emotions (confidence, enjoyment, enthusiasm, pride, puzzlement, suspicion, fear, panic, and the instinct for self-preservation). He has human habits and vices (he sticks out his tongue, blows bubbles, wears sunglasses, uses the telephone, uses bathrooms, blames others for his mistakes, keeps secrets, hatches plots, and tells lies). He is a chess player, an art critic, and a clinical psychologist. He is mortal. And before dying, he lapses into childlike senility, singing "Daisy, Daisy, give me your answer do."

A Dash of Divinity

A god who is the image of man still needs a little divinity to identify him as a deity. Hence, in addition to his human qualities, Hal displays *divine* qualities that identify him as the God whom Nietzsche condemns. Like the God who drove the Ugliest Man to murder him—the God who sees into man and spies all man's hidden secrets and shame—Hal uses his red eye to see into the pod where Bowman and Poole are trying to hold a secret conversation. Hal lip-reads the secrets the astronauts are trying to hide. Again like the Zarathustran God, who tries to kill man (figuratively, by killing his spirit)—and who literally does kill in the rope dancer parable—Hal tries to kill the five crewmen. And he largely succeeds, killing all but Bowman.

Hal might also answer prayers; I'm not sure. Consider the scene where Poole receives a birthday transmission from his parents. Every other scene in part 2 ("Jupiter Mission") contains symbolism, so this one should too. Without symbolism, the scene is almost pointless: it does nothing to advance the surface story's plot. At best it provides minor visual entertainment by displaying only slightly futuristic technology—a movable, adjustable, voice-actuated recliner lounge. Here's what happens. Hal tells Poole the birthday transmission is coming in. Poole replies: "Would you put it [TV] on here please? Take me in a bit [closer to the TV]." Hal obliges. He turns on the TV screen and slides the lounge closer to the screen.

Gods spend an inordinate amount of time doing favors for humans. But to get these favors, humans must take the initiative: they must pray for them. Perhaps when Poole asks Hal to adjust the lounge, Kubrick is symbolizing prayer. And perhaps when Hal grants Poole's request, Kubrick is showing Hal doing what gods do best. You decide.

In the next scene, Hal beats Poole in a game of chess. At the very least, this symbolizes the idea that Hal was created in the image of man: Hal plays chess. But it might also symbolize the idea that God is supreme. At any rate, he is supreme vis-à-vis lower man, Poole. Maybe it is significant that the losing astronaut is not Bowman, who proves to be a higher man. Ultimately, it is Bowman who becomes supreme.

Peering into people to learn their secrets, answering prayers, and acting supreme are certainly godlike characteristics. But let us not forget the divine attribute that, from Nietzsche's point of view, is the most important of all. In Nietzsche's rope-dancer parable, the God character—the buffoon—comes onto the rope *after* the rope dancer begins his crossing. The rope dancer symbolizes man; *man comes first*. Nietzsche is symbolizing, among other things, his idea that man created God (in this instance by letting the buffoon leap over him and thus become supreme). Hal-Discovery is created by a man, Heywood Floyd; the created comes *after* the creator.

Other Evidence That Hal-Discovery Is God

The HAL-IBM connection is additional evidence that Hal-Discovery is God. Recall that retreating each letter of IBM one notch backwards down the alphabet produces HAL. In the man-machine symbiosis allegory, the derivation of HAL from IBM symbolizes a synthesis of man (Hal) and machine (IBM). In this synthesis, a symbiotic being (Hal-Discovery) symbolizes a race of such beings that attempts to replace humanity. The HAL-IBM connection provides slightly different symbolism in the Zarathustra allegory. It now symbolizes God, as interpreted by Nietzsche. Nietzsche says God (1) was created by man and (2) is the image of man. IBM (a machine's name) symbolizes that Hal-Discovery was (1) created by man, as all machines are; Hal (a man's name) symbolizes that Hal-Discovery is (2) the image of man.

Finally, we come to some truly esoteric evidence. Shortly after Hal's death—no, make that *beyond* Hal's death—we see on the screen the title of *2001*'s last part: "Jupiter and Beyond the Infinite." Note the word "beyond." It suggests a spatial meaning—this movie is about space travel—but it actually has a temporal meaning. "Beyond" refers to what happens *after* God dies. But to know this, you have to know a little about theology: you have to understand what "the infinite" means in this context. "Beyond the Infinite" *seems* like a high-sounding abstraction whose only meaning lies in the mood it conveys—the mood of depth, expanse, and mystery. But "infinite" is not just a hollow victory of sound over substance; it does have meaning. It means God.

"Infinite" is a word sometimes used by philosopher-theologian Paul Tillich as a synonym for God. Tillich says, for example: "The finite cannot force the infinite; man cannot compel God."[34] He also says there is "essential unity of the finite [man] and the infinite [God]."[35] Still, "man is actually separated from the infinite [God]."[36] Who is infinite? "God is the infinite."[37] Also: "Man must ask about the infinite [God] from which he is estranged."[38] Again: "If man and his world are described as finite, God is infinite in contrast to them."[39] And: "The name of this infinite and inexhaustible ground of history is *God*."[40] Once more: "Being-itself [another Tillichian synonym for God] transcends every finite being infinitely; God in the divine-human encounter transcends man unconditionally."[41]

We see, then, that "the infinite" is God. And "beyond the infinite" means beyond God—after God, *after God's death*. Kubrick is alluding to the death of God. And who is it that has just died? Hal. Conclusion: Hal (really Hal-Discovery) is God.

The evidence is compelling. Like Nietzsche's version of God, Hal-Discovery comes after man and is created by man. He has many qualities that identify him as having been created in man's image. He has the necessary dash of divinity, particularly his seeing into men to learn their deepest secrets and his sneaking up behind the rope dancer to kill him. He has a name whose hidden meaning describes him as being a creation of man (IBM) and the image of man (Hal). He dies, which agrees with "God is Dead!" And he is "the infinite," which is another name for God. No doubt about it: Hal-Discovery is God.

NOTES

1. Strauss's opening fanfare, used by Kubrick at the beginning and end of *2001*, depicts man's climb from ape (low C) to overman (high C, three full octaves above low C). To avoid ambiguity concerning which octave a note is in, I will number the whole notes (white keys on the piano) from 1 (low C, one octave below middle C) through 8 (middle C) and 15 (one octave above middle C) to 22 (two octaves above C). Strauss uses only one sharp or flat, E-flat in the second octave; it is numbered 9½ (and provides an ominous tone suggesting failure). The three sets of five heraldic notes and the crescendo are as follows:

1st Set:	1 - 5 - 8	10 - 9½	(C, G, C, E, Eb)
2nd Set:	1 - 5 - 8	10 - 11	(C, G, C, E, F)
3rd Set:	1 - 5 - 8	11 - 12	(C, G, C, F, G)
Crescendo:	12 - 13 - 15	16 17 - 18 - 19	(G, A, C, D, E, F, G)
	17 - 18 - 19	20 - 21 - 22	(E, F, G, A, B, C)

The pattern of ascension suggests a man scaling a steep slope, starting at 1 (bottom), and becoming overman when he reaches the top. On the first try, with a running start, he advances 4 units (1 to 5), then 3, and then 2 before slipping back a half unit (to 9½) and then to the bottom. On the second try, his advance goes 4-3-2-1—this time the fourth step brings further progress—but he again loses purchase and slides back. Undaunted, he puts forth greater effort (the will to power) on his third try, reaches his previous best, 11, in just three steps, and is able to struggle on to 12 and obtain a handhold before stopping—no backsliding this time. Now the crescendo: After pausing for breath at 12, he makes two more quick advances (to 15), then a third, and three more in quick succession (to 19). He momentarily slips back two notches but quickly recaptures the lost elevation, then slowly but triumphantly continues on the last three steps to the top. Overman!

Strauss probably didn't intend to depict the emergence of higher man at a specific point, but conceivably he did so intend. If so, that point would be at the end of the third set of five notes, at note 12, where man finally gets a handhold and the backsliding to low C ends.

2. Many people have the misconception that 2000 (the thousandth year of the second millennium) rather than 2001 is the first year of the third millennium. But whereas the first thousand-mile interval on an automobile odometer begins at *zero* and ends at 1,000, history has no year zero. The first millennium began on January 1, 1 (i.e., 0001), and ended on December 31, 1000. Consequently, the beginning date of the second millennium was January 1, 1001, and the last day of the millennium will be December 31, 2000. So the beginning date of the third millennium will be January 1, 2001; the year 2001 is the start of the third millennium. For further discussion see Forum (letters to the editor), *National Geographic* 193, no. 5 (May 1998), unpaginated front matter, and "'2001' Writer Disputes Millennium's Turn" (public statement by Arthur C. Clarke), *Washington Post*, 9 January 1999, C12.

3. Friedrich Nietzsche, *Thus Spake Zarathustra*, trans. Thomas Common, rev. with introduction and notes by H. James Birx (Buffalo: Prometheus, 1993), 56 (my italics).

4. Ibid., 281.

5. Ibid., 35.

6. Ibid., 163.

7. Ibid., 224–25.

8. Ibid., 225.

9. Ibid.

10. Ibid., 162.

11. Ibid., 99 (my italics).

12. Ibid., 38.

13. Ibid.

14. H. James Birx, introduction to *Thus Spake Zarathustra*, by Friedrich Nietzsche, trans. Thomas Common (Buffalo: Prometheus, 1993), 23.

15. Ibid.

16. John Allen, untitled 1968 review of *2001*, in Jerome Agel, ed., *The Making of Kubrick's* 2001 (New York: New American Library, 1970), 233; Joseph Gelmis, untitled 1969 re-review of *2001*, in Agel, ed., *Making* 2001, 269; David G. Hoch, "Mythic Patterns in *2001: A Space Odyssey*," *Journal of Popular Culture* 4, no. 4 (Spring 1971), 961; and Carolyn Geduld, *Filmguide to* 2001: A Space Odyssey (Bloomington: Indiana University Press, 1973), 35.

17. Thomas J. Bogdewic, http://www.underview.com/2001/viewpoints.html. Note that the home page title, "Underman's 2001," is a pun-by-allusion that suggests

the home page creator's awareness that *2001* has Zarathustran connections. "Underman" alludes to both (1) "Down Under," or Australia, where Underman lives, and (2) Underman's opposite, overman, who is the goal of Zarathustran evolution.

18. Arthur Clarke, co-author of *2001*'s screenplay, would certainly seem to agree that superstition is what produces gods and goddesses. In his novel *Childhood's End* (which, incidentally, has a superficially Zarathustran plot), Clarke equates religion with superstition. The chief of the Overlords (equivalent to God) addresses mankind: "In the centuries before our coming, . . . you had put superstition behind you: Science was the only real religion of mankind." Arthur C. Clarke, *Childhood's End*, in *Across the Sea of Stars* (Clarke collection) (New York: Harcourt, Brace & World, Inc., 1959), 402.

19. Nietzsche, *Zarathustra*, 35, 37, 42.

20. Ibid., 56 (my italics).

21. Ibid (Neitzsche's italics).

22. Ibid., 34.

23. Ibid., 35.

24. Ibid., 341 (my italics).

25. Ibid., 51–53.

26. Gen. 1:27 Revised Standard Version.

27. Arthur C. Clarke, *The Lost Worlds of* 2001 (Boston: Gregg Press, 1979), 39.

28. According to the Bible, Jesus was God incarnate (John 1:14) and was conceived when the Holy Spirit impregnated Mary (Matthew 1:18–20, Luke 1:34–35). Thus, in effect and possibly by intent, the space shuttle symbolizes the Holy Spirit and the space station symbolizes Mary in the Zarathustra allegory. The Holy Spirit and Mary are not characters in *Zarathustra*, so if this symbolism is intentional rather than accidental it is not Zarathustran symbolism in the narrow sense. But it is Zarathustran in the broad sense, because it relates to God, who *is* a character in Zarathustra. As just implied, I am uncertain whether Kubrick intended to symbolize the Holy Spirit and Mary. But since he later intentionally symbolizes the Christian doctrine of The Fall (see chapter 6), which is not in *Zarathustra,* I am inclined to think that the symbolization of the Holy Spirit and Mary is likewise intentional.

29. Gen. 2:21–22 RSV.

30. Foster Hirsch, introduction to *The Lost Worlds of* 2001, by Arthur C. Clarke (Boston: Gregg Press, 1979), xi.

31. Paul Wallich, "Remembrance of Future Past" (book review), *Scientific American* 276, no. 1 (January 1997), 114.

32. Arthur C. Clarke, *2001: A Space Odyssey* (New York: Signet, 1968), 148–49, 159.

33. Alexander Pope (1688–1744), in John Bartlett, *Familiar Quotations*, 16th ed., rev. by Justin Kaplan (Boston: Little, Brown and Company, 1992), 299.

34. Paul Tillich, *Systematic Theology*, vol. 3 (Chicago: University of Chicago Press, 1963), 112–13.

35. Ibid., 113–14.

36. Paul Tillich, *Systematic Theology*, vol. 2 (Chicago: University of Chicago Press, 1957), 9.

37. Ibid., 10.

38. Paul Tillich, *Systematic Theology*, vol. 1 (Chicago: University of Chicago Press, 1951), 206.

39. Ibid., 252.

40. Paul Tillich, *The Shaking of the Foundations* (New York: Charles Scriber's Sons, 1948), 59.

41. Paul Tillich, *The Courage to Be* (New Haven: Yale University Press, 1952), 172.

Chapter 6

The Zarathustra Allegory: The Action

With the cast introduced, we can proceed with the action. The subtitle of this chapter is slightly misleading, because some of the action—the events preceding God's death—was covered in chapter 5. But this chapter does cover the most important action: the death of God and man's metamorphosis into overman. The events of both chapters occur in the context of an ape-man-overman evolutionary sequence. The middle stage of evolution, man, subdivides into (*a*) lower man (the believer, the masses, the crowd in the marketplace) and (*b*) higher man (the nonbeliever, he who would challenge God for supremacy). Between lower man and higher man stands God, who usurps the supremacy that rightfully belongs to man. Man must kill God to advance from lower man to higher man and thence to overman.

At the present stage of our drama, (1) ape has evolved into man (by acquiring intelligence and becoming a tool-user), (2) man—lower man—has created God (Heywood Floyd has symbolically acquired superstition and built Hal-Discovery), and (3) God stands in the way of further progress. The events that follow—the events analyzed in this chapter—are (4) the death of God, (5) the immediate aftermath of God's death, (6) the evolution of man into overman, and (7) eternal recurrence.

THE DEATH OF GOD

In writing *Thus Spake Zarathustra*, Nietzsche was portraying his vision of man's passage from ape to overman. The central part of this passage involves the rise and fall of God. Man creates God in his own image. While alive, God stands as an obstacle to man's reaching his goal: two beings cannot both be supreme. As we learned in the parable of the rope dancer, the Nietzschian God tries to kill man, tries to keep man from reaching his objective. Here Nietzsche is dramatizing the point that *belief* in God figuratively kills man by killing his creative spirit and suppressing his will to power. Because God stands in the way, God must die: man must stop believing in God. Or, to be more precise, *higher* man—the lion, he who seeks power—must kill God. Lower man—the camel, who submits to God's wishes—can and will go right on believing: "What the populace once learned to believe without reasons, who could—refute it to them by means of reasons?"[1]

For man to become overman, then, God must die. This is the meaning of the Zarathustran message for which Nietzsche is famous: "God is Dead!" That is, God *should* die, because he is an obstacle to human progress. And in Zarathustra's mind, which once created him ("that God whom I created"), God is already dead. (Nietzsche doesn't mean God once lived, then died; he means that *belief* in God once existed but died, at least in the minds of Nietzsche and other "higher" people.) The need for God to die—the oppressiveness and obtrusiveness of God, the wrongness of his doctrines—is a recurring theme in Zarathustra's teaching. Higher man must kill God; higher man must unleash the will to power.

In *Zarathustra* there is no scene in which God per se (as opposed to a God symbol in a parable) actually dies. But in one scene, God has been murdered offstage by the previously quoted Ugliest Man. His reason for murdering God is, to repeat, that God "looked with eyes which beheld *everything*."[2] Zarathustra puts it this way: "You could not *endure* him who beheld you—who always beheld you through and through, you ugliest man. You took revenge on this witness!"[3] This reason is highly relevant to *2001*, because in *2001* Hal's (God's) prying, all-seeing red eye is the foundation for the episode in which Dave Bowman symbolically kills God.

Before killing God, man must lose his faith. In *2001*, Bowman and Poole lose faith in Hal when they suspect he was wrong in predicting the failure of the AE-35 module. They realize that Hal is not what he, like God, is supposed to be: omniscient. And they retire to the interior of a pod to privately discuss (they think) cutting off Hal's higher brain functions. *This scene symbolizes loss of faith.* Hal's red eye sees into the pod and reads the astronauts' lips. And Hal reacts by doing what God often did to people who were unfaithful—for example, to the people of Sodom and Gomorrah and to Lot's wife.[4] He kills all the astronauts, except for Bowman, who fights back and kills Hal. The result: "God is Dead!"

One more symbol accompanies the death of god. After blasting himself back into the spaceship through the airlock, Bowman dons a *green* space helmet. It doesn't match the orange of his space suit. Is this some wardrobe designer's idea of color coordination? Hardly. Both in his earlier space walk and in the hotel room, Bowman has an *orange* helmet that matches his suit. Likewise, Poole's yellow helmet matches his space suit. The green is definitely symbolic. Or, rather, the green and orange *combination* is symbolic. Green and orange are the respective colors of the eternally feuding Catholics and Protestants in Northern Ireland. The Catholic color is green (probably from St. Patrick's shamrock emblem). The Protestant color is orange, taken from William of Orange, who became William III, king of England, Ireland, and Scotland. William, a Protestant, deposed James II, a Roman Catholic. William's color was adopted by Irish Protestants in the late eighteenth century. Although the green and orange combination could theoretically symbolize reconciliation, as it does in the flag of Ireland, the *2001* context is one of battle to the death. Kubrick is using green and orange as a battle symbol. More specifically, Bowman's donning the green helmet symbolizes his becoming, in terms of "the three metamorphoses," the lion: the green-and-orange Bowman is the lion—the battler—who "will struggle with the great dragon [God] for victory."[5]

THE IMMEDIATE AFTERMATH

Hal's death—the death of God—occurs near the end of Act 2, "Jupiter Mission: 18 Months Later." But the act has one more scene. Bowman has no sooner finished shutting Hal down than TV screens and loudspeakers cut in with the face and voice of Heywood Floyd. Floyd delivers a prerecorded briefing on the mission's purpose. It is intended for all five crewmen ("Now that . . . the entire crew is revived") but is, of course, heard only by Bowman. Floyd states that, "for security reasons of the highest importance," the contents of the briefing were previously known only to Hal. Bowman learns for the first time about the discovery of the moon monolith, the signal it beamed at Jupiter, and the purpose of the mission.

From the standpoint of the surface story plot, the timing of this briefing makes absolutely no sense (so look for symbolism). Even if there were a valid reason for keeping the public or the Russians uninformed about the moon monolith and about the mission's purpose, there would be no reason to keep the spaceship's *crew* in the dark. In wartime, does the need for secrecy require that fighter pilots and bomber crews and commandos be denied knowledge of their mission's purpose until they get to where they're going?

In the *2001* situation, dozens of other Americans on earth and on the moon obviously must already know the secrets that have been kept from

Discovery's crew. Technicians found the magnetic field that revealed the buried monolith's presence; workmen unburied the monolith; on arriving at the moon, Floyd attended a briefing with eleven other men who already knew what was going on; more technicians traced the radio signal to Jupiter; five men accompanied Floyd into the excavation to inspect the monolith, and you can be sure that others had inspected it first; all these men worked for supervisors and higher officials who had to be informed; the mission planners back on earth knew what was going on. Furthermore, all these people not only *knew* the facts that Discovery's crew was being kept in the dark about, they were in places—the earth and the moon— where they could get loose-lipped (perhaps after a few drinks) and blab to others. The five astronauts, in contrast, were sequestered in a spaceship millions of miles from earth, where they could talk to no one but themselves; three of the five were in hibernation.

And yet the crew of five carefully screened, highly trained, PhD astronauts couldn't be trusted with information they really had to know. The five couldn't be briefed even immediately before they departed or, in the case of the hibernating crew members, before they went into hibernation. Why not? Because they might talk to people back on earth that they were not in a position to talk to. Who's kidding whom?

Those aren't the only flaws in the scenario. Keeping the crew uninformed about their mission and their jobs creates a risk that they will not become informed—and that the mission will consequently fail. What if an accident or technical problem prevents the playing of the briefing recording? Even if it does get played, how can the crew get answers to questions about details that aren't clear? Are the questions supposed to be broadcast back to Mission Control so the Russians can intercept them—and the answers? Are Russian cryptographers to be viewed with scorn? If Hal has been given the answers to all possible questions, how were the people who gave Hal the answers able to anticipate all possible questions?

Everything about the prerecorded briefing is nonsensical. Whatever did Kubrick have in mind when he inserted this implausible and seemingly gratuitous scene?

It turns out that Kubrick did have something in mind: symbolism. When Floyd delivers his briefing, Bowman becomes *enlightened*. Which is to say, when higher man slays God, higher man becomes enlightened. Bowman's enlightenment symbolizes the enlightenment that Zarathustra (played by Bowman) acquires when God (played by Hal) dies. When Zarathustra realizes that God is dead—when he ceases to believe in God—the flame of his wisdom grows brighter: "A brighter flame I contrived for myself."[6] He sees all the errors in "the will of God," in religious doctrines and practices and beliefs, in piety, and so on. He is inspired to devote his life to criticizing religion and to expounding a new counterphilosophy of atheism, will to power, and overman.

It wouldn't do to have Zarathustra's vitriolic criticism of religion, his expounding of atheistic philosophy, taking place before he stopped believing—before he perceived that God was dead. So Kubrick made sure it didn't happen. In the symbolic surface story, Kubrick put Bowman's enlightenment in the right place—immediately *after* Bowman perceived that Hal was dead.

MAN INTO OVERMAN

In Nietzsche's philosophy, as spoken by Zarathustra, the death of God unleashes the will to power. The will to power, in turn, drives the evolution of man into overman. Some lower men—the populace, believers—become higher men, who kill God. The first higher men—nonbelievers—are but "a symbol that better ones are on the way."[7] Speaking to higher men assembled in his cave, Zarathustra cautions: "You signify steps: so do not upbraid him who ascends beyond you into *his* height!"[8] When higher man can climb no higher, he will become overman:

> God has died! You higher people, this God was your greatest danger.
> Only since he lay in the grave have you again risen. Now only comes the great noontime, now only does the higher man become [evolve into]—master [overman]! . . . Only now is the . . . human future in labor [ready to give birth]. God has died: now do *we* [but not the populace, lower man] desire—the overman to live.[9]

In this quotation, "the great noontime" is a combined climbing metaphor and illumination metaphor. Noon, when the sun has climbed to the *highest* point in its daily cycle, is the *brightest* part of the day: full illumination (the intellectual and moral illumination of overman) occurs at high noon, when man (the sun) has climbed above—*over*—the highest higher man to become *over*man. The sun at dawn is the ape. The next stages of the climbing sun are lower man and a series of ever-higher higher men—stair steps to overman. (Recall that Zarathustra said to the first higher men, "You signify *steps*." And earlier he promised to show "all the stairs to the overman."[10]) The noontime sun—at the top of the stairs (to mix metaphors)—is overman.

The sun's climb to the great noontime—man's climb up the stairs to overman—is intensely symbolized in the final part of *2001*, titled "Jupiter and Beyond the Infinite." There Kubrick depicts lower man, higher man, the will to power, overman, and related Zarathustran concepts and events in six sets of symbols: (1) Jupiter, its moons, and the last two monoliths, (2) an extended series of sexual reproduction symbols, (3) the Last Supper (Zarathustra's) symbols, (4) the black-white-radiant trio of symbols, combined with the broken wine glass, (5) the worm symbol and updated ape symbol, and (6) the "great noontime" symbols.

Jupiter, Its Moons, and the Last Two Monoliths

Arriving at Jupiter after killing Hal, Bowman sees the giant planet's five moons and something else—another black monolith. Unlike the two previous monoliths, which were stationary and upright, this one floats horizontally and (according to Clarke's novel) is in orbit. Bowman gets into the last pod and departs from the spaceship to investigate the monolith. The monolith lures Bowman toward the five moons, which mysteriously have moved into vertical alignment above Jupiter: the six bodies are stacked vertically, one above the other, with Jupiter on the bottom.

The monolith disappears in the distance, and the camera—Bowman's gaze—begins to pan upwards along an invisible perpendicular line passing through Jupiter and the moons above it. Bowman's gaze moves higher, higher, ever higher, until the highest moon disappears off the bottom of the screen. And there, well above the highest moon but still in alignment with the moons, the Star Gate opens. Bowman shoots through it and into the tunnel of lights.

What does the alignment of the six celestial bodies symbolize, and what does the Jupiter monolith symbolize? Geduld implies that this Jupiterian alignment is just another instance of "magical alignment" that Kubrick depicts "every time something strange or decisive is about to occur."[11] But Geduld is wrong about the alignment's being just an anticipatory announcement. The alignment is a multifaceted symbol, based on Nietzsche. Kubrick is symbolizing specific concepts from *Zarathustra.* Jupiter, on the bottom of the stack (*lowest*), symbolizes *lower* man, the populace, the crowd in the marketplace. The planet's gigantism symbolizes the overwhelming numerical superiority of lower man, who worships God. The five moons stacked above Jupiter symbolize the successive generations of higher man, each of which has climbed higher than the one before. And the four highest moons are the higher men Zarathustra has in mind when he says to the first higher men (lowest moon), "Do not upbraid him who ascends beyond you to *his* height!"

Earlier, Zarathustra promised himself, "I will show them the *rainbow*, and all the *stairs* to the overman."[12] There they are! Jupiter, with its rainbow-colored bands, is the rainbow. And its moons are the stairs to the overman.

Although Jupiter's color bands make it visually impressive, Kubrick apparently tried to provide an even better rainbow—the rings of Saturn. Saturn's rings would have presented more rainbowlike concentric curves—rainbow curves—with the appropriate spectrum of color bands. Without recognizing (or at least without acknowledging) that Nietzsche's rainbow was at stake, Clarke summarizes Kubrick's Saturn project: "Stanley and his special-effects team spent a great deal of time working on Saturn before it was decided to stick to Jupiter. There can be little doubt that Saturn, with its glorious system of rings, is the most spectacular of all the planets, and personally I was rather sorry when we abandoned it."[13] But, as Agel explains, Saturn was not to be: "After months of unsuccessful attempts at designing Saturn, Kubrick decided that Jupiter might be visually more interesting and possibly easier to produce. More months were [nevertheless] spent in an unsuccessful attempt to produce Saturn."[14]

Still, Bowman does see the promised rainbow, and above it the ascending stairs to the overman. When Bowman's gaze climbs upward beyond the highest moon—the top step—Kubrick is symbolizing Zarathustra's will to power. Zarathustra (Bowman) is aspiring to climb far above the height of the highest higher man. Zarathustra's will to power will drive him upward until he is above—over—the highest man, where overman belongs.

How does the Jupiter monolith relate to Jupiter and its moons? The monolith symbolizes *power*. In this respect it is analogous to the first two monoliths, which symbolized (1) intelligence and (2) superstition. In each case, the monolith's symbolic content is a human attribute that ape or man acquires. And in each case, acquisition of the attribute leads to the creation of a new being—first man, then God, and finally overman. If Bowman (higher man) can acquire power—if his "will to power" can become strong enough—he will become the first of a new species, overman.

But at Jupiter this doesn't happen: Bowman does not become overman—not yet. At Jupiter he pursues the power monolith, but he can't reach it. It disappears from sight. Bowman is not yet ready to become overman; he is not, as Zarathustra puts it, ripe. (On the final page of *Zarathustra*, the prophet says, "Zarathustra has grown ripe, my hour has come."[15]) He must evolve further; he must climb higher.

His further evolution takes place in the hotel room on the planet of the aliens. In the final scene before overman appears, the power monolith comes before Bowman once more. This time, however, it is no longer in motion, no longer elusive, no longer unattainable. It is upright, stationary. It is like the first monolith (intelligence) and the second (superstition), which were upright when earlier beings reached out to them and absorbed their essences.

Very old and very feeble, Bowman (Zarathustra) has evolved as far as man can evolve and still be man. At Jupiter he wasn't ready. But now he is. "Only now is the . . . human future in labor."[16] Bowman reaches out toward the monolith at the foot of his bed. Though it is physically out of reach, Bowman is now in full command of the will to power. His will asserts itself, and he metaphysically grasps the monolith. Power flows into his feeble body, and he evolves into the first member of a new species. Symbolically, Bowman has become overman.

Sexual Reproduction

The preceding moons-and-monoliths analysis glosses over what happens between the Jupiter monolith and the hotel-room monolith. Bowman isn't ready to grasp power at Jupiter. But he somehow matures and is able to grasp power when the last monolith appears. How does this transformation—this Zarathustran ripening—occur?

What happens is that Bowman, in the surface story, undergoes gradual metamorphosis, which symbolizes evolution. This surface story metamorphosis is symbolized by the Jupiter-and-beyond sexual reproduction symbolism that was explained in connection with the man-machine symbiosis allegory. The sexual reproduction symbolism uses fetal development—the maturing of a fetus—to symbolize metamorphosis. Here things get a little complicated, because fetal development is itself symbolized. It is symbolized by (1) Bowman's aging and (2) Bowman's seeing his next self. One Bowman's becoming two symbolizes cell division—fetal growth. The sexual reproduction symbolism serves the Zarathustra allegory as well as the symbiosis allegory. A quick review of this symbolism is therefore in order.

Bowman sees and decides to investigate the orbiting Jupiter monolith. He exits from the front tip of his elongated spaceship in one of the spherical pods. The monolith pulls him through the Star Gate and into the tunnel of lights. At the far end he zooms out across the cosmos and then skims over the surface of a planet. All of a sudden the pod, with Bowman inside, is sitting in a strange surrealistic hotel room with no door or windows. All illumination comes from below, through a translucent glass floor.

Three times in a row, one Bowman sees—and then becomes—an older version of himself: one Bowman becomes two. The final monolith appears in front of the last and oldest Bowman, bedridden and seemingly (but not actually) near death. Bowman reaches out toward the monolith, straining to reach it, and is transformed into the star-child. The star-child then moves into the universe.

In this procession of symbols, the elongated spaceship, originally God's body, is reconceptualized as a phallus. The spherical pod that emerges from its tip is ejaculated sperm. The trip through the tunnel of lights is the sperm's trip through a cosmic fallopian tube. The planet at the far end of the journey—the alien planet—is the ovum. The pod in the hotel room is the sperm cell immediately after entering the egg. Bowman inside the pod is the male chromosomes, the human input to the hybrid being that is going to be born. On leaving the pod and exploring the room—mingling with the chromosomes of the egg—Bowman becomes the fetus. The pod dissolves and disappears: the sperm cell ceases to be once its contents mix with the egg's. The windowless, doorless hotel room, a haven with no exits, is the amnion, or fetal sac. The translucent glass floor symbolizes the translucency of the amnionic membrane, and the light shining up through the floor represents light coming up through the birth canal, located below the fetus. The scenes where one Bowman becomes two depict the repeated cell division that occurs as the fetus grows. And Bowman's aging is the aging, hence growth, of the fetus.

Bowman's final self—aged, bald, bedridden—does not divide and therefore symbolizes the mature fetus, ready to be born. Here Kubrick is depicting the end of *Zarathustra*, where in the previously quoted statement about ripeness Zarathustra says, "Zarathustra has grown ripe, my hour has come." The monolith appears, Bowman acquires power, and the fetus becomes the star-child, symbolizing overman.

Just as we witnessed the birth of God, we witness the birth of overman. Recall the birth symbolism used with God. After an eighteen-month gestation period (fetal growth), Hal-Discovery (God) *emerged slowly into the black universe*, horizontally and headfirst, from the side of the screen. With the star-child, Kubrick uses parallel symbolism. The star-child on the bed has not yet been born; he is still in the room (the amnion); his birth is just beginning. As he moves through the birth canal, the camera lens moves slowly from the bed into the black monolith, which gradually fills the screen and becomes the black universe: as God did, overman *emerges slowly into the black universe.*

The sperm's trip to the egg raises a side issue. The most baffling symbol in the entire movie (except for the soap-bubble-like membrane in the cosmic wonders sequence) is Bowman's blinking eye. As Bowman exits from the tunnel of lights, we see the first of ten bitone, surrealistically colored, changing-color-scheme shots of one of Bowman's eyes, blinking. These shots, interspersed among views of celestial and then planetary wonders, increase in frequency, where frequency apparently represents intensity. The last six blinking eyes, augmented by a seventh in natural color (the eleventh in total), are consecutive and culminate in Bowman's first view of the hotel room: that final series of rapid blinks seems to bring the sperm inside the egg. What does the blinking eye symbolize?

I have a highly speculative hypothesis. The word *eye* is sometimes substituted for the upper-case letter *I* to avoid the latter's being misread as a Roman numeral. For example, Washington, D.C., has twenty-two lettered streets, including I Street, but some of the street signs for I Street read "Eye Street." Substitution of *eye* for *I* has also occurred in the absence of Roman numerals. In the title of Toni Morrison's novel *The Bluest Eye*, both *Bluest* and *Eye* have double meanings.[17] The title's second meaning is *the saddest I*, where *I* refers to the protagonist.

Could it be, then, that Kubrick is depicting the sperm's ego, represented by the word *I*? And could the blinking eye represent the word *eye*, which in turn symbolizes the word *I*? Is the particular sperm cell's determination to be the one that fertilizes the egg expressed in constant repetition of "I, I, I, . . ."? And does this expression of determination, escalating in frequency—intensity, excitement—as the sperm cell enters the egg, symbolize the will to power? I don't know the answers. But the context, as well as the lack of a better explanation, makes me inclined to think the hypothesis is correct. The blinking eye is the sperm's ego. The ego is saying, "I will be the one!"—an expression of the will to power. The blinking eye probably symbolizes the will to power.

The Last Supper

Near the end of *Zarathustra* is a chapter titled "The Last Supper." As the title suggests, this last supper is patterned after that of Jesus; Zarathustra becomes the counterpart of Jesus. The site is Zarathustra's cave. Zarathustra has as his guests twelve "disciples": two kings, an ass belonging to the kings, a magician, a pope, a voluntary beggar, Zarathustra's shadow, an intellectually conscientious man, the Ugliest Man, a soothsayer, Zarathustra's eagle, and Zarathustra's serpent. Zarathustra tells those assembled that they are "higher people" but that still higher ones—"always more, always better ones of your type"—must come and succumb before "the great noontime" witnesses the appearance of the overman.[18]

The Last Supper is preceded by an interlude during which Zarathustra is drawn into a brief expedition by a far-off "cry of distress."[19] Searching for its origin, Zarathustra encounters all but the last three of the disciples. He sends them on to his cave. Later, returning to his cave without having found the source of the cry, Zarathustra hears the cry once more. It is coming from his own cave. Although from a distance it had seemed to come from one mouth, the cry is now clearly that of many voices. The voices belong to those whom Zarathustra encountered while searching. Sudden insight tells Zarathustra that these represent higher man and that their collective despair is grounded in ignorance of the wisdom of Zarathustra.

In *2001*, Bowman's last supper symbolizes Zarathustra's Last Supper. Shortly before becoming the star-child, Bowman sits in the hotel room at a fully set table. (The table is that room-service dining cart whose two wheels tell us this is a hotel room, not a bedroom.) Bowman is eating. Then he seems to hear something in the bathroom. Getting up, he walks slowly over to the bathroom, looks around, sees nothing, returns to the dinner table, and resumes eating.

This symbolization of Zarathustra's Last Supper is extremely abstract, lacking both relevant detail and detailed meaning. There are no symbolic disciples, no words of wisdom. Bowman does break a wine glass, and the broken glass does have symbolic meaning; but that meaning does not relate to the Last Supper. For the most part, Kubrick is content simply to symbolize broadly one more significant incident from *Zarathustra*. But if you are familiar with Nietzsche's book and know the context of Zarathustra's Last Supper, there *is* meaning. The arrival of Bowman's last supper is a signal that overman is very close.

Bowman's investigatory trip to the bathroom appears to symbolize Zarathustra's short journey in search of the source of the cry of distress. If so, the incident's timing—Bowman's search occurs *during* the supper— does not jibe with the timing of Zarathustra's journey: in *Zarathustra*, the "cry of distress" incident comes *before* the Last Supper. The probable reason Kubrick combines the bathroom search with the supper is that doing so facilitates his condensing voluminous material from the book.

Black, White, Radiant, and Broken Glass

Bowman's last supper is also the beginning of an independent pattern of symbols, not part of the Last Supper symbolism. In the dinner-table sequence, Bowman is dressed all in *black*—robe, jersey, trousers, shoes. While eating, he knocks a wine glass to the floor; it breaks. He stares at the broken glass, and then slowly shifts his gaze to the bed. There he sees his next self, a feeble old man in *white* apparel. The perspective shifts; the black Bowman disappears. From nowhere, the last monolith materializes at the foot of the bed before the white Bowman. Grasping for it, he is transformed into the star-child, encased in a transparent globe and *radiant*—surrounded by light.

The black garb, the broken wine glass, the transformation from black to white and then to glowing radiance—these clearly are related symbols. But what is symbolized?

A parable told by Zarathustra provides the answers. Zarathustra describes how one day he saw on the ground a writhing, choking shepherd with a *black* serpent dangling from his mouth—head inside, tail outside. Unable to remove the serpent by pulling on it, Zarathustra commanded the shepherd: "Bite! Bite!" The shepherd obeyed. He bit off and spat out the head of the serpent. He then sprang up laughing, "*no longer man* [but] a *transformed* being, a *light-surrounded* being." Zarathustra asks, "Who is the man into whose throat all the heaviest and blackest *will* had crawled?"[20]

The answer isn't hard to deduce. The shepherd, writhing *on the ground* (hence literally *low*), is lower man; the upright, transformed, light-surrounded being is overman. Higher man (white) is Zarathustra, representing the transitional stage between lower man (black) and overman (radiant). The black serpent, alias the "blackest will," is God; the pain of its bite is the pain of subjugation to the will of God. The serpent's dangling from the shepherd's head symbolizes Nietzsche's idea that God exists only in man's head and that belief in God comes from (dangles from) man's head: man creates both God and the will of God. "Blackest will" (the will of God) implicitly contrasts with a white will, the will to power. By biting off and spitting out the serpent's head, the shepherd kills God—stops believing. Springing *up*, the former shepherd (no longer low, "no longer shepherd") ceases to be lower man; by implication he momentarily becomes another higher man. Higher man's will to power—the implied white will—transforms him into the "light-surrounded being."

Bowman's black garb symbolizes the black serpent, God, who torments lower man with his black will. The broken wine glass is the "broken" (decapitated) serpent, and the breaking of the wine glass is the death of God. When the glass breaks—when the concept of God is spat out of lower man's head—the white Bowman appears. Kubrick uses Bowman's gaze to establish a cause-and-effect connection between the broken glass and the white Bowman: after breaking the glass (killing God), Bowman stares at it (the cause), then shifts his gaze to the white Bowman (the effect) in bed. This new Bowman's white apparel represents a transitional stage—higher man—between the black of lower man and the radiant glow of overman. The white Bowman's reaching out toward the monolith is, we saw, his will to power; the monolith symbolizes power. Finally, the light-surrounded star-child is the "transformed . . . light-surrounded being," the overman. Black–white–radiant = lower man–higher man–overman. Broken glass = "God is dead" (having died between black and white).

Why does Kubrick resymbolize the death of God, previously symbolized by Hal's death? Kubrick needed a symbol for the overman. He got it—the infant surrounded by light and snuggled in a globe—by *combining* three metaphorical images that Nietzsche provided: (1) a light-surrounded being, from the shepherd-and-serpent parable, (2) a child, from Nietzsche's "three metamorphoses of the spirit" metaphor, and (3) the "great noontime" sun (a globe), from Nietzsche's dawn-to-noon climbing-sun metaphor. But the light-surrounded-being imagery came with some other imagery—the black serpent, biting off the serpent's head—that was too good to pass up. So Kubrick did what Nietzsche did: he resymbolized a previously symbolized concept. The redundancy stems from Kubrick's desire to symbolize as much of *Zarathustra* as practical.

The "three metamorphoses" metaphor was presented in chapter 5 in connection with the point that Bowman symbolizes the older Zarathustra. A brief recapitulation seems advisable. The three metamorphoses are (1) human spirit into *camel*, God's docile load-bearer, (2) camel into *lion*, the rebel who slays God, and (3) lion into *child*, the new beginning. Camel, lion, and child represent lower man, higher man, and overman. When Bowman fights and kills Hal, he is the lion. When he changes into the star-child, he is—who can doubt this?—the child. The child, obviously, is overman.

The third of the three metaphors Kubrick borrows from Nietzsche for designing the star-child is the "great noontime" sun. This metaphor has already been previewed and will be discussed in detail shortly. For the moment, all you need to understand is that the globe encasing the star-child is there to make him spherical, like the sun. The globe is not a womb or, as Sobchack believes, an amnion.[21] Neither does it signify that the star-child is still a fetus. The star-child is (while in the room) in the process of being born; he is a baby, a child.

Before leaving the "Black, White, Radiant, and Broken Glass" subtopic, we must return to the broken wine glass and view it from another angle. Before breaking, it *falls* from the table. Originally, it was Adam and Eve who fell (from God's grace): they ate the forbidden fruit, got themselves kicked out of the Garden of Eden, and in doing so gave rise to the doctrine of "The Fall." Just as Kubrick turned "in his own image" upside down, he turns "The Fall" upside down—by having God be the one who falls. *The wine glass's fall from the table symbolizes God's fall from man's grace.*

The Worm in the Fetus

Whatever became of Mr. Worm? You may recall that Nietzsche described evolution as progressing from worm to ape to man to overman. Specifically, Zarathustra told the crowd in the marketplace (rope-dancer parable): "You have made your way from the worm to man, and much within you is still worm. Once you were apes, and even yet man is more of an ape than any of the apes."[22] (He means that apes are stupid but not so stupid that they create gods.) There you have it: the worm as the first stage of evolution. Yet, so far, Kubrick seems to have ignored the worm. For example, in the Dawn of Man sequence from part 1, evolution begins with the ape.

The worm's being slighted is due partly to Nietzsche's famous rope metaphor. Zarathustra tells the crowd that "humankind is a rope stretched between the animal [ape] and the overman—a rope over an abyss."[23] No mention of worm. But, in any event, the worm *is* part of Nietzsche's scheme. And when we count the worm, and also count lower man and higher man as two separate stages, evolution has five stages: (1) worm, (2) ape, (3) lower man, (4) higher man, and (5) overman. But again, where in Kubrick's symbolism is the worm?

The answer to this question emerges from two clues. The first is that the hotel-room sequence has another five-stage progression: (1) Bowman in the pod, (2) Bowman wandering around the room in his orange space suit, (3) Bowman dressed in black, eating dinner, (4) Bowman dressed in white, lying in bed, and (5) Bowman metamorphosed into the radiantly illuminated star-child. The second clue is that the last three of these Bowman stages—black, white, and radiant—cover, in the proper sequence, the last three of the five stages of evolution. Extrapolating backwards, can we infer that the first two hotel-room Bowmans represent the first two stages of evolution—worm and ape?

I'm sure we can. The first Bowman is inside the Pod. As previously observed, he symbolizes the chromosomes inside the sperm cell (the pod). The *American Heritage College Dictionary* defines chromosome as "a *threadlike* [= wormlike] *linear* strand of DNA and associated proteins in the nucleus of animal and plant cells that carries the genes and functions in the transmission of hereditary information." (See the picture on page 250 of the third edition.) Aha! A chromosome has a linear shape—threadlike or wormlike. (In the picture it looks much more like a worm than a thread.) What we seem to have is indirect symbolization of the worm. Bowman symbolizes chromosomes, and the chromosomes symbolize worms.

If that interpretation is correct, there is no room for doubt that the second Bowman—the chap in the orange space suit—symbolizes the only remaining stage of evolution: ape. The logic is solid: Bowman's second stage symbolizes evolution's second stage. And we have more than that to go on. An orangutan is an ape, and orangutans have orangish fur. Does Kubrick intend that the orange color of Bowman's external covering, the space suit, represent the orange color of the orangutan-ape's external covering? Almost certainly, the answer is yes; otherwise we would have nothing but sequence to identify the symbolism. One more consideration, highly speculative, is that a space suit is sometimes facetiously called a "monkey suit." Apes aren't monkeys, I realize, but people sometimes refer to them as such. Kubrick probably didn't but possibly did have this in mind.

It seems, then, that the five Bowmans in the hotel room serve five symbolic purposes (collectively, not one purpose per Bowman). First, they complete the sexual reproduction chain of symbols by symbolizing the aging (growth) of the fetus and then the birth of the child: Bowman's aging symbolizes the fetus's aging. Second, as a corollary, they symbolize cell division: when one Bowman sees the next, the cell has divided—again signifying growth of the fetus. Third, they symbolize the five stages of evolution: worm, ape, lower man, higher man, and overman. Fourth—this applies only to the last three Bowmans—they collectively symbolize Zarathustra's parable of the shepherd, the black serpent, and the light-surrounded being. Fifth, the last three Bowmans also symbolize Nietzsche's three metamorphoses (camel, lion, and child).

In chapter 1, I wrote that "Kubrick's symbolization of evolution is . . . detailed, intricate, complicated, multifaceted, and subtle." The above summary shows what I meant.

The Great Noontime

At the beginning of this "Man into Overman" section, Nietzsche's concept of "the great noontime" was introduced. A crucial declaration by Zarathustra bears repeating: "Now only [i.e., now that God is dead] comes the great noontime, now only does the higher man become—master [overman]."[24] The great noontime, we saw, combines a climbing-sun metaphor with a solar-illumination metaphor. Starting with dawn, the sun climbs steadily until noon, when it is highest and brightest: maximum height brings maximum illumination—at noon. The height is the *over* in *overman*. The illumination is the intellectual and moral illumination of overman—expressed as the star-child's glowing radiance in Kubrick's symbolism. The climbing metaphor uses the idea that successive generations of higher men will go higher and higher until man evolves into overman. At that point—it's time for some more mixed metaphor—the chasm separating ape from overman will have been crossed, the stairs to the overman will have been climbed, and the spirit will have metamorphosed from camel to lion to child.

If you think that exhausts the metaphors, you are mistaken. Zarathustra also uses a lightning metaphor to express the association between overman, on the one hand, and illumination and climbing on the other. Addressing the higher people at his Last Supper, Zarathustra pontificates: "Always more, always better ones of your [higher] type shall succumb. . . . Then only grows man aloft to the height where the lightning strikes and shatters him: high enough for the lightning!" But man will climb still higher, until "the lightning no longer does harm." Then man will command the lightning ("it shall learn—to work for *me*"). Its illumination will be overman's.[25]

Having thus reinforced the more abstract concepts of climbing and illumination, Zarathustra returns in the last two sentences of Nietzsche's book to the concrete idea of the great noontime:

> "This is my morning, my day begins: *arise now, arise, you great noontime!*"—
> Thus spake Zarathustra, and he left his cave, glowing and strong, like a morning sun coming out of gloomy mountains.[26]

Where in *2001* is the great noontime—the ending of *Zarathustra*—depicted? Appropriately, it is depicted at the end of the movie. But to understand the final scene, you must go back to the first, the prologue. Recall the dramatic opening of *2001*. To the accompaniment of Richard Strauss's inspiring music, the opening bars of "Thus Spake Zarathustra," the sun climbs slowly from behind the earth to shine on the cratered moon. We are witnessing an ecliptic dawn, a dawn that symbolizes *the dawn of evolution*. Here evolution refers to Nietzschean evolution (as simplified by omission of the worm): the transition from ape to man to overman.

The first scene beyond this prologue echoes the lunar dawn by presenting an earthly one: the sun creeps up over the horizon and starts to shine on the African desert, while the words "The Dawn of Man" flash onto the screen. The overall process of evolution begins with ape's evolution into man.

Compare these opening scenes with *2001*'s final scene and you can grasp the Zarathustran metaphorical structure of the movie. *2001* begins at dawn and ends at noon; the sun climbs from the morning horizon to its highest point. But in the process of climbing, the sun undergoes a striking transformation. Starting out as a *literal* sun at dawn, it becomes a *figurative* sun—

the light-surrounded star-child — at noon. The final scene of *2001* shows the radiant star-child, encased in a metaphysical globe (hence spherical, like the sun), shining down on the earth — and then on the audience. The wisdom of the star-child is illuminating the earth — and mankind (the audience). Overman has arrived. It is the great noontime!

ETERNAL RECURRENCE

The star-child really symbolizes *two* Nietzscheian concepts: the overman and eternal recurrence. Eternal recurrence was an extremely important concept to Nietzsche. But this curious theory of metaphysical determinism fails to support — indeed, it greatly weakens — his theory of evolution. Kubrick nevertheless gives the idea obligatory attention and even shows considerable imagination in symbolizing it.

The concept of eternal recurrence views time as an ever-repeating cosmic circle. Every thing and every being and every situation that ever existed in history or will exist in the future existed in previous histories and will exist again in an eternity of subsequent histories. After the climactic great noontime, the sun will slowly set until the last man disappears. Then the cycle will begin anew. Time is a circle.

Zarathustra elucidates — no, make that obfuscates — this idea when he recounts his vision of an encounter with a dwarf.[27] The dwarf sits oppressively on Zarathustra's shoulder, dripping painful thoughts like molten lead into the prophet's ear. (The dwarf symbolizes troubling ideas.) The two come to a gateway inscribed "This Moment," and Zarathustra forces the dwarf off. (Zarathustra has accepted an idea; it is no longer painful.) Two roads — we would view them as one — begin within the gateway and run in opposite directions. One runs backward into the past, the other forward into future. Zarathustra asks the dwarf whether the roads, if followed far enough, are "eternally antithetical."

"Everything straight lies [is not truthfully 'straight']," replies the dwarf. "All truth [each road] is crooked [circular]; time itself is a circle."

Zarathustra treats the dwarf's idea — the implicit idea that the far ends connect to form a circle — as his own (which it really is). He elaborates by calling attention to the gateway. In an incredible outburst of corrupt logic, he argues, "If everything [in the past] has already existed, . . . must not this gateway [the present, inscribed 'This Moment'] also — have already existed?" He then deduces, by truly specious reasoning, "This slow spider which creeps in the moonlight . . . and you and I in this gateway whispering together . . . must we not all have already existed?" Hence: "Must we not eternally return?"

The argument is fallacious; appendix A to this chapter explains why. But the fallacy is beside the point. The point is that Nietzsche, through Zarathustra, is espousing the idea that time runs in a circle. Everything that occurs over time—every fly caught in a spider web, every brief conversation, the whole process of evolution—repeats again and again.

How does Kubrick symbolize the idea of time as a circle, or eternal recurrence? He does it in four, possibly five, ways. The first is early in *2001*, where we see the wheel-shaped space station. Walk straight ahead in the interior (outer circumference) and you eventually return to where you started. The second way eternal recurrence is symbolized involves the telephone bay within the space station. While Heywood Floyd talks to his daughter "Squirt" back on earth, we see the earth through the phone bay window. As the space station revolves while seeming not to, the earth seems to move in a circle (optical illusion); it returns repeatedly to where it was earlier in time. (Now you can see why this scene, which does nothing to advance the surface story plot, was inserted.) The third symbolization of eternal recurrence occurs in part 2 ("Jupiter Mission"). In the first scene inside the spaceship, Frank Poole jogs around the exercise centrifuge. He keeps coming back to where he was before and then repeating the circle all over again.

The fourth symbol of eternal recurrence departs from the concept of circular movement and substitutes the concept of beginning anew. When the star-child appears, Bowman is reborn, symbolically at any rate. He is (still symbolically) going to live his life all over again—even if in doing so he is a radically different person than before and is not truly going to repeat everything the original Bowman did. If you think the star-child fails to capture Nietzsche's idea of *exact* repetition, be aware that Kubrick has taken the child symbol from Nietzsche. The flaw in the symbol comes from Nietzsche, not Kubrick. Nietzsche's idea is that the child, unaware of the past, represents a new beginning: "Innocence is the child, and forgetfulness, a new beginning."[28]

The three upright monoliths, viewed collectively, are probably intended as a fifth symbol of eternal recurrence. The monoliths are much like the child. The child represents a new beginning. Each monolith likewise represents a new beginning (in the second and third allegories). The first new beginning is the beginning of man; the second is the beginning of *Homo machinus* (second allegory) or God (third allegory); the third is the beginning of *Homo futurus* (second allegory) or overman (third allegory). We might even count the nonupright Jupiter monolith and treat it as the beginning of higher man.

Doubt about whether the monoliths are a fifth symbol stems from the fact that each beginning is something different. You have to abstract man, God, overman, and possibly higher man into the general (abstract) concept of *a* new being before you can say the monoliths collectively symbolize the recurring appearance of a new being. But Nietzsche abstracts when he uses the child, a symbol for overman in particular, to also symbolize eternal recurrence, a general concept. So, by Nietzsche's rules, Kubrick is entitled to treat certain things abstractly in order to have them repeat.

When the five eternal recurrence symbols are counted, and assuming that the monoliths *are* another symbol for eternal recurrence, the Zarathustra allegory has 160 symbols, not counting any I have overlooked. (Appendix B to this chapter lists and counts the 160 symbols.) Since the movie is 139 minutes long, 160 symbols comes to more than one symbol per minute— actually one every 52 seconds, on the average—for this allegory alone. Let it not be said that Kubrick's treatment of *Zarathustra* is only superficially allegorical.

APPENDIX A: FALLACIES IN ZARATHUSTRA'S ETERNAL RECURRENCE ARGUMENT

Although Zarathustra presents no explicit syllogistic argument for eternal recurrence, such an argument is unmistakably implied in the way he draws conclusions from a set of supposed facts. The "facts," as set forth in the parable of the dwarf, are that (1) the present is part of the past and (2) the present is part of the future. When Zarathustra asks, "Must not [the present] . . . have already existed?" and "Must we not eternally return?" the questions are rhetorical;[29] they amount to *conclusions* that are phrased as questions. The reader is expected to discern the implicit logic by which the conclusions flow from the facts.

Zarathustra's (Nietzsche's) implicit argument for eternal recurrence boils down to this: The past and the future (the two roads) come together at the present (the gateway, "This Moment"). Therefore, the present is in both the past and the future. Since everything in the past has already happened and the present is part of the past, the present must have happened before. And since the present is also part of the future and the present has happened before, all the rest of the future has also happened before.

The argument can be formalized as two syllogisms, A and B, the second of which is a two-link chain syllogism wherein the conclusion of one syllogism becomes the major premise of the next. The syllogisms are as follows:

A. *Present Linked with Past*
   1. Major Premise: All events of the past have already happened.
   2. Minor Premise: The present is an event of the past.
   3. Conclusion: The present has already happened.

B. *Present Linked with Future*
   1. Major Premise: All events of the future have the same has-happened-before or hasn't-happened-before status.
   2. Minor Premise: The present is an event of the future.
   3. Conclusion and New Major Premise: The present has the same has-happened-before or hasn't-happened-before status as all events of the future.
   4. Minor Premise: The present has has-happened-before status (Conclusion A3).
   5. Conclusion: All future events have has-happened-before status (= all future events have happened before).

Both syllogisms—A and B—embody the same flaw in their logic. This flaw is called "the flaw of the ambiguous middle term"; the middle term is the minor premise. The flaw involves using one definition or meaning for a term in the first premise but then switching to a different definition in the second premise. Take this example: (1) All reds are Communists; (2) All Cincinnati baseball players are Reds; (3) Ergo, all Cincinnati baseball players are Communists. The fallacy is that the first premise uses a political definition of reds whereas the second premise uses a baseball definition. Because the two definitions differ, the argument is fallacious and the conclusion invalid.

In syllogism A, Nietzsche implicitly excludes the present from his definition of the past when suggesting that—this amounts to an axiom—all events of the past have already happened. (The present is still in the process of happening.) But in the minor premise he switches to a different definition of the past: it now includes the present (on the assumption that the metaphorical road from the past ends *within* "This Moment," the present). Since premises A1 and A2 don't use the same definition of the past, conclusion A3 is invalid.

In the first stage of syllogism B, Nietzsche excludes the present from the future when he says (B1) that all events of the future have the same status. The premise is true because all future events have hasn't-happened-before status. But minor premise B2 makes the present part of the future, creating an ambiguous middle term. Conclusion B3 is therefore invalid. And that means that major premise B3 is untrue, or at least unproven—and definitely untrue if the present has already happened, as A3 claims. Premise B4 is also false, because it is the invalid conclusion from A3. Conclusion B5 is false because it is deduced from two false premises, the falsity of either of which would invalidate the conclusion.

Another fallacy in Zarathustra's implicit argument is that it confuses definitions with facts. A person can define a term in a certain way for purposes of argumentation. But a definition is just that, a definition. It is not necessarily a statement of fact or truth. I can define an elf as a small, mischievous creature with magical powers. And I can use that definition in an argument, even a logically valid argument, involving elves. But my use of the definition does not establish that elves truly exist. By the same token, if Zarathustra implicitly defines the present as part of the past, that definition doesn't prove that an event now happening (at "this moment") actually occurred previously, either in an earlier stage of history or in an earlier history. Defining the present as part of the past doesn't make it so.

A devil's advocate could apply Nietzsche's logic in reverse to "prove" that the events of the past never happened. He would first argue that all events of the future have never happened, that the present is part of the future, and that the present therefore has never happened. He would next argue that all past events have the same status, that the present is part of the past and has never-happened status, and that therefore the events of the past never happened. So much for eternal recurrence.

APPENDIX B: LIST OF THE
ZARATHUSTRA ALLEGORY'S 160 SYMBOLS

The 160 symbols I have counted for the Zarathustra allegory are as follows:

General Symbols Pointing to Nietzsche's *Thus Spake Zarathustra*

1. *2001* (the film's title) = the time of Zoroaster's (Zarathustra's) arrival, namely at the beginning of a new millennium (after the first 9000 years of Zoroastrian history).
2. 9000 (from "HAL-9000 Computer") = $3 \times 3,000 = 9,000$ years, the combined length of the first three 3,000-year periods in Zoroastrian history. After 9,000 years, Zoroaster (Zarathustra) arrives to lead man in the battle against Angra Mainyu, the evil spirit.
3. Opening bars of Richard Strauss's "Thus Spake Zarathustra" = Friedrich Nietzsche's book *Thus Spake Zarathustra* (a bold hint that *Zarathustra* is being allegorized).

4.   Celestial dawn (beginning of movie) = the beginning of ape-man-overman evolution, hence also the beginning of the sun's climb to *Zarathustra*'s "great noontime," when overman arrives.

5.   Radiant globe encasing the star-child = the "great noontime" sun.

6.   Star-child radiating above the earth = "the great noontime" (i.e., overman's arrival).

7.   Sun's climb from dawn to high noon = the climb from ape to man to overman.

Monoliths, Characters, and Names

8.   First monolith (Africa) = intelligence (abstract quality that beings can acquire).

9.   Second monolith (moon) = superstition (another abstract quality, the basis of gods).

10.   Third monolith (Jupiter) = power, not yet attained (another abstract quality, the object of Nietzsche's "will to power," the force that causes man to evolve into overman).

11.   Fourth monolith (hotel room) = power again, this time attained.

12.   Non-tool-using apes = ape, the precursor of man.

13.   Tool-using apes = man (second character in Nietzsche's ape-man-overman sequence).

14.   Star-child = overman (third character in the ape-man-overman sequence).

15.   Heywood Floyd = young Zarathustra and lower man, who create God.

16.   Hal-Discovery = God (Hal = brain and central nervous system; Discovery = body).

17.   Frank Poole = the rope dancer, who is killed by God (represented by the buffoon).

18.   Dave Bowman = older Zarathustra and higher man, who kill God.

19.   David (Dave Bowman's first name) = biblical David, who slew Goliath by attacking his forehead = Zarathustra, who slays God (Hal-Discovery) by attacking his forehead.

20.   [F]rank Poole = [W]alk on rope (anagram alluding to the rope dancer, the character from *Zarathustra* who Frank Poole symbolizes).

21.   HAL = IBM with a one-letter lag, symbolizing a combination of (*a*) the image of man, or Hal (man's name) and (*b*) created by man, or IBM (machine's name): Nietzsche's upside down version of God is created by man in his (man's) own image.

The "Dawn of Man" Episode

22. African dawn = the Dawn of Man.
23. Moonwatcher's touching the monolith = ape's acquisition of intelligence.
24. Bone = tool (also weapon).
25. Act of clubbing with bone-weapon = tool use, which marks the evolution of man.
26. Orbiting bombs = space-age tool-weapons.
27. Bone-to-bomb transition = primitive tool's transition to space-age tool.
28. Earth shuttle *Orion* = male machine (phallic symbol), father of God.
29. Rotating, slotted space station = female machine, mother of God.
30. Penetration of space station by *Orion* = sexual intercourse that begets God.
31. Moon lander *Aries* = sperm cell that fertilizes ovum (moon).
32. *Aries'* trip to the moon = sperm's trip up invisible fallopian tube.
33. Moon = ovum that gestates into God.
34. *Aries'* entry into moon through hangar door = fertilization of ovum.
35. Heywood Floyd's touching the moon monolith = man's acquisition of superstition, the human quality that causes man to create gods.
36. Lunar dawn (sun peeking over moon monolith) = the Dawn of God.

The "Jupiter Mission: 18 Months Later" Episode

37. "18 Months Later" (subtitle) = God's eighteen-month gestation period (twice that of man).
38. Hal-Discovery's cruising slowly into view, headfirst, horizontally = the birth of God.
39. The combined 8 stages in the creation of God (bone to birth) = God was made from a bone (Kubrick joke, alluding to woman's being made from Adam's rib).
40–53. Symbols that use Discovery's characteristics to describe God (Hal-Discovery) as the *physical* image of man ("created [by man] in his own image"): (1) spherical crew cabin = head, (2) pod bay doors = mouths, (3) pod launching ramps = tongues, (4) cabin window strip = mod sunglasses, (5) red eye = eyes, (6) tapered link behind cabin = neck, (7) fuel and storage modules behind neck = vertebrae, (8) rocket engine module at rear = sacrum, (9) rocket nozzles = excretory orifices, (10) pods = shoulders, (11)

pod arms = arms, (12) pod hands = hands, (13) sexual origin = sexual procreation, and (14) ultimate death = mortality.

54–68.   Symbols that use Hal's characteristics to describe God as the *mental* image of man: (1) consciousness, (2) cognition, (3) confidence, (4) enjoyment, (5) enthusiasm, (6) pride, (7) secretiveness, (8) puzzlement, (9) blaming, (10) suspicion, (11) treachery, (12) lying, (13) fear, (14) panic, and (15) senility.

69–81.   Other image-of-man characteristics: (1) extending pod launching ramp = sticking out tongue, (2) launching pod = blowing a bubble, (3) three-dish antennae array = using a telephone, (4) rear hexagons enclosing pairs of rocket nozzles (excretory orifices) = traditional hexagonal white bathroom tiles = using bathrooms to answer the call of nature, (5) spying on Bowman and Poole = seeing, (6–7) conversing = talking and hearing, (8) helping Poole in sunbathing scene = serving as valet, (9) playing chess = playing chess, (10) complimenting Bowman on his sketches = acting as art critic, (11) preparing crew psychology report = acting as clinical psychologist, (12) using pod to kill Poole = being a tool-user, and (13) being wrong about impending failure of AE-35 unit = making an error ("To err is human").

82–87.   Divine characteristics: (1) responding to Poole's "prayer" requests = answering prayers, (2) defeating Poole at chess = acting supreme, (3) lip-reading the conversation taking place inside the pod = seeing inside "the Ugliest Man" (from *Zarathustra*), (4) sneaking up behind Poole to kill him = buffoon's (God symbol from *Zarathustra*) coming up behind the rope dancer and causing the latter's death, (5) Hal's being killed by Bowman = God's being killed by higher man, and (6) "the infinite" in the subtitle "Beyond the Infinite" = one of theologian Paul Tillich's names for God = God.

88–89.   First pod = (1) the buffoon (from *Zarathustra*) and (2) a tool (used to kill Poole).

90.   Poole's jogging and shadowboxing on centrifuge = rope dancing.

91.   Bowman and Poole's pod conversation about shutting down Hal = loss of faith.

92.   Hal's killing Poole = the buffoon's killing the rope dancer.

93.   Bowman's grasping Poole's body = Zarathustra's picking up the rope dancer's body.

94.   Bowman's releasing Poole's body = Zarathustra's disposing of the rope dancer's body.

95. Bowman's orange and green spacesuit-and-helmet combination = combat colors of Northern Ireland's Protestant (orange) and Catholic (green) combatants = combat.
96. Bowman's determination to kill Hall = the will to power.
97. Hal's voice winding down = the death of God ("God is dead!").
98. Recorded briefing heard by Bowman after Hal's death = higher man's enlightenment.

The "Jupiter and Beyond the Infinite" Episode

99. "Beyond" in "Beyond the Infinite [God]" = after (temporal rather than spatial meaning), which signifies that "Beyond the Infinite [God]" means "*after* the death of God"—additional symbolic evidence that Hal-Discovery is God.
100. Discovery when it launches the last pod = a phallus, the source of the sperm that fertilizes the ovum (planet of the aliens) that develops into overman.
101. Third pod = the sperm cell that fertilizes the ovum.
102. The launching of the last pod from Discovery's tip = ejaculation.
103. Jupiter, at the bottom of the stack when its moons come into vertical alignment above the planet = lower man.
104. Jupiter's low position = lower man's evolutionary position (below higher man).
105. Jupiter's huge size = lower man's numerical dominance relative to higher man.
106. Jupiter's colored bands = the rainbow (from Zarathustra's promise, "I will show them [higher men] the rainbow, and all the stairs to the overman").
107. The five moons aligned above Jupiter = successive generations of higher man.
108. The high positions of the moons relative to Jupiter = higher man's evolutionary position (above lower man).
109. Small size of the moons = higher man's numerical inferiority.
110. Vertical stack (Jupiter + five moons) = "the stairs to the overman."
111. Point above the stack where the Star Gate opens = overman's position (*over* lower man and higher man, at the top of the stairs to the overman).
112. Bowman's chasing the Jupiter monolith (power) = the will to power.
113. Bowman's gaze climbing up the "stairs to the overman" to the overman position at the top of the stairs = the will to power.

114.   Tunnel of lights = a cosmic fallopian tube.

115.   Pod's trip through the tunnel = the sperm's trip through the fallopian tube.

116.   Planet of the aliens = the ovum that gestates into overman.

117.   Bowman's blinking eye = "I" (rhymes with eye) = the sperm's ego ("I [eye] will be the one to fertilize the ovum; I will become overman, the being who attains power.") = the will to power.

118.   Last seven eye blinks, in rapid succession = I, I, I, I, I, I, I = sperm's explosion of ego ("I have won!") as it enters the ovum.

119.   Pod's entry into the hotel room = fertilization.

120.   Pod's disappearance = the sperm's disappearance when its chromosomes merge with those of the ovum.

121.   Hotel room = amnion (fetal sac).

122.   Absence of doors and windows in hotel room = absence of openings in the amnion.

123.   Glass floor = translucency of the amnion.

124.   Light from below the floor = light coming in through the birth canal (allow artistic license here).

125.   Bowman's seeing his next self (one self becomes two) = cell division = fetal growth.

126.   Bowman's aging = fetus's aging = fetal growth (parallel symbolism).

127–28. First hotel-room Bowman (inside the pod) = (1) the chromosomes of mankind and (2) the worm from Nietzsche's five-stage (worm–ape–lower man–higher man–overman) evolutionary sequence. (Chromosomes are threadlike or wormlike in appearance.)

129–30. Second hotel-room Bowman (in orange space suit) = (1) the ape, the second creature in the five-stage evolutionary sequence (orangutans are apes and have orangish fur) and (2) the immature fetus (also symbolized by the third and fourth Bowmans).

131–34. Third hotel-room Bowman (black clothing) = (1) the writhing-on-the-ground (low) shepherd (afflicted by the black serpent) from Zarathustra's shepherd-and-serpent parable, (2) lower man (on the ground, afflicted by God), (3) the camel from "The Three Metamorphoses," and (4) the immature fetus at a more advanced stage.

135–37. Fourth hotel-room Bowman (white clothing) = (1) higher man, intermediate between black and radiant, (2) the lion from "The Three Metamorphoses," and (3) the almost-mature fetus.

138–39. Fifth hotel-room Bowman (radiant, the star-child) = (0) overman, previously counted as symbol 14, (1) the "light-surrounded being" from the shepherd-and-serpent parable, and (2) the child from "The Three Metamorphoses."

140.   Bowman's black clothing = the blackness (evil) imposed on man by the black serpent, which represents God.

141.   Wine glass = the serpent from Zarathustra's shepherd-and-serpent parable = God.

142.   Bowman's last supper = Zarathustra's "Last Supper" (based on that of Jesus).

143.   Bowman's hearing something in the bathroom = the "cry of distress" heard by Zarathustra before his last supper.

144–45. Bowman's knocking over the wine glass = (1) the shepherd's biting off the head of the serpent and (2) man's killing of God.

146.   Wine glass's fall from the table = "The Fall" (God's fall from man's grace, or the Garden of Eden myth turned upside down).

147.   Broken wine glass = "God is dead!"

148.   Bowman's shifting his gaze from the broken glass to white Bowman = the cause-and-effect relationship between the wine glass's breaking and Bowman's transformation to white (the death of God transforms lower man [black] to higher man [white]).

149.   Second (orange, ape), third (black, lower man), and fourth (white, higher man) Bowmans collectively = the maturing fetus that will become overman.

150–51. Third (black), fourth (white), and fifth (radiant) Bowmans collectively = (1) "The Three Metamorphoses" of the spirit (camel, lion, and child) and (2) Zarathustra's parable of the shepherd and serpent.

152.   Bowman's white clothing = the goodness and moral superiority of higher man.

153.   White Bowman's reaching out toward the monolith = man's acquisition of power (supremacy), culmination of the quest motivated by "the will to power."

154.   Camera lens's zooming from the bed into the black monolith = the birth of overman (overman's passage from the hotel-room womb into the black universe, analog of God's [Hal-Discovery's] earlier passage from an offscreen womb into the black universe).

155.   Star-child's turning to face (shine on) audience = overman conveying wisdom to (figuratively shining on) mankind.

156-60. Eternal recurrence symbols: (1) walking ahead in the rotating space station on a path that leads in a circle back to the starting point, (2) the earth's moving in circles outside the phone booth window, returning repeatedly to its starting point, (3) Frank

Poole's jogging around the exercise centrifuge, passing the same points repeatedly, (4) man's rebirth as the star-child, and (5) the recurring four monoliths, collectively.

NOTES

1. Friedrich Nietzsche, *Thus Spake Zarathustra*, trans. Thomas Common, rev. with introduction and notes by H. James Birx (Buffalo: Prometheus, 1993), 305.

2. Ibid., 281.

3. Ibid., 279.

4. Gen. 19:24–28.

5. Nietzsche, *Zarathustra*, 52.

6. Ibid, 56.

7. Ibid., 296.

8. Ibid., 297.

9. Ibid., 301.

10. Ibid., 46.

11. Carolyn Geduld, *Filmguide to* 2001: A Space Odyssey (Bloomington: Indiana University Press, 1973), 35. Geduld has apparently borrowed the term "magical alignment" either from Jerome Agel, ed., *The Making of Kubrick's* 2001 (New York: New American Library, 1970), 139, or from Alexander Walker, *Stanley Kubrick Directs* (New York: Harcourt Brace Jovanovich, 1971), 245. Walker, in turn, is paraphrasing the phrase "*mystical* alignment," which Kubrick used in the following sentence, quoted by Walker: "The mystical alignment of the sun, the moon, and the earth, or of Jupiter and its moons, was used throughout the film as a premonitory image of a leap forward into the unknown" (245). Here Kubrick, who does not give away his allegorical secrets, is tossing us a red herring.

12. Nietzsche, *Zarathustra*, 46 (my italics).

13. Arthur C. Clarke, *The Lost Worlds of* 2001 (Boston: Gregg Press, 1979), 126.

14. Agel, ed, *Making* 2001, 134.

15. Nietzsche, *Zarathustra*, 341.

16. Ibid., 301.

17. Toni Morrison, *The Bluest Eye* (New York: Holt, 1969).

18. Nietzche, *Zarathustra,* 298–303.

19. Ibid., 256-57.

20. Ibid., 180–81 (my italics).

21. Vivian Sobchack, *Screening Space: The American Science Fiction Film*, 2d and enl. ed. (New York: Ungar, 1993), 91.

22. Nietzsche, *Zarathustra*, 36.
23. Ibid., 38.
24. Ibid., 301.
25. Ibid., 303–4.
26. Ibid., 341 (Nietzsche's italics).
27. Ibid., 178–79.
28. Ibid., 53.
29. Ibid., 179.

Chapter 7

Evaluation

I hesitate to use the cliché, but *2001* is indeed in a class by itself: it is an allegorical movie that embodies more than one allegory. And each allegory is genuine, thorough. No one could ever call *2001* semiallegorical or only superficially allegorical. *2001* does not simply change the names, times, and settings but otherwise use the original narratives for the surface story. Likewise, *2001*'s symbols are not transparent imitations of the things they symbolize: Homer's cyclops monster was not a computer, a sperm cell is not a space pod, and Nietzsche's stairs to the overman was not built from a planet and its moons. Neither does *2001* gloss over important details, symbolizing the original narrative only in broad outline. Kubrick pays scrupulous attention to detail. Elements of the original are omitted—left unsymbolized—only to the extent necessary for condensing. Moreover, each allegory is developed with originality, inventiveness, beauty, and wit. Plus a little roguish teasing. (I still haven't figured out some of the cosmic-wonders symbolism.)

To appreciate fully the enormousness and artistry of Kubrick's achievement, we need to look more closely at (1) the stature of *2001* among critics before allegory was factored into the evaluation calculus and (2) the quality of *2001*'s allegory and related symbolism.

2001'S CRITICAL STATURE IN THE ABSENCE OF ALLEGORY

A good starting point for analyzing *2001*'s previous critical stature is Geduld's nonjudgmental 1973 assessment, made five years after *2001* was released. She writes: "Currently, *2001*'s reputation rests, in part, on its technical achievements. The special effects work in the film is often original, often novel, certainly an extension of basic cinema vocabulary."[1] Her second sentence surely

understates the magnificence of those special effects. *Time* said it better:
Kubrick's special effects "provide the screen with some of the most dazzling
visual happenings and technical achievements in the history of the motion picture."[2] But just how good those special effects are isn't quite the point. The
point is, rather, that by 1973 Kubrick's movie had developed a favorable reputation that rested heavily on its wondrous visual displays.

By 1982, when Roger Ebert drew up for *Sight and Sound* his list of the
ten best films of all time, things hadn't changed. Ebert prepared for separate publication a capsule appraisal of each film on his list. In his
appraisal of *2001*, he wrote, "What is important here is the sense of wonder."[3] When the *2001* video was released, Ebert provided a more detailed
review. His high estimation of the film continued to rest on *2001*'s special effects: "The fascinating thing about this film is that it fails on the
human level but succeeds magnificently on a cosmic scale. . . . What
remains fascinating is the fanatic care with which Kubrick has built his
machines and achieved his special effects. There is not a single moment,
in this long film, when the audience can see through the props. . . . This
is how it would really be, you find yourself believing."[4] Still later, in a
1997 "Ebert's Great Movies" website review, the emphasis is still on
2001's visual grandeur, as complemented by classical music: "Alone
among science-fiction movies, '2001' is not concerned with thrilling us,
but with inspiring our awe."[5] Using the docking sequence at the space
station as an example, Ebert lauds "the sheer wonder of the visuals."[6]
And as a prelude to his conclusion that *2001* is one of only a few films
that are "transcendent," Ebert observes that "the film creates its effects
essentially out of visuals and music."[7]

My point in relating these details is that Ebert is able to judge *2001* "transcendent" and one of the ten best films of all time without any reference to
or knowledge of the film's being an allegory. The film's visual-musical
artistry and the awe it inspires are sufficient. What I'm driving at, of course,
is that when *2001*'s other powerful virtue—its brilliantly designed allegorical material and supporting symbolism—is recognized, an already great
film becomes that much greater.

When Piers Bizony published *2001: Filming the Future* in 1994, *2001*'s
eminence still rested on its visual achievements. Bizony does not have a
best-ten list, but his praise of the film is unbounded. Both his evaluation of
2001 and the basis for that evaluation can be found in this sentence: "Today,
Kubrick's epic space drama stands as the epitome of science fiction film-
making, and as an extraordinary exercise in *totally visual cinema*."[8] As
though to underscore his point about "totally visual," Bizony also says this:

"Reading the library copies of 1968 newspaper reviews and articles about the film, I saw at last that my childhood judgement had been essentially correct. 'You're just meant to *watch* it.'"[9] Plot, characters, suspense, allegory—these don't enter his appraisal.

In another 1994 book, *Radical Visions: American Film Renaissance, 1967–76*, Glenn Man joins those who express strong admiration for *2001*. He calls the nine months from August 1967 through April 1968 "The Wonder Year," so named because it spawned three films—*Bonnie and Clyde*, *The Graduate*, and *2001: A Space Odyssey*—that "stand as fountainheads for the films of the [renaissance] period," 1967–76.[10] What distinguishes these films is a combination of "technical innovation, reflexivity, genre transformation, and radical themes."[11] In *2001*'s case, Man emphasizes the film's "modernist ambiguity" (genre transformation) and its "stunning visual sets and effects" (technical innovation).[12] He appreciatively acknowledges the presence of considerable figurative material but sees no allegory. Man's praise of *2001* is strongest where visual effects are concerned:

> More than any previous film, [*2001*] creates convincingly a complete world of future space. One may describe the film's plot as overly simple and its theme as pretentious, but one can only marvel at the film's unqualified success in creating the world of *2001* in meticulous visual detail. The scenes in space and on spaceships are as much performed for their authenticity as for their contribution to plot or theme. Some would say even more so. . . . Kubrick's fashioning of a complete world of the future, grandly announced by Richard Strauss's *Thus Spake Zarathustra* and gracefully inhabited by waltzing spaceships to the tune of *The Blue Danube*, testifies to the glory of man's achievements at this stage of his evolutionary development.[13]

We don't know what criteria were applied by the international critics who, in the 1992 decennial *Sight and Sound* poll, ranked *2001* the tenth best film of all time. But one thing is clear: nobody gave any credit for *2001*'s allegorical material, because the allegories were not yet recognized. A severely limited understanding of *2001*'s symbolism *was* available, it is true. Some of the earliest reviews mentioned the Nietzscheian character of the film's ape-man-overman theme, and some people almost certainly recognized snippets of Odyssean symbolism (e.g., the death of all crewmen). Yet no one went beyond these superficial points to develop the thesis that *2001* was a full-blown allegory. Presumably, then, most of the international critics who gave *2001* its high ranking were swayed by the same sort of things that swayed Ebert, Bizony, and Man and, in some instances, by the few symbols that have been recognized. I think it is fair to anticipate that, when *2001*'s allegorical themes become better understood, the film will be even more highly regarded.

THE QUALITY OF THE ALLEGORY AND SYMBOLISM

My point is not that allegory automatically enhances a film's stature. The allegorized subject matter must be significant or intriguing, the coverage of that subject matter reasonably thorough and satisfying, the allegorical material continuous, and the symbolism well conceived. *2001* meets these tests. Where significance of subject matter is concerned, Homer's *The Odyssey* and Nietzsche's *Thus Spake Zarathustra* (first and third allegories) are widely recognized as literary classics. Clarke's idea of man-machine symbiosis (second allegory) is not particularly significant, but it sure is intriguing: it provides an engaging mental exercise that adds considerably to Kubrick's achievement. Some specific aspects of Kubrick's allegorical symbolism that acknowledge the other tests of good allegory are (1) the pervasiveness of Kubrick's allegorical material, (2) the thoroughness of the coverage of material in *The Odyssey* and *Thus Spake Zarathustra*, (3) the well-developed structure of the man-machine symbiosis allegory, (4) the variety of the symbols, (5) the versatility—the ability to symbolize several things at once—of some of the symbols, and (6) the imaginativeness and cleverness of the symbols.

Pervasiveness of Allegorical Material

Appreciation of the quality of *2001*'s allegories begins with recognition of how pervasive the allegorical material is. Whereas "allegorical tendency" involves only occasional references to the narrative or idea being symbolized, Kubrick's *2001* has what true allegory requires: a continuous stream of allegorical symbols. Except for (*a*) the plight-of-the-apes sequence between the opening African dawn scene (symbolizing the dawn of man) and the first monolith (symbolizing three things) and (*b*) the hilarious zero-gravity toilet scene, inserted purely for comic effect, no scene in 2001 lacks allegorical symbolism.[14] (I am admittedly *assuming* that every scene in the "cosmic wonders" sequence beyond the tunnel of lights symbolizes something; I have been unable even to guess at the meaning of the cosmic wonder that resembles bubble surfaces, and most of my "cosmic wonders" interpretations have some degree of uncertainty.)

The earth-to-moon episode—the second of *2001*'s four episodes—illustrates the pervasiveness of Kubrick's symbolism. In quick succession, the screen displays six symbolic space vehicles: four orbiting nuclear bombs (the three goddesses and Zeus), the rotating space station (female space machine), and the phallic earth shuttle *Orion* (male space machine). Overlaid on these symbols are the golden sun (the golden apple marked "For the Fairest") and two symbolic transitions: the bone-to-bomb (primitive weapon to space-age weapon) transition and the non-self-propelled to self-propelled (and nonsexual to sexual) transition. The two transitions are stages 2 and 3 in the eight-stage evolution of both humanoid machines and God. On the earth shuttle, Heywood Floyd symbolizes Paris, who is on his way to Sparta to meet Helen. Floyd-Paris receives a phallic gift, the floating pen—Aphrodite's gift of ecstasy with Helen. The shuttle then penetrates the rotating space station, thereby completing the sexual context for Paris's meeting with Helen (Odysseus allegory) and depicting stage 4 in the eight-stage evolution (symbiosis and Zarathustra allegories).

Floyd leaves the shuttle and goes through voiceprint identification. This action might seem like nothing more than a showy display of futuristic technology, but it is actually a means of introducing the highly symbolic name Heywood R. Floyd (complete with middle initial). Decipher the name ("*He*len *y* [= and] *Wood*en Horse *Re*flect Tr*oy*'s *D*ownfall") and you can deduce that Dr. Floyd represents someone connected with Helen of Troy and with the fall of Troy. The next two scenes show Floyd walking along the *circumferential* space-station corridor and then making a phone call while the earth *circles* outside the window. Both scenes symbolize Zarathustran eternal recurrence. Floyd then meets Elena (Russian for Helen): Paris meets Helen (better known as Helen of Troy). Elena mentions that her husband is off in the Baltic: symbolically, Helen's husband is off in the Mediterranean (on Crete). The coast is clear: Paris and Helen can enjoy each other.

The symbols come one after another in the remaining part 1 scenes. The spherical moon lander's trip to the moon symbolizes both the return from Crete of Menelaus, who is the second of *two* Odysseian characters represented by Dr. Floyd, and the sperm's trip to the ovum, stage 5 of the eight-stage evolution of God. The spherical moon's opening up to take the lander inside symbolizes stage 6: the ovum's taking the sperm inside and becoming fertilized. When Floyd is briefed about developments on the moon, Menelaus is being briefed on Helen's elopement with Paris. When Floyd glides to the crater Tycho (symbolizing Troy) in the *many-footed* moon bus (symbolizing a millipede, a *thousand-footed* crawler), Menelaus and his army are sailing to Troy on the recently launched *thousand* ships. On the moon bus, a chart showing TMA-1 (= TMA-ONE) is presented to the tune of "Ham, ham, ham, ham" (= meat, meat, meat, meat). Kubrick is hinting that the moon monolith (TMA-ONE) has "No Meat" (anagram): the monolith symbolizes the meatless wooden horse, the Trojan Horse. The walls of the excavation at Tycho are the walls of Troy; the Trojan Horse has been brought inside the walls. Floyd (now symbolizing the young Zarathustra) touches the monolith, thereby absorbing superstition (symbolized by the monolith in the Zarathustra allegory) and becoming motivated to create God (Hal-Discovery, who is born—slowly and headfirst—in the next scene after eighteen months of gestation). Suddenly, a signal beams from the monolith: Greeks sneak out of the Trojan Horse to let the Greek army into Troy. The space-suited men fall back in pain: the Trojans die, and Troy falls. The final shot in the earth-to-moon episode shows the sun peeking over the top of the monolith. The lunar dawn symbolizes both the dawn of *Homo machinus* (second allegory) and the dawn of God (third allegory).

My point again: the symbolism is continuous.

What is especially remarkable is the way Kubrick has been able to juggle three allegories at once—yet still create an engrossing surface story that incorporates all the necessary allegorical material. And he has done all this while simultaneously creating some of the most dazzling and entrancing special effects ever seen on the screen.

Thoroughness of Coverage

Kurbick has done a masterful job of providing broad, comprehensive coverage of events and ideas from *The Odyssey* (first allegory) and *Thus Spake Zarathustra* (third allegory). No coverage issue arises with the second allegory, because Kubrick himself is creating the narrative being allegorized, the narrative that fleshes out Clarke's idea of man-machine symbiosis.

Coverage of The Odyssey

Look first at the Odysseus allegory. In chapter 1, I provide a numerical list of the events that preceded Odysseus's homeward voyage and that occurred during and after the voyage. Kubrick symbolizes *all eleven* of the numbered events that preceded the voyage. The events and event elements symbolized are (1) the Great Bow's being given to Odysseus, (2) the tossing-out of the golden apple, (3a) the three goddesses' asking (3b) Zeus to judge, (4) the gift-bribe Aphrodite gives to Paris (substitute judge) for awarding her the golden apple, (5) Paris's being given Helen as his reward for making Aphrodite the winner, (6a) Paris's seduction of

Helen while (6b) Menelaus is off in the Mediterranean, (7) Menelaus's return to Sparta, (8) Menelaus's being briefed on what has happened, (9) Menelaus's launching of a thousand ships, (10) the siege of Troy, and (11a) the Greeks' use of the Trojan Horse to (11b) conquer Troy by killing its defenders.

Of the 25 numbered events that occurred during and after Odysseus's voyage, 17 (more than two-thirds) are represented in the Odysseus allegory. The 17 events are (1) the sacking of Ismarus, including (1a) the attack, (1b) the looting, and (1c) the counterattack that "burns" Odysseus; (2a) the disabling of (2b) the three *survey* crewmen who eat lotus; (3) the encounter with the cyclops, an encounter having symbols for (3a) the cyclops's giant size, (3b) his eye, (3c) his killing of several crewmen, (3d) the fight, (3e) Odysseus's attacking the monster's forehead, (3f) Odysseus's using a stake as a weapon, (3g) Odysseus's plunging the stake into the monster, (3h) Odysseus's twisting the stake, (3i) the monster's screaming in pain, and (3j) the monster's being disabled; (4) the rock attack by the Laestrygonians; (5a) the beckoning of and (5b) the trip past the Sirens; (6a) the escape from and (6b) the exploding sound of the raging surf; (7) the escape from the whirlpool Charybdis; (8) the loss of six men to the six-headed monster Scylla; (9) the antagonizing of the sun god Hyperion by Odysseus's men; (10) the loss of Odysseus's last ship in the attack by Zeus; (11a) Odysseus's nine days of drifting to Calypso's island, where he (11b) spends seven years as her love slave; (12) Zeus's intervention, which frees Odysseus from Calypso's grasp; (13a) the Phaeacian's help in escorting Odysseus home to Ithaca, after which (13b) they depart in their ship; (14) Penelope's despair; (15) Athene's helpful presence; (16) Odysseus's regaining the Great Bow; and (17) Odysseus's reunion with Penelope. An eighteenth event, the slaying of Penelope's suitors, is there in spirit (and is in Clarke's novel); it can also be read into Odysseus's regaining of the Great Bow. And I'm reasonably sure that still other events are buried in some of that inscrutable cosmic-wonders symbolism, beyond the tunnel of lights.

Still more symbols referring to *The Odyssey* can be found in (*a*) *2001*'s subtitle, *A Space Odyssey*, (*b*) Heywood R. Floyd's name, (*c*) the moon monolith's "scientific" label, TMA-1, (*d*) the "Ham, ham, ham, ham" hint that TMA-1 is a symbol relating to meat, (*e*) the crater Tycho's semianagrammatic name, (*f*) Dave Bowman's last name, (*g*) Dave Bowman's first name, and (*h*) the death of all of Bowman's crewmen. All told, I count fifty-five Odyssean symbols; I surely overlooked others. Considering the magnitude of the task of allegorizing not just *The Odyssey* but pre-*Odyssey* events as well, I'd say that Kubrick has done a splendid job of condensing the original epic to movie length, depicting the most important elements, and also depicting most of the remaining elements.

Coverage of Zarathustra

Now look at the Zarathustra allegory. Here the symbolism is even more extensive—and complex. It begins with the title, *2001*, which alludes to Zoroastrian mythology wherein the prophet Zoroaster (a.k.a. Zarathustra) appears at the beginning of *a new millennium*. Next, the opening bars of Richard Strauss's "Thus Spake Zarathustra" reiterate that the movie relates to Zarathustra. The title of *2001*'s first part, "The Dawn of Man," and the African dawn scene that follows coordinate with the final scene's "great noontime" (overman's arrival) symbolism. Together, dawn and high noon provide an overarching dawn-to-high-noon metaphor that is straight from Nietzsche's book.

Thus Spake Zarathustra is basically a story of evolution. Simplified, the story is one of movement from ape to man to overman, who is a mentally and morally superior being. God, created by man *in his own image* (the biblical doctrine stood on its head), comes between man and overman; God must die for man to become overman. There are thus three main creations: (1) man, created from ape through *intelligence*, (2) God, created by man through *superstition*, and (3) overman, created from man through "the will to *power*." Kubrick uses human contact with the three upright monoliths—these symbolize intelligence, superstition, and power—to symbolize the acquisition of the creative substances by predecessor beings. The resulting creations—man, God, and overman—are respectively symbolized by the tool-user apes (no longer apes but men), Hal-Discovery, and the star-child. Hal-Discovery's many human characteristics, both mental (Hal) and physical (Discovery), symbolize Nietzsche's idea that God was created in the image of man. The child symbolizes the third of Nietzsche's "three metamorphoses" (camel, lion, and child), and the globe-enclosed star-child's shining down on earth symbolizes "the great noontime," meaning the arrival of overman.

That's the simplified story. The more detailed version subdivides man into (1) lower man (the believing masses, who create God) and (2) higher man (the nonbelieving exceptions, who kill God and exercise the will to power). Heywood Floyd, who creates Hal-Discovery after touching the moon monolith, symbolizes the young Zarathustra, who creates God after acquiring superstition. Like Nietzsche's version of God, who is created by man in man's own image, Hal-Discovery comes after man and is created by man. And he has all sorts of human physical and mental characteristics that signify that he is man's image.

Dave Bowman, who effectively kills Hal, symbolizes the older Zarathustra, the nonbeliever, who kills God and asserts the will to power. Loss of faith, symbolized when Bowman and Poole climb into a pod to privately discuss shutting Hal down, precedes the death of God. Hal's lip-reading of the "private" Bowman-Poole conversation symbolizes God's peering into the Ugliest Man (a *Zarathustra* character) to learn his innermost secrets. When Bowman becomes the lion (from Nietzsche's camel-lion-child metaphor) and prepares to do battle with the dragon (also from the metaphor), the green and orange colors of his "battle uniform" use Northern Ireland's Catholic-Protestant "combat colors" to symbolize his determination to fight.

The illogically timed, prerecorded mission briefing Bowman hears after killing Hal symbolizes enlightenment—the rekindling of lower man's ashes into higher man's flame (another of Nietzsche's metaphors). "Beyond the Infinite," a phrase in the title of *2001*'s last part, means "after the death of God": "the infinite" is one of philosopher-theologian Paul Tillich's names for God. Bowman's initially unsuccessful (Jupiter) but later successful (hotel room) effort to acquire power (last two monoliths) symbolizes the transformation of man into overman. The camera's moving into the black monolith symbolizes overman's birth.

Nietzsche's higher man passes through a series of increasingly higher stages; Zarathustra describes these metaphorically as the stairs to the overman. In a beautifully designed symbolic mosaic, Kubrick uses a mysterious vertical alignment of Jupiter and its five moons to symbolize lower man, the series of ever-higher higher men, and the stairs to the overman. Jupiter's *position* at the bottom of the stairs—the lowest position—symbolizes the concept of lower man; Jupiter's huge *size* symbolizes the idea that the masses constitute lower man; and Jupiter's colored bands symbolize "the rainbow" that Zarathustra promised to show mankind. The smallness of the moons symbolizes the scarcity of higher men. When Bowman pursues the Jupiter monolith (power), he is asserting "the will to power." And when he sets his sights above the highest moon, he is symbolically aspiring to become overman.

As a further complication, Zarathustran evolution has a pre-ape stage: worm. The result is five stages of evolution: (1) worm, (2) ape, (3) lower man, (4) higher man, and (5) overman. These five stages are symbolized by the five Bowmans who appear in sequence in the hotel room. The first Bowman, inside the sperm-pod, symbolizes the sperm's threadlike or wormlike chromosomes, which in turn symbolize the worm. The next Bowman, outside the pod in an orange space suit, has the orange color of an orangutan—an ape—and thus symbolizes the ape. Bowman in black (explained below but also reflecting the idea that the bad guy wears a black hat) symbolizes lower man, who is also the camel of "the three metamorphoses"; the camel is the bearer of God's burdens. Bowman in white (the cowboy hero wears a white hat) symbolizes higher man, who is also the lion; the lion is the slayer of God. The "light-surrounded being" (Nietzsche's words), the star-child, symbolizes overman, who is also the child of the three metamorphoses. The last three Bowmans also symbolize one of Nietzsche's parables, discussed below.

Two parables in *Zarathustra* are especially important. These feature (1) the rope dancer and (2) the shepherd, the serpent, and the light-surrounded being the shepherd becomes. Frank Poole, who is killed by Hal, symbolizes the rope dancer (tightrope walker), who is killed by God. Poole's name is a "90 percent anagram": the last 9 of the 10 letters of "[F]rank Poole" are derived from the last 9 of the 10 letters of "[W]alk on Rope." Bowman's picking up Poole's body and later releasing it symbolizes Zarathustra's picking up the rope dancer's body and later disposing of it.

The second parable features a writhing-on-the-ground shepherd (lower man), a black serpent (God) dangling from the shepherd's mouth, and the transfigured, light-surrounded being (overman) the shepherd becomes when he bites off and spits out the serpent's head (kills God). The black-white-radiant sequence in the hotel room symbolizes this parable. Bowman in black (supper table) is the serpent-afflicted shepherd, lower man; the broken wine glass is the decapitated serpent, the "God is dead" image; Bowman in white (in bed) is a postserpent transitional stage, higher man; and the light-surrounded star-child is the light-surrounded being, overman, that the shepherd becomes. Bowman's staring at the broken wine glass and then shifting his gaze to the white Bowman symbolizes the cause-and-effect connection between the breaking of the glass (the death of God) and the emergence of higher man (dressed in white).

As an extra touch, not part of the parable, Kubrick uses the glass's falling to the floor to symbolize *God's* falling from *man's* grace. This is Kubrick's upside down version of the Christian doctrine of "The Fall" (man's fall from God's grace, or expulsion from the Garden of Eden). In *Zarathustra*, it is man who becomes disenchanted with the other party.

Eternal recurrence, or time as a circle, is another important Zarathustran concept. It is loosely related to the ape-man-overman evolutionary scheme. Kubrick symbolizes eternal recurrence with (1) the circumferential space-station corridor, where walking straight ahead gets you back to where you started, (2) the earth's moving in circles outside the phone booth window,

(3) the circumferential exercise centrifuge, (4) the reborn star-child, and—probably (but not certainly)—(5) the recurring *upright* monoliths, each of which symbolizes a new beginning (man, God, and then overman).

All told, *2001* has at least 160 Zarathustran symbols. Again, my purpose in reviewing this Zarathustran symbolism is to show how thoroughly Kubrick covers the material of *Zarathustra*. Thoroughness of coverage is one of the tests of good allegory.

Structure of Man-Machine Symbiosis Allegory

In the man-machine symbiosis allegory, Kubrick is dealing with a relatively simple idea rather than with a narrative (*The Odyssey*) or with a system of ideas displayed on a narrative framework (*Zarathustra*). So thoroughness of coverage is not an issue. Kubrick's task is not to represent symbolically a preexisting narrative or a philosophical system. Rather, it is to *develop* an idea, man-machine symbiosis, into a story that can be told allegorically.

Clarke's idea is that man and machine will one day become so interdependent—so symbiotically related—that they will function as a single entity, one being. Kubrick fleshes out this skeleton by caricaturing the symbiotic being as a new species that evolves from man. But Kubrick isn't going to let this new species go anywhere; it will be an evolutionary dead end. The new species will die—it will be killed by man—so that man can evolve in a more attractive direction. Kubrick fits the dead-end species into the context of a Nietzscheian evolutionary scheme that runs from (1) ape to (2) man to (3a) man-machine symbiotic species, the dead end, then back to man and on in a new direction to (3b) a more worthy new species that will supersede man. The new species is analogous to Nietzsche's overman, but its chief characteristic is benevolence: it doesn't attack the old species as its two predecessors did.

To turn symbiosis into an allegory, Kubrick creates Hal-Discovery. In one sense, Hal is the "man" side of man-machine symbiosis and Discovery is the "machine" side. But in another sense, Hal and Discovery are *both* humanoid ("man") yet also *both* machines. The symbolism begins with the name Hal, based on HAL, which is derived from IBM by retreating each letter of IBM one notch backwards down the alphabet. Hal (a human name) symbolizes man, IBM (a machine name) symbolizes machine, and the union of man and machine in one humanoid machine symbolizes symbiosis.

To carry the symbolization further, Kubrick lets his marvelous sense of comedy run wild. Hal-Discovery has a humanoid body: a big round head, a segmented spine ending in a sacrum, and excretory orifices (rocket nozzles) at the rear. The head has three mouths (pod bay doors), each of which has a tongue (pod launching ramp) that can be stuck out, and is bedecked in wide-band mod sunglasses (command module windows). The excretory orifices come in three pairs, one pair for each mouth. And each pair has its own private bathroom, symbolized by a hexagonal enclosure patterned after the hexagonal white bathroom tiles that were so popular before World War II. Hal-Discovery also has arms and hands (the pod arms and hands) and what amounts to shoulders (the pods)—detachable shoulders (he's triple-jointed, I guess). The new humanoid is a telephone-user: mounted on his back is a dish-antenna array that, viewed from a certain angle, looks just like a standard 1968 (*2001*'s release year) telephone. Members of the new species can talk, see, and hear.

That's just the physical side of the symbolism. On the mental side, Hal has all sorts of human mental traits. Chapter 4 has evidence of fourteen: consciousness, cognition, confidence, enjoyment, enthusiasm, pride, secrecy, puzzlement, blaming others, treachery, fear, panic, lying, and senility. Hal also has human skills: he is a valet, a chess player, an art critic, a clinical psychologist, and—the definitive human skill—a tool-user. Finally, lest there be any doubt about his essential humanity, he makes a mistake (predicting the failure of the AE-35 unit). Why the mistake? Because "to err is human."

As a *humanoid* machine, Hal-Discovery comes into being through sexual reproduction. He is conceived when the male earth shuttle copulates with the female space station and sends a spermlike moon lander onto the ovum-moon, initiating an eighteen-month gestation period that culminates in his birth. And at the end of his life he does what many humans do: he becomes senile, singing "Daisy, Daisy," the song he learned when he was a child being educated (programmed).

Kubrick uses the monoliths to place the symbiotic race in the context of evolution. For purposes of the man-machine symbiosis allegory, the monoliths symbolize milestones along the road of humanoid evolution. Each *upright* milestone marks the evolution of a new species—first man (African monolith), then humanoid machine (moon monolith), and finally future man (hotel room monolith). When the middle species dies, we backtrack along the dead-end detour and go back to the main road. There lies a toppled milestone (Jupiter monolith), no longer upright.

A postmonolith battle is part of the pattern of monolith symbolism. When ape evolves into man after touching the first monolith, he attacks and kills the old species (Battle at the Waterhole). When man creates humanoid machine after touching the second monolith, the new race (symbolized by Hal-Discovery) attacks and almost kills off the old species (Battle in Outer

Space). Fortunately, the old species wins the second battle: evolution can proceed in a more promising direction. At the end of the road of evolution, man evolves into future man after touching the third upright monolith. But this time no battle follows; the new race does not try to kill off the old. Here the *absence* of a battle is the symbol. It signifies that the new race is benevolent, something better than man.

The foregoing man-machine symbiosis symbolism is impressive. It is clever, it is imaginative, it is variegated, it is thoughtful, and it is extensive. Furthermore, it reflects considerable storytelling skill. Kubrick has taken a simple idea and developed it into a complete story, then told the story symbolically. In 1968, when the humanoid machine allegory was the only allegory I recognized and when I missed about one-third of this allegory's physical-mental symbols (and mistook the no-door, no-windows hotel room for a cocoon), I regarded the product as first-class allegory. Today, when I see much more (but not all) of the symbolism, I am even more impressed. This is *splendid* allegory.

Variety of the Symbols

The quality of Kubrick's allegorical symbols is, in general, outstanding. One impressive aspect of the symbols is their variety. Kubrick can turn almost anything into a symbol. You never know where to look. Or, I should say, you know you must look everywhere. Kubrick's symbols fall into fourteen categories:

1. *Names with Hidden Meanings:* Heywood R. Floyd, David Bowman, Frank Poole, Hal, 9000 (part of "HAL 9000 computer"), Elena, TMA-1 (= TMA-ONE), and Tycho.
2. *Characters:* The apes, Moonwatcher, Heywood Floyd, Dave Bowman, Frank Poole, Hal-Discovery, Elena, the six persons at Tycho (including Floyd), and the three hibernating astronauts.
3. *Screen Titles and Subtitles:* "2001," "A Space Odyssey," "18 Months Later," and "Beyond the Infinite."
4. *Spoken Words:* Elena's statement that her husband is off doing research in the Baltic, the BBC announcer's reference to the hibernating "survey team" (alluding to Odysseus's survey team in Lotus-eater land), Michaels' saying "Ham, ham, ham, ham," Poole's "take me in a bit" symbolized prayer (?) to Hal, many words spoken by Hal that reveal human traits (e.g., "I'm sorry, Dave, I don't have enough information" [lying]), and Hal's mimicking the cyclops's cries of pain ("I can feel it! I can feel it!").

5. *Music and Other Sounds:* Strauss's "Thus Spake Zarathustra," the signal beam from the moon monolith, the Sirens' call at Jupiter, the raging surf sound (cosmic wonders sequence), the "Help me!" cry near the bathtub, and "Daisy, Daisy."

6. *Colors and Lighting:* The green-orange (helmet-spacesuit) Northern Ireland "battle" combination, Jupiter's "rainbow" of colors, orange (space suit), black (Bowman's dinner-table clothing), white (Bowman in bed), the hotel room's beneath-the-floor lighting, and the star-child's radiance.

7. *Shapes and Sizes:* The phallic pen; the elongated (again phallic) earth shuttle; the circular space station and exercise centrifuge; the spherical moon lander, moon, pods, and star-child's globe; the moon bus "feet"; the skeleton-shaped spaceship; the tonguelike pod launching ramps; the hexagons at Hal's rear end; the elongated key-stake; the big (Jupiter) and small (moons) heavenly bodies in alignment; the V-formation flown in by the alien escorts; the worm-shaped chromosomes; and the Palladian arches on the hotel-room wall recesses, paintings, and bathroom door.

8. *Other Features:* Abstracted gun turrets on top of first three bombs (goddesses) to differentiate them from the fourth (Zeus), the absence of an exterior door and windows in the hotel room, Bowman's aging in the hotel room (brown-haired and young, graying and wrinkled, white-haired and more wrinkled, bald and withered).

9. *Abstractions:* The four monoliths, the tunnel of lights, the cosmic wonders beyond the tunnel, and the octahedra (representing aliens).

10. *Motion:* The shuttle's approach to the space station, the space station's rotation, the earth's apparent circular motion outside the phone booth window, the jabbing and twisting of the stake-key, and the climb of Bowman's gaze at Jupiter.

11. *Transitions:* The sun's movement from dawn position in the opening scene to high-noon position (symbolized by the shining, sphere-enclosed star-child) at the end, the bone-to-bomb transition, black Bowman shifting his gaze from the broken wine glass to white Bowman, and the star-child's (overman's) turning to shine on the audience.

12. *Events and Actions:* Almost every scene (e.g., sunrise, Moon-walker's using the bone-club, the shuttle's docking, Floyd's meeting Elena, the lander's entering the moon, the Jupiter signal, the moon-monolith inspection party's retreating in pain, Poole's jogging and shadowboxing on the centrifuge, Bowman's burning his fingers,

Hal's making a mistake, Hal's using a tool (a pod), Bowman's picking up Poole's body, the trip through the tunnel of lights, the vanishing of the pod from the hotel room, one Bowman seeing the next,
and the breaking of the wine glass).

13. *Objects:* A huge variety of items, including the bone-club, the orbiting
    nuclear weapons, the space vehicles and space station, the floating pen
    on the earth shuttle, the earth and moon, the moon bus's feet, the pods,
    the pod bay doors, the pod launching ramps, the set of dish antennae,
    the rocket nozzles, the food-dispensing machine, Hal's red eye, the
    brain shutdown key-stake, Jupiter and its moons, the sperm-pod, the
    exploding star, the spiral galaxy, the necklace of stars, the octahedra
    (aliens), the other cosmic wonders, the planet of the aliens, Bowman's
    blinking eye, the hotel room without doors and windows, the translu-
    cent glass floor, and the broken wine glass.

14. *Positions:* The nuclear bombs' (goddesses') position in the sky (where
    gods and goddesses hang out), Jupiter's (lower man's) alignment posi-
    tion *below* its moons, the moons' (higher man's) position *above* Jupiter,
    the alien-octahedra flying in V-formation (escort position), and the star-
    child's "great noontime" (noontime sun) position shining on the earth.

Versatility of the Symbols

In addition to being widely varied, Kubrick's symbols are often versatile. By
versatile I mean they are used to symbolize more than one thing or to symbolize the same thing in two different allegories. Ordinarily, I would not say
that versatility is a virtue in a symbol. It can be confusing, especially if you are
not expecting more than one referent or meaning. But when three allegories
must be developed and movie length is a constraint, some economizing in the
form of multiple meanings can be a virtue. I can't help but admire the way
Kubrick has gotten extra mileage from some of his symbols by having them
represent two, three, or even four different things. Kubrick has done this with
the monoliths, surface story characters, the orbiting nuclear bombs, the moon
lander's trip to the moon, the tunnel of lights, the eight stages of Hal-Discovery's evolution, the many human characteristics of Hal-Discovery, Jupiter, the
Jupiter-to-hotel-room sexual reproduction symbolism, the disappearance of
the pod from the hotel room, and the five Bowmans in the hotel room. Let's
review those multiple meanings:

- **The African monolith** symbolizes (1) the Great Bow in the Odysseus
  allegory, (2) a milestone—the birth of *Homo sapiens*—along the road

of evolution in the man-machine symbiosis allegory, (3) intelligence in the Zarathustra allegory, and possibly also (4) eternal recurrence in the Zarathustra allegory.

- **The moon monolith** symbolizes (1) the Trojan Horse in the Odysseus allegory, (2) another milestone—the birth of *Homo machinus*—in the symbiosis allegory, (3) superstition in the Zarathustra allegory, and possibly (4) eternal recurrence.
- **The Jupiter monolith** symbolizes (1) the Sirens in the Odysseus allegory, (2) a toppled milestone—the death of *Homo machinus*—in the symbiosis allegory, (3) power—not yet attainable—in the Zarathustra allegory, and possibly (4) eternal recurrence.
- **The hotel-room monolith** symbolizes (1) the Great Bow in the Odysseus allegory, (2) another milestone—the birth of *Homo futurus*—in the symbiosis allegory, (3) power—now attainable—in the Zarathustra allegory, and possibly (4) eternal recurrence.
- **Heywood R. Floyd** symbolizes (1 and 2) both Paris *and* Menelaus in the Odysseus allegory and (3) the young Zarathustra, the creator of God, in the Zarathustra allegory.
- **Dave Bowman** symbolizes (1) Odysseus in the Odysseus allegory, (2) humanity—Moonwatcher and others share this role—in the symbiosis allegory, and (3) the older Zarathustra, who is the slayer of God, in the Zarathustra allegory.
- **Frank Poole** symbolizes (1) one of the crewman devoured by the cyclops in the Odysseus allegory, (2) the exterminated part of humanity in the symbiosis allegory, and (3) the rope dancer in the Zarathustra allegory.
- **Hal-Discovery** symbolizes (1) the cyclops in the Odysseus allegory, (2) *Homo machinus*—the new species of humanoid machines—in the symbiosis allegory, and (3) God—the God created by man in his own image—in the Zarathustra allegory.
- **The three hibernating astronauts** symbolize in the Odysseus allegory both (1) the three crewmen in irons (out of action) who ate lotus and (2) three of the crewman devoured by the cyclops monster.
- **The orbiting nuclear bombs** symbolize (1) the three beauty contest goddesses plus Zeus near the beginning of the Odysseus allegory and (2) Penelope's suitors in the originally planned ending of the Odysseus allegory (the ending still found in Clarke's novel and still present in spirit in the movie).
- **The moon lander's trip to the moon** symbolizes (1) Menelaus's return from Crete in the Odysseus allegory and (2) the earth shuttle's

sperm's trip to the ovum that, once fertilized, symbolically develops into Hal-Discovery in the last two allegories.

- **The tunnel of lights** symbolizes (1) the trip past the deadly Sirens in the Odysseus allegory and (2) a cosmic fallopian tube up which the sperm-pod travels in the symbiosis and Zarathustra allegories.
- **The eight stages of evolution** serve both (1) *Homo machinus* in the symbiosis allegory and (2) God in the Zarathustra allegory.
- **Hal-Discovery's many human characteristics** serve both (1) *Homo machinus* in the symbiosis allegory and (2) the God created in man's image in the Zarathustra allegory.
- **Jupiter** symbolizes both (1) Zarathustra's promised rainbow, which the planet's colored bands represent, and (2) Zarathustra's lower man, at the bottom of the stack.
- **The Jupiter-to-hotel-room sexual reproduction symbolism** serves both (1) *Homo futurus* in the symbiosis allegory and (2) overman in the Zarathustra allegory.
- **The disappearance of the pod from the hotel room** symbolizes both (1) the departure of the Phaeacian ship after the Phaeacians put Odysseus safely ashore at Ithaca in the Odysseus allegory and (2) the dissolving of the sperm cell when it fertilizes the ovum in the other two allegories.
- **The five Bowmans in the hotel room** (just three or four Bowmans in some instances) collectively symbolize (1) the aging (maturation) and birth of the fetus, (2) cell division (first four Bowmans), (3) the five stages of evolution (worm, ape, lower man, higher man, and overman), (4) Zarathustra's parable of the shepherd, the black serpent, and the light-surrounded being (last three Bowmans only), and (5) Zarathustra's three metamorphoses (camel, lion, and child) metaphor (last three Bowmans).

Had Kubrick not made these symbols versatile, he would have needed many more symbols to get the same comprehensiveness of allegorical coverage. Working the extra symbols into the surface story would have inevitably resulted in undesirable plot complications and—worse—extra length in an already very long movie (139 minutes). Kubrick deserves lots of credit for devising a highly efficient surface story to serve his three allegories.

Imaginativeness and Cleverness of the Symbols

The third principal virtue of Kubrick's symbols—variety and versatility are the first two—is their imaginativeness and cleverness, often combined with humor. Others have found humor in overt details, such as the signs for the

Howard Johnson's restaurant and the Hilton hotel inside the space station. But Kubrick's best humor is covert, hidden in symbols—sometimes interconnected symbols, as with the first example below. Just about every Kubrick symbol, humorous or not, shows considerable imagination. I can't discuss every symbol in the movie, so I'm going to resort to an old movie critics' stratagem: the best-ten list. Below, ranked in order of merit (1 = best), are my choices for Kubrick's ten most imaginative and clever symbols (extra credit is given for humor):

1. *God Made from a Bone: 2001* is full of humor. But surely the funniest joke of all is the one that pokes fun at the biblical idea that God made woman from Adam's rib. In a subtle 41-minute evolutionary process that starts when Moonwatcher picks up an animal bone, Kubrick makes God (Hal-Discovery) from a bone! The concept—God made from a bone—is itself inspired, but what is truly marvelous is the way it is executed. The work of a genius can be seen in such details as (*a*) the transformation of a bone into a tool-weapon, (*b*) the transformation of a primitive weapon into a space-age weapon, (*c*) the progression from a space weapon to a sexual space vehicle, the earth shuttle, (*d*) the space-machine copulation and fertilization process, (*e*) the eighteen-month gestation period, and (*f*) the slow, headfirst birth of God.

2. *Hal:* The real star of *2001* is—I'm not the first to say this—Hal, the conscious, proud, thinking, talking, seeing (and lip-reading), hearing, error-making, sinister, ultimately terrified—in a word, *human*—computer. You can't overstate the imagination that went into Hal's design; his sheer complexity is enough to put him on the list. His red eye, predatory ways, and vulnerability to jabbed-and-twisted stakes (the brain key) make him the perfect one-eyed cyclops for the Odysseus allegory. His many human qualities, complemented by those of Discovery and including sexual conception, make him a superb comic symbol for the new humanoid species in the symbiosis allegory. And those same qualities, as well as his (and Discovery's) being made from a bone, make him an apt symbol for the Zarathustra allegory's upside down God, the mortal God who is created by man in man's own image (rather than vice versa).

3. *The Bathroom Tiles:* For a long time I was baffled by the three hexagons enclosing the rocket nozzles on Discovery's rear end. They had to be symbolic: Discovery was not a legitimate scientific design—the design was based on human anatomy—and the hexagon shape had no conceivable engineering purpose. (Nothing comparable to honeycomb wing

tanks or structural triangulation is involved here.) I knew the exhaust nozzles symbolized excretory orifices and that there was a pair for each of Discovery's three mouths. But somehow I didn't see the hexagon connection. Then I remembered the hexagonal white bathroom tiles in homes where I lived as a child. And I cracked up: each pair of orifices — number one and number two — has its own private bathroom! Kubrick would have made a fantastic astronautical engineer.

4. *Blowing a Bubble:* Just as using bathrooms symbolizes Hal-Discovery's essential humanity, so does his impishly human act of opening his mouth (pod bay door), sticking out his tongue (pod launching ramp), blowing a bubble (spherical pod), and watching it rise up over his head. Once again, Kubrick sees the humor in human behavior and uses it to symbolize — imaginatively and cleverly — a central Nietzscheian concept: God was made by man *in his own image.* Like man, God blows bubbles.

5. *The Monoliths:* The monoliths cannot be denied recognition. Along with Hal, they have become science-fiction institutions. Two features explain my admiration. First, in the Zarathustra allegory, they use abstract shapes to symbolize abstract concepts: intelligence, superstition, and power. Second, they are collectively the most versatile of all of Kubrick's symbols: they symbolize ten or eleven things and concepts, depending on whether Kubrick intends that eternal recurrence be an eleventh referent.

6. *The Tunnel of Lights:* Kubrick's light show — Bowman's whizbang ride through the intergalactic corridor of multicolored lights — would be on this list even if it symbolized nothing. It has thrilled and beguiled millions. But it is more than a thrilling ride, or "ultimate trip" as it came to be called. It is also a symbol, a *double* symbol. It symbolizes Odysseus's harrowing trip past the seductive-but-deadly Sirens, and it also symbolizes the sperm's (pod's) trip up the fallopian tube to fertilize the ovum (planet of the aliens), which will mature into overman (the star-child).

7. *The Hotel Room:* In order to depict the development and maturation of the fetus after the ovum's fertilization, Kubrick needed to symbolize the amnion, or fetal sac. His answer was the surrealistic hotel room. To decipher this symbol, you must notice that the room has no windows or external door (because the amnion has no openings) and has a glass floor through which all illumination comes from below (because the amnion is a translucent membrane that, in artistic theory if not in fact, admits light from the outside world through the birth

canal, located below the fetus in humans). Windowlike wall recesses, a bathroom door, and distracting furnishings and ornamentation create the illusion that the room does have a door and windows. Lots of imagination went into this one: beneath-the-floor lighting would be an inspired surrealistic concept even without being symbolic.

8. *The Stairs to the Overman:* Kubrick is determined to help Zarathustra keep his pledge to show society's higher people "the rainbow" and "all the stairs to the overman."[15] The help comes at Jupiter. There we are treated to a spectacular display of building materials—Jupiter and its orbiting moons—and then shown the finished product: a staircase formed by Jupiter, at the bottom, and a succession of ever-higher moons above it. In addition to symbolizing the staircase, the heavenly bodies symbolize the rainbow (Jupiter, with its rainbow-colored bands), lower man (Jupiter again), and the promised series of higher men (the moons). A superb combination of beauty and imagination.

9. *The Moon Bus:* One of the most enduring vestiges of Homer's *Iliad* and *Odyssey* is Helen of Troy's image as "the face that launched a thousand ships." Since Kubrick's Odysseus allegory is intended to include the events leading up to the hero's homeward voyage, the allegory would not have been complete without the thousand ships. But how do you symbolize them in a scenario that has no place for a huge fleet of spaceships? Kubrick again turns loose his imagination. He imagines a bug-eyed (front windows) moon bus that lands on clusters of mechanical feet. The bus symbolizes a millipede, whose "thousand" legs in turn symbolize the thousand ships. As a bonus, the moon bus is associated with the most hypnotizing, entrancing scenes in the movie—the scenes where the moon bus glides above the haunting moonscape.

10. *The Designation TMA-1:* This list definitely must include the best example of Kubrick's names with hidden meanings (Heywood R. Floyd, Dave Bowman, Frank Poole, Hal, Elena, TMA-1, and Tycho). The choice is almost a toss-up between two that are anagrams—Frank Poole and TMA-1. But TMA-1 wins, because (*a*) it's not just a 90 percent anagram like [F]rank Poole, (*b*) interpreting it is a two-step process, which makes it more complex, and (*c*) it embodies humor. By "two-step process" I mean you must first respell TMA-1 as TMA-ONE. Only then can you (step 2) rearrange the letters to get "NO MEAT," which jokingly hints at TMA-1's identity: the meatless (wooden) Trojan Horse.

I'm also going to award an honorable mention. It goes to a symbol that, though not exactly clever, does reflect imagination and, in addition, significance. (Granted, significance is not an official criterion for recognition under the present subheading.) Nietzsche, to repeat, is famous for the words "God is Dead!" These words come from the book Kubrick is allegorizing, and no allegory depicting *Zarathustra* would be complete without a "God is Dead!" symbol. Kubrick actually symbolizes the death of God twice—first, by having Hal's voice gradually wind down like a phonograph record coming to a halt as he sings "Daisy, Daisy"; second, by having Bowman break the wine glass. The broken wine glass is the symbol I have in mind. Unlike Hal's silenced voice (intangible), the broken wine glass provides a tangible symbol of the dead God: it directly symbolizes the decapitated serpent, which in turn represents the *fallen* God. The glass literally falls from the table.

What is especially imaginative here is Kubrick's performing a third upside down trick. The first such trick is where he turns "in his own image" upside down by having man create God in his own image, in accordance with Nietzsche, instead of having God create man in his own image, in accordance with the Bible. The second is where Kubrick turns "made from a bone" upside down by having God evolve from a bone instead of having God make woman from a bone (Adam's rib). With the wine glass, Kubrick inverts a third biblical concept, the concept of "The Fall." "The Fall" refers to the temptation and disobedience of Adam and Eve, who fall from God's grace and are expelled by God from the Garden of Eden. In Kubrick's version, it is *God* who falls—from *man's* grace. And it is *man* who "punishes" the other party—by knocking the wine glass (God) off the table, causing it to fall. Imitating Zarathustra, who said it first, the broken wine glass declares, "God is Dead!"

Monumentally Unimaginative?

Among *2001*'s detractors, Pauline Kael is particularly venomous. Writing in 1994, she summarizes and reaffirms her earlier harsh criticism of the film. In essence, she says *2001* is all special effects and no substance. "The special effects . . . are good and big and awesomely, expensively detailed." But "Kubrick never really made his movie" and "he doesn't seem to know it." The movie suggests "Kubrick really doing every dumb thing he wanted to do, building enormous science-fiction sets and equipment, never even bothering to figure out what he was going to do with them." The result is "a monumentally unimaginative movie."[16]

In truth, however, *2001* is a monumentally *imaginative* movie. The quality of the allegorical symbolism—and the allegories—amply supports this conclusion. Contrary to what Kael says, Kubrick knew exactly "what he was going to do with" those special effects. They all have a purpose; the special effects are the movie's servant, not its master. This point is nowhere better illustrated than in Kubrick's unsuccessful effort to use Saturn's rings, colored to resemble a rainbow, to symbolize Zarathustra's promised rainbow. Kubrick had to settle for second best, a color-banded Jupiter, but he stuck with the rainbow concept. He did so not to provide beauty for the sake of beauty but because he *needed* the symbolic rainbow.

Similarly, the tunnel of lights was not designed merely as a visual treat, then patched into the story. Kubrick wanted to symbolize both (1) Odysseus's trip past and exposure to the alluring voices of the Sirens and (2) a sperm cell's trip up a fallopian tube. He told special-effects designer Douglas Trumbull to develop concepts that would make the camera appear to "go through something."[17] The tunnel of lights was the result. The allegorical need came first; the special effects came second.

And how about that pen floating in the gravity-free cabin of the earth shuttle? Kael implies that it is purely a special-effects gimmick that contributes nothing to the narrative. (Even if that were true, the pen would be justified as a device for developing the setting: defining the setting and establishing mood can be as important as developing a character.) What Kael doesn't realize is that the narrative is an allegory and that the pen is an allegorical symbol. It represents Aphrodite's erotic gift to Paris in the Odysseus allegory.

Though Kael believes otherwise, *2001* has substance right down to the core. The substance is allegory—three allegories in one movie. And the special effects, which she thinks are all there is to the movie, are part of the symbolism used to construct the three allegories. Kael can be excused for missing the allegories. Everybody else did too. But being excused is one thing; being right is another. In suggesting that *2001* is all special effects and no substance, and that it lacks the imagination to put those special effects to good use, Kael is dreadfully wrong.

ONE MAN'S OPINION

Stanley Kubrick's *2001* is, in my judgment, the grandest motion picture ever filmed. If the plot seems to develop too slowly, that is because Kubrick is giving us time to savor the strangeness and wonder of space travel—and giving *himself* time to weave in essential allegorical threads and symbols. If character development seems neglected, it is because the surface story characters are merely design elements in Kubrick's symbolic tapestry: the movie is not about the surface story characters. It is true that *2001* is weakened by unexplained events and by the surface story's ambiguous, cryptic, symbolically told ending. Casual filmgoers ought to be able to understand at least the surface story. But *2001*'s powerful—utterly absorbing—visual effects, intelligent story line (rare in science-fiction films), scientific realism (up to a point), and sly humor are more than enough to compensate. Besides, the challenge of smashing the ambiguity, wiggling through the symbolism, and solving the puzzle is part of what makes watching—and later contemplating—*2001* such a satisfying experience.

The above virtues are by themselves enough to put *2001* among the all-time top-ten films; *Sight and Sound*'s 1992 international poll of film critics substantiates this point.[18] Add even one well-designed allegory to the pattern and you've boosted *2001* to a place among the top three. At any rate, when I first saw *2001*—twice—in 1968, I put it on my personal list of the three best movies of all time.[19] My appraisal was based on (*a*) the intellectually stimulating *Homo sapiens–Homo machinus–Homo futurus* (or humanoid-machine-as-an-evolutionary-dead-end) allegory, which is the only allegory I recognized at the time, (*b*) the marvelously imaginative symbolism, particularly that used to portray Hal-Discovery as a humanoid, hence a qualified evolutionary successor to man, (*c*) those awesomely believable special effects, (*d*) the uplifting space conquest theme, unfettered by the hackneyed postapocalyptic nihilism that soils so much science fiction, and (*e*) the sophisticated plot, free from the escapism and hamminess of so much other science fiction.

My early appraisal assumed there was just one allegory. But *2001* isn't just one allegory. It's three. And the humanoid machine (man-machine symbiosis) allegory is the least important of the three; the Odysseus allegory and the Zarathustra allegory are weightier—more complex, more literary, more infused with symbols. Interweave in one plot *three* well-designed allegories, two of which depict literary classics, and you have achieved film supremacy. Kubrick's feat is unparalleled. What other film or literary work has attempted even a double allegory, let alone a triple allegory? By augmenting the film's other virtues with three simultaneously revealed allegories, Kubrick has done more than weave an intricate masterpiece. He has transformed himself into cinema's overman.

NOTES

1. Carolyn Geduld, *Filmguide to* 2001: A Space Odyssey (Bloomington: Indiana University Press, 1973), 77.

2. New Movies, "2001: A Space Odyssey," *Time*, 19 April 1968, 92.

3. Roger Ebert, *Roger Ebert's Movie Home Companion*, 1st ed. (Kansas City, Mo.: Andrews, McMeel & Parker, 1984), 390.

4. Roger Ebert, *Roger Ebert's Video Companion* (Kansas City, Mo.: Andrews and McMeel, 1996), 897–98.

5. Roger Ebert, "2001: A Space Odyssey," www.suntimes.com/Ebert/old_movies/space_ odyssey.html, 1.

6. Ibid., 2.

7. Ibid., 3.

8. Piers Bizony, 2001*: Filming the Future* (London: Aurum Press, 1994), 21 (my italics).

9. Ibid., 9.

10. Glenn Man, *Radical Visions: American Film Renaissance, 1967–76* (Westport, CT: Greenwood Press, 1994), 7, 5.

11. Ibid., 5.

12. Ibid., 53, 62.

13. Ibid., 62–63.

14. I am not entirely certain that the zero-gravity toilet scene lacks symbolism. Kubrick may have intended that the scene represent Menelaus's predicament, wherein Menelaus is being cuckolded by Helen.

15. Friedrich Nietzsche, *Thus Spake Zarathustra*, trans. Thomas Common, rev. with introduction and notes by H. James Birx (Buffalo: Prometheus, 1993), 46.

16. Pauline Kael, *For Keeps* (New York: Dutton, 1994), 222–23.

17. Bizony, *Filming the Future*, 115.

18. Roger Ebert, ed., *Roger Ebert's Book of Film* (New York: W. W. Norton, 1997), 779–80.

19. *2001: A Space Odyssey* (1968), *Snow White and the Seven Dwarfs* (1937), and *Lili* (1953).

Bibliography

Abrahamson, David. "Creatures of Invention." *National Wildlife* 23, no. 2 (February–March 1985): 24–28.

Agel, Jerome., ed. *The Making of Kubrick's* 2001. New York: New American Library, 1970.

Alexander, Caroline. "Echoes of the Heroic Age." *National Geographic* 196, no. 6 (December 1999): 54–78.

Allen, John. Untitled *Christian Science Monitor* review of *2001: A Space Odyssey*. In *The Making of Kubrick's* 2001, edited by Jerome Agel, 229–34. New York: New American Library, 1970.

Baxter, John. *Stanley Kubrick: A Biography*. New York: Carroll & Graf, 1997.

Bernstein, Theodore M. *The Careful Writer: A Modern Guide to English Usage*. New York: Atheneum, 1985.

Birx, H. James. Introduction to *Thus Spake Zarathustra*, by Friedrich Nietzsche. Translated by Thomas Common, with revisions by H. James Birx. Buffalo, N.Y.: Prometheus, 1993.

Bizony, Piers. 2001: *Filming the Future*. London: Aurum Press, 1994.

Blades, Joe, and the Editors of Consumer Reports Books. *Guide to Movies on Video Cassette*. Mount Vernon, NY: Consumers Union, 1986.

Champlin, Charles. Untitled *Los Angeles Times* review of *2001: A Space Odyssey*. In *The Making of Kubrick's* 2001, edited by Jerome Agel, 215. New York: New American Library, 1970.

Clarke, Arthur C. *2001: A Space Odyssey*. New York: Signet, 1968.

——. *The Lost Worlds of 2001*. Boston: Gregg Press, 1979.

——. Foreword to *2001: Filming the Future*, by Piers Bizony. London: Aurum Press, 1994.

Cohn, Victor. "Idea for New Space Movie Came from a Fertile Mind." *Washington Post*, 31 March 1968: G2.

Conod, Kevin. "Astronomical Gaffes." *Science News* 152, no. 14 (4 October 1997): 211.

Ebert, Roger. *Roger Ebert's Home Movie Companion*. Kansas City, Mo.: Andrews and McMeel, 1988.

————, ed. *Roger Ebert's Book of Film*. New York: W. W. Norton, 1997.

Friedman, Norman. "Allegory." In *Princeton Encyclopedia of Poetry and Poetics*, edited by Alex Preminger. Princeton, N.J.: Princeton University Press, 1974.

Geduld, Carolyn. *Filmguide to* 2001: A Space Odyssey. Bloomington: Indiana University Press, 1973.

Gelmis, Joseph. "Understanding the Message of *2001*." In *The Making of Kubrick's* 2001, edited by Jerome Agel, 268–69. New York: New American Library, 1970.

Gilliatt, Penelope. "After Man" (*New Yorker* review of *2001: A Space Odyssey*). In *The Making of Kubrick's* 2001, edited by Jerome Agel, 209–13. New York: New American Library, 1970. Also in *2001: Filming the Future*, by Piers Bizony. London: Aurum Press, 1994, 64–65.

Greenberg, Harvey R. *The Movies on Your Mind*. New York: Saturday Review Press/E. P. Dutton, 1975.

Hamilton, Edith. *Mythology: Timeless Tales of Gods and Heroes*. New York: New American Library, 1953.

Hirsch, Foster. Introduction to *The Lost Worlds of 2001*, by Arthur C. Clarke. Boston: Gregg Press, 1979.

Hoch, David G. "Mythic Patterns in *2001: A Space Odyssey*." *Journal of Popular Culture* 4, no. 4 (1971): 960-65.

Homer. *The Odyssey*. Translated by E. V. Rieu. Baltimore, Md.: Penguin, 1946.

Kael, Pauline. *For Keeps*. New York: Dutton, 1994.

Kempley, Rita. "American Film Institute's Pick of the Flicks." *Washington Post*, 17 June 1998: D1 and D8.

Man, Glenn. *Radical Visions: American Film Renaissance, 1967–1976*. Westport, Conn.: Greenwood Press, 1994.

Morgenstern, Joseph. "Kubrick's Cosmos" (review of *2001: A Space Odyssey*). *Newsweek* 71, no. 16 (15 April 1968): 97, 100.

Nietzsche, Friedrich. *Thus Spake Zarathustra*. Translated by Thomas Common, with revisions by H. James Birx. Buffalo, N.Y.: Prometheus, 1993.

Ordway, Frederick I. "Perhaps I'm Just Projecting My Own Concern about It." In *The Making of Kubrick's* 2001, edited by Jerome Agel, 193–98. New York: New American Library, 1970.

Schwam, Stephanie. *The Making of* 2001: A Space Odyssey. New York: Modern Library, 2000.

Severin, Tim. "The Quest for Ulysses [Odysseus]." *National Geographic* 170, no. 2 (August 1986): 197–225.

Sobchack, Vivian. *Screening Space: The American Science Fiction Film*, 2d, enl. ed. New York: Ungar, 1993.

Stork, David G. *HAL's Legacy: 2001's Computer as Dream and Reality*. Cambridge, Mass.: MIT Press, 1997.

Tillich, Paul. *The Courage to Be*. New Haven, Conn.: Yale University Press, 1952.

————. *The Shaking of the Foundations*. New York: Charles Scribner's Sons, 1948.

————. *Systematic Theology*, vol. 1. Chicago: University of Chicago Press, 1951.

————. *Systematic Theology*, vol. 2. Chicago: University of Chicago Press, 1957.

———. *Systematic Theology*, vol. 3. Chicago: University of Chicago Press, 1963.

"'2001' Writer Disputes Millennium's Turn." *Washington Post*, 9 January 1999: C12.

Walker, Alexander. *Stanley Kubrick Directs*. New York: Harcourt Brace Jovanovich, 1971.

Wallich, Paul. "Remembrance of Future Past" (review of *HAL's Legacy*). *Scientific American* 276, no. 1 (January 1997): 114–15.

Watson, Russell and Corie Brown. "The 100 Best of 100 Years." *Newsweek Extra: 2000* (June 1998): 17–20.

Wheat, Leonard F. *Paul Tillich's Dialectical Humanism: Unmasking the God above God*. Baltimore, Md.: Johns Hopkins Press, 1970.

Index

acronyms, 71, 72, 73–74
Adam's rib, 102, 131, 156, 159
AE-35 unit, 24, 25, 34, 96, 102, 110, 132
Aeolus, 5, 53–54
Agel, Jerome, 11, 60, 115
aging, 36, 77, 79, 116, 117, 123, 134, 152, 155
Ahriman, 87
Ahura Mazdah, 87
airlock, 26, 78, 82, 96
Alex, as discarded name for Dave Bowman, 42
aliens, 102; Clarke on, 30, 31, 32, 39; at the hotel room, 33, 36, 37, 38; as installers of the monoliths, 22, 30–33, 38, 43, 65; octahedra as symbols representing, 9, 58, 152, 153; uncertainty about existence of, 17, 29. *See also* planet of the aliens
alignment (of Jupiter and its moons). *See* magical alignment
allegorical tendency, 9, 41, 127, 142
allegory, 3, 8–13, 85, 139, 140, 160; in Clarke's novelization of *2001*, 37; defined, 8–9, 41;

depicting *The Odyssey*, 3–5, 34, 41–62; depicting man-machine symbiosis, 3, 5–7, 63–86, 92; depicting *Thus Spake Zarathustra*, 3, 7–8, 37, 38, 43–44, 87–137. *See also* allegorical tendency
Allen, John, 91
ambiguity, 1, 2, 9, 13, 14n12, 29, 141, 161
American Film Institute, 1
amnion, 77, 80, 117, 121, 134, 157
anagrams, 13, 22, 95, 130, 148, 158
Angra Mainyu, 87
answers, to questions about *2001*, 2, 14n12, 36–39
anthropomorphism, 24, 25, 68–71, 75, 100–103
ape, 42; as a stage of evolution, 3, 7, 18, 19, 22, 67, 81, 122; symbolized, 113, 123, 134; used as symbols, 9, 10, 11
Aphrodite, 4, 44, 45, 47, 48, 62n7, 144, 160; as briber of Paris, 4, 44, 47, 48, 144, 160; symbolized by orbiting bomb, 45
arches. *See* Palladian arches

167

Aries. See moon lander
art-deco styling, 35
asteriods. *See* meteoroids
atheism, 7, 92, 96, 97, 101, 113
Athene, 59, 72; competes for
   golden apple, 44, 45, 144; helps
   Odysseus, 5, 57, 60, 145
Australopithecus, 6, 65, 66, 75

baby. *See* child, star-child
Baltic, 20, 48, 143,151
bathrooms: Hal-Discovery's, 7,
   70–71, 132, 150, 156–57; hotel
   room's, 28, 35, 59, 77, 84, 119,
   135, 158
Battle in Outer Space, 6, 18,
   25–26, 64, 65, 75–76, 150–51
Battle at the Waterhole, 6, 19–20,
   64, 65, 75, 150
BBC telecast, 23–24, 84, 102
beauty contest (three goddesses), 4,
   42–43. *See also* Aphrodite,
   golden apple
Bernstein, Theodore, 8
"beyond" (meaning of in "Beyond
   the Infinite"), 104–5, 133, 151
Bible, 7, 100
birth: of God, 12, 23, 67, 93, 97,
   101, 102, 131, 144, 156; of the
   star-child, 28–29, 78, 79, 117
birthday transmission, received by
   Frank Poole, 24, 103
Birx, H. James, 10, 91
Bizony, Piers, 1, 20, 22, 64, 70, 71,
   140
black. *See* color
black slabs. *See* monoliths
blackest will. *See* will of god
Bogdewic, Thomas J., 10, 91,
   106n17

bombs. *See* nuclear bombs
bone-club, 9, 19, 75; as a stage in
   evolution of God, 66, 101–2,
   152; as a tool, 10, 31, 65, 93,
   98, 131; transition of into
   modern weapon, 20, 45, 66.
   See also intelligence, tool-use
books about *2001*, 1, 14n1
Bowman, Dave, 23–29, 34, 35–39,
   83, 85, 110, 155; battle with
   Hal, 18, 25–26, 53, 75–76,
   110–11; blinking eye of, 9, 27,
   84, 117–18, 134; as Odysseus,
   3, 4, 41–42, 53, 54, 55, 56, 57,
   58, 59, 60, 97, 154, 157; as
   overman, 93, 99, 100, 116–17,
   121, 123, 126, 148; in the
   symbiosis allegory, 69, 70,
   76–80; as a symbolic name, 4,
   13, 41–42, 46, 49, 61n1, 95; as
   the older Zarathustra, 8, 10, 91,
   96, 97, 98–99, 100, 110–11,
   112–13, 114–16, 130, 132, 133,
   147, 154
brain shutoff key. *See* key, for
   lobotomizing Hal
"breakdown" of Hal. *See* Hal,
   "breakdown" of
briefing, 9, 21, 44, 49
British Film Institute, 1. *See also*
   Sight and Sound
bubble, Hal-Discovery's blowing a,
   7, 25, 82, 103, 132, 156
buffoon, 94–95, 96, 104, 130, 132
burned fingers, Dave Bowman's,
   23, 51–52, 152

Calypso, 5, 56–57, 59, 145
camel, 37, 99, 110, 121, 123, 124,
   134, 148

cave, Zarathustra's, 97, 119

cell division, 78, 79, 116, 117, 123, 134, 155

centrifuge, 23, 52, 95, 96, 126, 132, 136, 149

Charybdis, 5, 55, 56, 145

chess, 24, 70, 86n11, 103, 132

child, 8, 28, 37, 82, 99, 121, 123, 124, 126, 134

chromosomes, 77, 78, 79, 117, 122–23, 134, 147

Cicones, 51

Circe, 5, 54, 55

Clarke, Arthur, 1, 26, 30–33, 72, 83, 92; on Kubrick's efforts to use Saturn, 115; and man-machine symbiosis, 3, 5–6, 12, 63, 64, 75, 142, 149; his novel *2001*, interpretations and differences in, 20, 22, 29–30, 32, 33, 36, 39, 40n8, 61, 80, 96, 98, 102; on superstition, 107n18; on symbols in the movie, 4, 71–75; on *2001*'s "theme," 101

Clavius, 21, 49

club. *See* bone-club

color, 27, 118; black, 9, 28, 35, 79, 119, 120, 121, 122, 123, 134, 135, 148, 152; green-orange combination, 110–11, 133, 147, 152; orange, 28, 35, 122, 123, 134, 148, 152; two-tone objects, 27, 118; white, 9, 28, 35, 79, 120, 122, 123, 134, 148, 152

comet, 57

conception: on the moon (humanoid machine and God), 12, 21, 23, 67, 68, 97, 131, 156; on the planet of the aliens (overman), 77, 78, 117–18, 122–23, 133, 134. *See also* copulation

confusion. *See* ambiguity

Consumer Reports, readers ratings of *2001*, 1

copulation, of space shuttle with space station, 9, 47, 48, 66, 80, 101, 131, 150, 156

cosmic wonders (beyond Jupiter), 17, 27, 55–58

crew: of Odysseus, 4, 5, 10, 24, 41, 51, 53, 84, 145, 154; of spaceship Discovery, 24, 53, 103, 111, 112

critics, 1, 33–34, 80–85, 139–41. *See also* Ebert, Roger; Kael, Pauline; *Sight and Sound* poll; and *Time*

cry of distress, 59, 119, 135

cyclops, 5, 41, 52–53, 54, 139, 145; disabled by stake, 11, 12, 26, 42; symbolized by Hal, 10, 11, 12, 53, 151, 154, 156

"Daisy, Daisy," sung by Hal, 26, 39n6, 70, 103, 150, 152, 159

Darwin, Charles, 7, 89

David, as a symbolic name, 41–42, 61n1, 130

Dawn of Evolution, 124, 130

Dawn of God, 100, 101, 131, 144

Dawn of Homo machinus, 67

Dawn of Man, 6, 19, 31, 42, 63, 65–66, 67, 84, 122, 131, 146

dining cart-table, 27, 28, 79, 118–19

disciples, Zarathustra's, 118–19

Discovery, the spaceship, 6, 9, 10–11, 18, 53, 81; as humanoid,

12, 70–71, 102, 149–50; as a
phallus, 77, 116, 133. *See also*
Hal-Discovery
divinity, of Hal-Discovery, 103–4
doors and windows, missing in the
hotel room, 77, 116, 134, 152,
153, 157
Dr. Strangelove, 60, 70
dragon, God as the, 99, 111, 147
dwarf, 125, 127

earth, 3, 9, 24, 25, 32, 152; in
earth-to-moon trip, 18, 20–21,
66, 97; orbited by nuclear
bombs, 20, 38, 39, 61, 80; as
Penelope, 10, 60, 61; star-child
shining on, 17, 19, 29, 37, 125,
130, 185
earth shuttle. *See* space shuttle
Ebert, Roger, 1, 48, 140
Eden, Garden of. *See* the Fall
eight steps in evolution of Homo
machinus and God, 67–68, 85,
101–2, 131, 155
"18 Months Later," 12, 19, 67,
131, 151. *See also* gestation
eight-part circles, 67–68, 85
Elena, 3, 9, 13, 20, 46, 48, 49, 72,
95, 152. *See also* Helen of Troy
emergency airlock. *See* airlock
enlightenment, 97, 98–99 112–13,
133, 147
Eris, 44
escorts, Phaeacians and octahedra
(aliens) as, 58
eternal recurrence, 88–89, 90, 91,
109, 125–27, 127–29, 135, 143,
148, 154
evolution, 7; ape's, 18, 20, 43, 65;
five stages of, 122, 123, 134,

147; man's, 33, 36, 60, 113–25;
Nietzschean, 6, 11, 88, 89, 91,
109, 122, 123, 124, 134, 146,
147; in the symbiosis allegory,
3, 63–86, 150
exercise centrifuge. *See* centrifuge
exhaust nozzles. *See* rocket
nozzles
extraterrestrials. *See* aliens
eye. *See* red eye of Hal; Bowman,
Dave, blinking eye of

faith, loss of, 110, 132
the Fall, Christian doctrine of, 11,
107n28, 121–22, 135, 148, 159.
See also upside down religious
doctrines
fallopian tube, 10, 78, 82, 117, 131,
134, 155, 157, 160
fertilization. *See* conception
fetal sac. *See* amnion
fetus, 36, 77–80, 116–18, 121, 134,
135
Floyd, Heywood R., 9, 22, 83; as
builder of Hal-Discovery, 98,
101, 109, 146; as Menelaus, 10,
49–50, 97, 154; as Paris, l0, 45,
47–48, 97, 143, 154; recorded
message from at Jupiter, 26,
111–12; as a symbolic name, 5,
13, 46, 49, 72, 95, 143, 145; trip
to the moon by, 18, 19, 20–21,
84, 126; as the young
Zarathustra, 8, 96–98, 100, 130.
See also "Squirt"
food dispensing machine, 23, 52,
85, 153
Forbidden Planet, 63
Freud, Sigmund, 64, 80–82, 85
Friedman, Norman, 9

Garnette, Louis, 72. *See also* "The Sentinel"

Geduld, Carolyn, 2, 4, 11, 33, 91, 114, 136n11, 139; Freudian-Jungian interpretation by, 64, 80–85

Gelmis, Joseph, 91

gestation: in the hotel room, 77, 78–79, 117, 134, 157–58; in the moon, 12, 23, 67, 93, 97, 101, 102, 117, 131, 150, 156. *See also* amnion, birth, conception, fetus

glass floor, 9, 27, 35, 76, 77, 117, 134, 153, 157

globe enclosing the star-child, 19, 28, 38, 80, 121, 124, 130, 152. *See also* the "great noontime"

God: as a barrier to evolution, 3, 8, 89, 146; birth of, 12, 23, 67, 93, 97, 101, 102, 131, 144, 156; creation of, 44, 89, 92, 93, 97, 101, 104, 115, 131; death of, 8, 10, 11, 88, 93, 96, 98–99, 109–111, 113, 135, 159; as the image of man, 7, 10, 91, 98, 100–103, 109, 130, 131–32, 146, 157, 159; made from a bone, 101–102, 156, 159; symbolized by the buffoon, 94–95, 96, 104, 130, 132; symbolized by the dragon, 99, 111; symbolized by Hal-Discovery, 7, 91, 100–105, 110, 111, 130, 131, 133, 144, 156, 157; symbolized by "the infinite," 27, 104–5, 133, 147; symbolized by wine glass, 11, 28, 119–22, 135, 148, 159; will of, 90, 113, 120. *See also* the Fall, "God is dead!," wine glass

"God is dead!," 112, 123; as Nietzsche's most famous words, 3, 7, 110, 159; spoken by Zarathustra, 8, 89, 99, 113; symbolized, 26, 105, 121, 133, 135, 148. *See also* God, death of

golden apple, 4, 45, 46, 47, 143, 144

Goodall, Jane, 66

gravity, 20, 47

Great Bow of Odysseus: given to Odysseus, 4, 42, 43, 144; regained by Odysseus, 5, 42, 43, 59–61, 145; symbolized, 43, 65, 92, 153, 154

"great noontime," 8, 118; as a Nietzsche symbol for overman, 37, 38, 113, 121; symbolized by Kubrick, 10, 60–61, 123–25, 130, 146, 153. *See also* overman, star-child

green-orange color combination. *See* color, green-orange combination

Grego (a.k.a. Gregori), 48. *See also* Menelaus

Hades, 5, 54

Hal, 6, 10, 23, 24, 34, 84, 91, 103–4, 156; as an acronym, 71, 72, 73–74; "breakdown" of, 29, 102; as the cyclops, 53, 154, 156; as a killer, 18, 25, 29, 34, 69, 70, 75, 96, 103, 105; as omniscient ("incapable of error"), 24, 34, 110; as a symbolic name, 13, 46, 49, 69, 71–75, 95, 104, 130, 149. *See also* Hal-Discovery; mistake, made by Hal; red eye of Hal

Hal-Discovery, 7, 9, 64, 98, 100, 146; anthropomorphism of, 24, 66, 68–75, 98, 100–103; 131–32, 156–57; birth of, 23, 67, 77, 93, 97, 101, 131, 144; built by Heywood Floyd, 98, 101, 109, 146; why combined (hyphenated), 100; as God, 8, 22, 91, 99, 100–105, 130, 131, 133, 146, 154; as Homo machinus, 6, 12, 64, 66–76, 149–151, 154; as a phallus, 117. *See also* God, Hal, Homo machinus

Halvorsen, Dr., 22, 49, 50

Hamilton, Edith, 44, 47

hangar doors, 21, 68, 131

Helen of Troy, 4, 43, 44, 45, 46, 47–48, 49, 62n7, 80, 143, 144, 158. *See* also Elena, Menelaus

Hera, 44, 45

Hermes, 57

hexagons, 70–71, 132, 152, 156

hibernation, 9, 24, 25, 52, 53, 70, 75, 81, 84, 112, 154. *See also* lotus

higher man: Bowman as, 91, 98–99, 103, 134; and evolution, 7, 8, 109, 120, 121, 123, 124, 134, 146, 147; as killer of God, 89, 110, 113; Jupiter's moons as, 114, 133, 147, 158; the lion as, 37, 99, 110, 111, 121, 124, 134, 147, 148; in Strauss's "Thus Spake Zarathustra," 106n1; Zarathustra as, 91, 94, 98–99, 100; in Zarathustra's cave, 118, 119

Hilton hotel, 20, 156

Hirsch, Foster, 66, 102

Hoch, David G., 33–34, 91

Holy Spirit, 96, 107n28

Homer, 3, 12, 41, 142

Homo futurus, 6, 75, 79, 80, 126, 154, 155

Homo machinus, 6, 66, 68, 75–76, 126, 154, 155

Homo sapiens, 6, 65, 66, 68, 71, 75

hotel room, 18, 27–28, 43, 76–80, 115–23; confusing, 10, 35, 76–77; provided by aliens, 30, 36, 58; as a symbol, 9, 77–80, 134, 153, 157–58

Howard Johnson's, 156

Howell, Dr., 20, 21

humanoids: God as a, 100–103, 156; as machines, 3, 6, 7, 10, 23, 63, 64, 66–76, 79, 92, 149, 150, 156; as post-human organic beings, 38, 77. *See also* God, as the image of man; Hal-Discovery; Homo futurus; star-child

humor, 3, 13, 23, 61n6, 139, 155–58; Discovery's physique, 70–71, 131–32, 149–50; gestation period of symbiots and God twice that of humans, 67, 101, 131; God made from a bone, 101–2, 131, 156, 159; God's bathrooms, 70–71, 103, 132, 150, 156–57; God's sticking out his tongue and blowing a bubble, 25, 103, 132, 157; God's wide-band mod sunglasses, 70, 102, 103, 131, 150; "no meat" on Trojan Horse, 50, 144, 158; zero-gravity toilet scene, 142. *See also* upside down religious doctrines

Hyperion, 5, 56, 145

IBM, 71–75, 104, 105, 130, 149

illumination: from beneath the hotel-room floor, 27, 35, 76, 77, 117, 134, 157; of Nietzsche's "light-surrounded being," 11, 120, 121, 123, 134–35, 148, 155; surrounding the star-child, 28, 35, 122

image of man. *See* God, as the image of man

"the infinite," 27, 113–14, 133; as God, 27, 104–5, 132, 147

intelligence, 109, 146; imparted to ape by first monolith in surface story, 31, 38, 43, 60, 65, 93, 98; imparted to man by fourth monolith in surface story, 33, 38, 43, 60; symbolized by first monolith in Zarathustra allegory, 92, 115, 116, 130, 131, 153–54

Iphitus, 43

Ismarus, 5, 51–52, 145

Ithaca, 4, 52, 58, 59, 79

jokes. *See* humor

Judgment of Paris, 44–45, 47, 48

Jung, Carl, 64, 80, 83–85

Jupiter, 17, 19, 84, 85, 93, 152; as target of moon monolith's signal, 18, 32, 76, 111; as a symbol, 9, 10, 114–15, 133, 147, 155, 157, 160

Jupiter mission, 18, 19, 23–26, 51–55, 67, 75–76, 98–104, 109–13

Kael, Pauline, 2, 159–60

key, for lobotomizing Hal, 9, 12, 26, 42, 53, 152, 153

Krusch, Barry, 61n1

Kubrick, Stanley, 1, 3, 5–7, 14n12, 29, 49, 71–72, 160–61; as an atheist, 92, 101; attention to details, 33, 38, 53, 139; as an optimist, 7, 63, 64, 80; imaginativeness and cleverness of his symbols, 100–101, 155–60; reasons for doing certain things, 19, 27, 31, 50, 66. *See also* humor, "Squirt"

last man, 125

Last Supper, 11, 35, 118–19, 124, 135

Laestrygonians, 5, 53–54, 145. *See also* meteoroids

Leda, 44

Leucothoe, 58

lightning, commanded by Zarathustra, 124

"light-surrounded being." *See* illumination, of Nietzsche's "light-surrounded being"

lion, 37, 99, 110, 111, 121, 123, 124, 134, 147, 148

logic, in eternal recurrence argument, 127–29

Louis XVI decor in hotel room, 76, 86n14

Lotus-eaters, 5, 12, 24, 52, 145, 154

lower man: the camel as, 37, 99, 110, 134, 148; as creator of God, 89, 109, 146; the crowd in the market place as, 7, 94, 109, 114, 122; and evolution, 7, 8, 89, 109, 113, 146; Frank Poole as, 103; Heywood Floyd as, 96–98, 100, 101, 109, 130, 146;

Jupiter as, 114, 133, 147, 155, 158; the shepherd as, 120, 134

magical alignment, 10, 27, 84, 114, 115, 136n11, 147
Man, Glen, 2, 141
mankind, star-child's shining on, 125, 135
man-machine symbiosis. *See* symbiosis
Mediterranean, 4, 44, 48
Menelaus, 4, 10, 44, 46, 47, 48, 62n7, 143, 145, 154
metamorphosis, 18, 36, 99, 109, 116, 122, 124
metaphor, 8, 14n12, 38, 63, 82, 94, 99, 113, 121, 122, 123, 146. *See also* sun, in Kubrick's climbing-sun metaphor
metaphysics, 33, 116, 125
meteoroids, 24, 54. *See also* Laestrygonians
Michaels, 22, 50
Michelangelo, 100, 101
milestones, 6, 63, 65, 67, 75, 92, 150, 153
millennium, 88, 129, 146
Miller, 20, 84
mission control, 24, 102, 112
mistake, made by Hal, 7, 9, 30, 39n6, 102, 132, 150, 153; as counterpoint to "incapable of error," 24, 34
Moisevitch, Dimitri, 72
monoliths, 17, 29, 31, 33–34, 83, 126, 152; in Africa, 18, 19, 31, 41, 42–44, 65, 92, 98, 130, 150, 153–54; in the hotel room, 28, 33, 35, 38, 60, 92, 93, 115–16, 120, 121, 130, 151, 154; at

Jupiter, 18, 27, 32, 55, 65, 76, 78, 92, 93, 114–15, 116, 124, 130, 150, 154; as milestones, 6, 63, 64, 66, 79, 150; on the moon, 18, 22, 26, 31–32, 36, 49–51, 67, 69, 79, 92–93, 97, 98, 110–11, 130, 131, 150, 154; as symbols, 9, 82, 91–93, 136, 149, 157
moon, 9, 83, 97; as an ovum, 12, 21, 23, 67, 77, 78, 81, 101, 131, 150; in the surface story, 18, 21–23, 49–51
moon bus: in the surface story, 21–22, 31, 49, 50, 84; as a symbol, 49, 143, 158
moon lander, 21, 68, 83, 84, 85; and Menelaus, 143, 154; as a sperm cell, 11, 21, 23, 48, 67, 77, 97, 131, 143, 150, 154
moons of Jupiter, 39n7; in the surface story, 27, 84, 85, 115; as symbols, 9, 10, 114–15, 133
Moonwatcher, 19, 20, 31, 37, 43, 75, 84, 93, 98, 131
Morrison, Toni, 118
mystical alignment. *See* magical alignment

National Council of Astronautics, 20, 21, 98
Nausicaa, 58
Nietzsche, Friedrich, 3, 7, 8, 13, 26, 87, 94, 142; as an atheist, 92, 101; his concept of evolution, 6, 10, 109, 122; his concept of God, 7, 100; his logic, 127–129; his message, 8, 103; his symbols, 37, 38, 81, 82, 99, 104, 118, 120, 121, 123–24, 125, 126, 127

nihilism, 161

9000, from HAL 9000 computer, 69, 88, 129, 151

nuclear bombs: in the bone-to-bomb transition, 19, 20, 66; in the surface story, 20, 45, 47; as symbols, 9, 45, 61n6, 131, 143, 153, 154

octahedra, as escorts to alien planet, 9, 58, 152, 153

odds against coincidence, in HAL-IBM alphabetic lag, 74–75

Odysseus, 4–5, 10, 38, 79, 145

The Odyssey, 1, 142; plot of, 3–5, 12, 24, 41–61, 87; symbolized, 41–61, 144–46

optical illusion, earth moving in circle as, 20

optimism and pessimism, 7, 63, 64, 80

orange Bowman. *See* color

orange-green (spacesuit-helmet) combination. *See* color

orangutan, 123, 134

Ordway, Frederick, 20, 32

Orion. See space shuttle

overman, 3, 6, 82, 89, 115–125; birth of, 117, 135, 147; and evolution, 3, 7–8, 81, 90, 91, 109, 110, 123–25; symbolized as a child by Nietzsche, 8, 28, 37, 82, 99, 121, 124, 126, 134–35; symbolized as "the great noontime" by Nietzsche, 8, 37, 38, 113, 118, 121, 130; symbolized as the "light-surrounded being" by Nietzsche, 11, 120, 121, 123, 134–35, 148, 155; as the attainment of power,

8, 90, 93, 117, 147; symbolized by Kubrick's star-child, 91, 99, 121, 124–25, 130, 148; symbolized by Richard Strauss's "Thus Spake Zarathustra," 105–6n1. *See also* supremacy

ovum. *See* moon, as an ovum; planet of the aliens, as an ovum

Palladian arches, 27, 35, 59, 76, 84, 152

Pallas Athene. *See* Athene

parable, 89, 94, 103, 104, 120, 121, 122, 127, 148, 155; of dwarf on Zarathustra's shoulder, 125, 127; of rope dancer, 10, 13, 30, 89, 94–96, 103, 104, 105, 122, 130, 132, 148; of shepherd and serpent, 11, 29, 120–21, 123, 134, 135, 148, 155

Paris, 4, 47–48, 49, 154; and Helen, 43, 44–45, 46, 80, 143; as beauty contest judge, 4, 46, 144, 160

pen, floating, 47, 48, 143, 152, 153, 160

Penelope, 5, 10, 42, 43, 45, 57, 59–61, 145

Phaeacians, 5, 57–58, 79, 145, 155

phallic symbol: Discovery, 77–78, 117, 133; floating pen, 47, 48, 143, 152, 160; space shuttle, 12, 20, 66, 77, 101, 131, 143, 150, 152

planet of the aliens: as hotel room's location, 33, 58, 59, 115; as an ovum, 78, 117, 133, 134, 153; in the surface story, 17, 18, 27, 76, 116

pod, utility, 9, 84, 150; as a bubble, 7, 25, 82, 103, 132, 156;

deposited in hotel room, 28, 35, 58, 117, 118, 122, 134; disappearance from hotel room, 28, 58, 78–79, 153, 155; on voyage to Jupiter, 24, 25, 26, 78, 82, 132; used for trip to planet of aliens, 18, 27, 55, 76, 77, 114, 117, 133, 134, 155; used as weapon, 70, 96

Poole, Frank, 23–26, 34, 51–52, 53, 75, 85, 103, 147; anagram, the name as an, 13, 50, 130; murdered, 18, 25, 53, 70, 75, 94, 103, 132; as the rope dancer, 13, 94–96, 98, 100, 130, 148, 154; as a symbol, 9, 10, 46, 49, 51, 72, 130, 158

Poseidon, 5, 57

power, 90, 92, 147; grasped, 8, 93, 117; symbolized, 92, 130, 154, 157. *See also* monoliths, in the hotel room and at Jupiter; supremacy; will to power

prayer, 103, 132, 151

prologue to *Thus Spake Zarathustra*, 94, 124

Proteus, 61n5

races (species), 64, 77, 79, 82, 104

rainbow, promised by Zarathustra, 115, 133, 155, 158, 160

red eye of Hal, 24, 25, 70, 103, 110, 153; as symbol of one-eyed cyclops, 4, 10, 12, 53, 156

red giant star, 56

Robby the Robot, 63

rocket nozzles, 70–71, 84, 102, 131, 132, 157. *See also* bathrooms, Hal-Discovery's

rocks. *See* meteoroids

rope across the abyss, 90, 91, 94, 122, 124

rope dancer, 89, 94–96, 103, 104, 105; killed, 94, 103, 104, 105, 132; symbolized, 10, 13, 30, 130, 132, 148. *See also* Poole, Frank

saoshyant, 88

Saturn, 32, 115, 160

science fiction, 2, 3, 32, 33, 63, 107n18, 140, 157, 161. *See also* "The Sentinel"

Scylla, 6, 55–56, 145

senility, of Hal, 26, 70, 103, 132

"The Sentinel," 5, 30, 31, 33, 72

serpent, 11, 29, 120, 121, 123, 134, 135, 148, 155. *See also* wine glass

sexual reproduction symbolism, 10, 12, 23, 64, 68, 77, 78, 80–82, 101, 116–18, 123, 155. *See also* amnion; birth, of God; birth, of the star-child; conception; copulation; Discovery, as a phallus; fallopian tube; fetus; gestation; moon, as an ovum; planet of the aliens, as an ovum; moon lander; pen, floating; phallic symbol; sperm; space shuttle; space station

shadowboxing, 51–52, 95, 132, 152

shepherd, 120–21, 123, 134, 135, 148, 155

shuttle. *See* space shuttle

Sight and Sound poll, 1, 140, 141, 161

signal from moon monolith, 18, 19, 22, 26, 31, 32, 76, 111, 112; as a symbol, 51, 144, 152 sirens, 5, 54, 145, 152; symbolized, 10, 33, 55, 92, 154, 155, 157, 160

slabs. *See* monoliths

Smyslov, Andrey, 20–21, 72, 86n11

snake. *See* serpent, wine glass

Sobchack, Vivian, 121

Socrates, as a discarded name for Hal, 72–73, 74

space pods. *See* pods, utility

space rocks. *See* meteoroids

spaceship. *See* Discovery, Hal-Discovery, space shuttle

space shuttle (*Orion*), 20, 47, 85; as a phallus, 12, 48, 66, 77, 81, 101, 131, 143, 150, 152; as symbolic, 9, 107n28, 153

space station, 9, 11, 20–21, 46, 126, 152, 153; as a symbol of eternal recurrence, 126, 135, 148, 150; as a woman, 12, 47, 48, 66, 67, 77, 81, 101, 131, 143

Sparta, 9, 44

special effects. *See* visual images

sperm. *See* chromosomes; conception; fallopian tube; moon lander; pod, used for trip to planet of aliens

sphere. *See* globe inclosing the star-child

"Squirt" (Heywood Floyd's daughter), 20, 84, 126

stairs to the overman, Nietzsche's, 113, 115, 124, 133, 139, 147, 158

stake, used against cyclops, 4, 11, 12, 53

statuettes, 27, 35, 59

star-child, 6, 8, 17, 19, 33, 39, 61, 64, 80, 82, 120–21, 134–35,

146; birth of, 18, 28–29, 79, 117; as the "great noontime" sun, 29, 38, 124, 130; as Odysseus, 10, 61; as overman, 91, 99, 121, 130, 148; as a symbol (in the abstract), 9, 35, 136, 149. *See also* "great noontime"; overman; sun, in Kubrick's climbing-sun metaphor

Star Gate, 32, 55, 114, 116, 133

Stork, David G., 30, 58

Strangelove. *See Dr. Strangelove*

Strauss, Richard. *See* "Thus Spake Zarathustra" (symphonic poem)

suitors, Penelope's, 5, 42, 45, 59, 60–61, 145, 154

sun, 9, 45; at dawn, 19, 22, 67, 113, 123, 124, 130; at "the great noontime," 8, 37, 38, 113, 121, 123, 130, 153; in Kubrick's climbing-sun metaphor, 81, 113, 121, 123, 124–25, 130, 146, 152

superman. *See* overman

supernaturalism, 33, 97

superstition, 93, 97, 107n18, 146; acquired by Heywood Floyd (young Zarathustra), 98, 109, 131; symbolized by moon monolith, 10, 92, 115, 116, 130, 154, 157

supremacy, 8, 90, 92, 94, 99, 103, 104, 109, 132

surf, the raging, 5, 55, 145

surrealism, 2, 13, 14, 17, 27, 34, 35, 36, 76, 116, 118

survey team, 12, 24, 52, 145. *See also* hibernation, Lotus-eaters

syllogisms, in the eternal
recurrence argument, 127–29
symbiosis, man-machine, 3, 5–7,
12, 23, 64, 75, 142

telephone: Hal's, 71, 150; on the
space station, 20, 126, 135, 143,
148, 152
The Terminator, 63
"a thousand ships," launched by
Helen's face, 4, 5, 49, 145, 158
the "three metamorphoses," 37, 84,
99, 111, 121, 124, 134, 135,
146, 148, 155
Thus Spake Zarathustra (book), 3,
7, 8, 13, 87, 88–89, 94, 97, 109,
129, 142
"Thus Spake Zarathustra"
(symphonic poem), 81, 87,
105–6n1, 124, 129, 146
tightrope. *See* rope across the
abyss, rope dancer
tiles, bathroom, 7, 70–71, 132, 150,
156–57
Tillich, Paul, 33, 104–5, 132, 147
time as a circle. *See* eternal
recurrence
Time magazine, 2, 90, 125, 126,
140
TMA-1, 22, 49–50, 144; as an
anagram, 13, 49–50, 149, 158;
as symbolic, 46, 95, 145. *See
also* monoliths, on the moon
tool-use, 10, 66; as that which
changes ape into man, 11,
19–20, 65, 109, 131; as the
result of contact with African
monolith, 31, 98; by Hal-
Discovery, 64, 70, 102, 132

transition, from bone to bomb, 19,
66, 102, 156
Trojan Horse, 4, 46, 48, 81, 145; in
the name Heywood R. Floyd,
46, 48; symbolized, 10, 22, 34,
50, 51, 92, 144, 158
Trojan War, 3, 4, 13, 43, 44, 51
Troy: in the name Heywood R.
Floyd, 46, 48; in *The Odyssey*,
3, 4, 42, 44, 46, 49, 143, 145;
symbolized, 46, 48, 51, 81, 144
Trumbull, Douglas, 160
2001, as a symbol, 87–88, 106n2,
129
tunnel of lights, 17, 40n8, 40n19;
in the surface story, 18, 27, 32,
39, 54–55, 76, 114, 116, 118; as
a symbol, 9, 10, 54–55, 78, 117,
134, 152, 153, 155, 157, 160
Tycho: in the surface story, 18,
21–23, 49, 50–51, 67, 84; as a
symbol, 9, 49, 51, 81, 144, 145

Ugliest Man, 89, 103, 110, 118,
132, 147
"ultimate trip," 157. *See also*
tunnel of lights
Ulysses. *See* Odysseus
Underman, 91, 106n17
universe, 12, 67, 79, 117, 135
upside down religious doctrines,
11, 100, 102, 121–22, 130, 135,
148, 156, 159

vacuum, survival in a, 26
vehicles. *See* Discovery, Hal-
Discovery, moon bus, moon
lander, pod, space shuttle
(*Orion*), space station

Vendy, Phil, 91, 106n17
visual images, 1, 2, 139–41, 158, 159–60
voiceprint identification, 46, 84, 143
Walker, Alexander, 20
Wallich, Paul, 64, 102
white. *See* color

will of God, 90, 113, 120
will to power, 7, 8, 88, 93, 110; defined, 9, 82, 89–90, 92, 113, 146; symbolized, 115, 116, 118, 121, 133, 134, 147. *See also* Bowman, blinking eye of; God, death of; magical alignment; monoliths, as symbols; power
Wilson (from "The Sentinel"), 72
windows (hotel room). *See* doors and windows
wine glass, 28; as a symbol (abstract), 9, 10, 35, 153; as a symbol (concrete), 29, 119–22, 135, 148, 152, 159. *See also* the Fall; parable, of shepherd and serpent
womb, 23, 81, 82. *See also* amnion, birth, conception, fetus, gestation

wooden horse. *See* Floyd, Heywood R., as a symbolic name; Trojan Horse
worm, 7, 122–23, 124, 134, 147
wormhole, 32, 39, 40n19. *See also* tunnel of lights

Zarathustra (the book). *See Thus Spake Zarathustra*; Nietzsche, Friedrich
Zarathustra (the character), 3, 7–8, 87–88, 89; as a believer (young), 8, 10, 44, 96–98, 100, 130, 146, 154; as higher man, 100, 120; as a nonbeliever (older), 8, 10, 43–44, 92, 94, 96, 97, 98–99, 112, 130, 147, 154; as overman, 99; quoted, 8, 97, 98, 99, 110, 112, 113, 114, 115, 120, 124, 125
zero-gravity toilet, 142, 162n14
Zeus, 5, 45, 56, 57, 59, 67, 145; refusal to judge the beauty contest, 44, 47, 144, 154
Zoroaster, 87
Zoroastrianism, 87–88

About the Author

Born in 1931, Leonard F. Wheat received his BA degree from the University of Minnesota at Duluth, his MPA from the University of Minnesota at Minneapolis, and his PhD in political economy and government from Harvard University. His early career included positions with the Minnesota Department of Taxation, the Office of Special Projects of the U.S. Department of the Navy, and the U.S. Bureau of the Budget. From 1966 until his retirement in 1997, he was an economist with the Economic Development Administration of the U.S. Department of Commerce.

Dr. Wheat is the author or (in one case) coauthor of four previous books—three economic studies and one book on philosophical theology. He is also the author of two book-length government economic studies, various shorter government studies, four refereed journal articles, and several articles and publications relating to hiking. His first book, *Paul Tillich's Dialectical Humanism: Unmasking the God Above God* (1970), bears striking similarities to the present book. Both identify cryptic symbolism in other works—coded messages, so to speak—and decipher the symbols to reveal hidden content.

Leonard Wheat is an associate editor of the *Journal of Regional Science* and a member of the American Economic Association, the Southern Economic Association, the Regional Science Association International, the Society for Cinema Studies, and numerous environmental groups. His hobbies include hiking, swimming, canoeing, playing chess, and raising daylilies. He lives in Fairfax County, Virginia, with his wife, Dr. Wei-hsiung (Kitty) Wheat, Professor Emerita of English at Bowie State University in Maryland.